FEDERAL COURTS STANDARDS OF REVIEW

Appellate Court Review of District Court Decisions and Agency Actions

Harry T. Edwards

Senior Circuit Judge
U.S. Court of Appeals for the D.C. Circuit

Visiting Professor of Law
New York University School of Law

Linda A. Elliott

Special Counsel to Judge Edwards
at the U.S. Court of Appeals for the D.C. Circuit

Adjunct Professor of Law
New York University School of Law

AMERICAN CASEBOOK SERIES®

THOMSON
™
WEST

Mat #40452569

© 2007 Thomson/West
      610 Opperman Drive
      St. Paul, MN 55123
      1–800–313–9378

Printed in the United States of America

ISBN: 978–0–314–16761–3

 *TEXT IS PRINTED ON 10% POST CONSUMER RECYCLED PAPER*

For Pamela, with my love and appreciation for your patience and support.

— HTE

In memory of Douglas W. Hillman, former Chief Judge of the United States District Court for the Western District of Michigan. I cannot thank him enough for teaching me how noble a profession the law can be.

And for John and Joey – "my best and my favorite" – with love.

— LAE

*

Preface

A number of years ago, during an oral argument before the U.S. Court of Appeals for the D.C. Circuit, an attorney was asked by a member of the bench, "What standard of review governs this issue?" Counsel looked confused, hesitated, and then finally said to the inquiring judge, "I am not sure that I understand what you mean." The judge tried again, asking: "How closely do we scrutinize the trial court's decision in determining whether to affirm or reverse? Do we give any deference to the trial judge or do we review the matter in dispute *de novo*?" The attorney hesitated again, then answered, "Your honor, if you think we're right, we win." Although this response garnered laughter from courtroom observers, the bench was understandably frustrated by the lawyer's failure to comprehend either the meaning or the importance of standards of review.

"Most people, if asked what judges do, would say they apply 'the law' to the facts. But there is an important step in between. Appellate courts have to decide what the 'standard of review' is, and that standard more often than not determines the outcome" of an appeal. Wald, *The Rhetoric of Results and the Results of Rhetoric: Judicial Writings*, 62 U. CHI. L. REV. 1371, 1391 (1995). This is because the standards of review determine the degree of scrutiny with which appellate courts will examine alleged errors in district court and agency decisionmaking. Judge Deanell R. Tacha, former Chief Judge of the United States Court of Appeals for the Tenth Circuit, once pithily described what is at stake: "I despise 'legalese,' and I know I am not alone. But I think that word gets overused, because there are some words with legal meaning that you simply cannot avoid. Take 'standard of review.' Now to the normal reader that is legalese. To the judge, it is everything."

Over the years—while teaching law, reading appellate briefs, and listening to oral arguments—we have been surprised by the number of law students and practicing attorneys who treat the standards of review as mere "legalese." What we have seen may be attributable to the short shrift that standards of review are sometimes given in legal teaching and publications. It may also reflect the somewhat cynical belief, shared by some members of the legal academy, that "the rules governing judicial review have no more substance at the core than a seedless grape." Gellhorn & Robinson, *Perspectives on Administrative Law*, 75 COLUM. L. REV. 771, 780 (1975). Our decision to write this book was spurred, in part, by our determination to counter this misguided view of federal appellate decisionmaking. It was also prompted by the dearth of easily manageable published materials on the topic. Standards of review may not be everything, but they are critically important in determining the parameters of appellate review and in allocating authority between trial courts and agencies, on the one hand, and the appellate bench, on the other. They are thus worthy of serious study.

Appellate scrutiny of district court decisions varies greatly depending upon whether the *de novo*, clearly erroneous, abuse of discretion, or plain error standard of review controls. Likewise, the scrutiny with which administrative agency actions are examined depends upon whether the appellate court is constrained by the arbitrary and capricious, substantial evidence, or *Chevron* Step Two standards of review or engages in *de novo* review under *Chevron* Step One. This book attempts to give definition to these various standards.

Part One covers appellate court review of district court decisions and Part Two addresses appellate review of administrative agency actions. This separate treatment is necessitated by the fundamentally different character of the decisionmaking performed by agencies and trial courts. Administrative agencies make law pursuant to congressionally delegated authority. It is relatively rare, however, that Congress, in delegating law-making authority, prescribes precisely how an agency should act in a given situation. Rather, Congress frequently permits agency officials to employ their expertise and exercise their political judgment to effect quasi legislative policymaking goals. Therefore, as a general matter, it has been determined that many administrative actions are most appropriately overseen by a politically accountable branch of the government. Tailored to take account of this reality, most of the standards governing judicial review of administrative actions tend to be deferential. No single principle similarly animates appellate review of trial court decisions. Instead, the deference owed is determined by a variety of factors, more than one of which may be at play with respect to any particular appellate issue. These factors include whether the appeal arises out of a civil case or a criminal prosecution; whether the various constitutional provisions protecting the decisionmaking authority of jurors or the due process rights of the parties are implicated; whether certain legislative and judicial directives giving effect to notions of fair play and the appropriate use of judicial resources are applicable; and, perhaps most fundamentally, whether trial judges or appellate judges are deemed better suited to decide the particular type of question at issue.

Our goal is to provide readers with easy to comprehend frameworks for understanding the effect of these considerations on the standards of appellate review governing challenges to trial court and agency decisionmaking. To this end, we have not taken the approach of a traditional casebook or treatise. Rather, in each of the two parts of the book, we first present an overview of the basic paradigm informing the applicable standards of review. We then describe the controlling standards, including those codified in Title 28, Section 2111 of the U.S. Code, the Federal Rules of Civil Procedure, the Federal Rules of Criminal Procedure, the Federal Rules of Evidence, and the Administrative Procedure Act, relying, whenever possible, on seminal Supreme Court decisions to give meaning to those standards. Only when important questions pertaining to the governing standards have not been addressed by the Supreme Court, do we look to circuit decisions to identify the prevalent norms. However, because our focus is on the "big picture," we do not detail every circuit split regarding such norms. Using the information presented here as a starting point, we leave to our readers the critical lawyering task of researching precisely how a challenge to a particular issue is reviewed within any individual circuit. In addition, we do not describe standards of review that are unique to particularized areas of the law. In other words, we do not purport to present a comprehensive guide to federal appellate review of, for example, arbitration decisions, bankruptcy proceedings, admiralty litigation, habeas corpus proceedings, patent litigation, or federal sentencing decisions. Moreover, substantive constitutional review standards (such as "strict scrutiny" and "rational basis" review), standards unique to Supreme Court litigation, the rules governing district court review of magistrate decisions, and the standards pursuant to which agencies review their own decisions or decisionmaking processes, are beyond the scope of this book.

Describing the substantial evidence standard of review, Justice Frankfurter once observed: "[T]he precise way in which courts interfere with agency findings cannot be imprisoned within any form of words . . . . The difficulty is that we cannot escape, in relation to this problem, the use of undefined defining terms." *Universal Camera Corp. v. NLRB*, 340 U.S. 474, 489 (1951). The same can be said of all standards of review. As Justice Frankfurter explained, however, "a standard leaving an unavoidable margin for individual judgment does not leave the judicial judgment at large even though the phrasing of the standard does not wholly fence it in." *Id.* This is because "[t]he ultimate reliance for the fair operation of any standard is a judiciary of high competence and character and the constant play of an informed professional critique upon its work." *Id.*

We hope that our book will be a useful resource for law students studying federal courts, administrative law, federal jurisprudence, and appellate practice, and a helpful tool for participants in trial and appellate clinics. It is also our hope that the book will be a good practical aid for law clerks assisting federal judges, as well as for lawyers engaged in federal practice. In other words, we hope that it will contribute to the ability of lawyers to participate in the "informed professional critique" to which Justice Frankfurter referred.

HARRY T. EDWARDS

LINDA A. ELLIOTT

*

Acknowledgments

We would like to extend our gratitude to Paul Berman, Joel Beauvais, and Daphna Renan for reading an early draft of the manuscript and offering helpful comments for our consideration. We also extend our thanks to Tabatha Abu El Haj, Kevin Chambers, Richard Kaplan, and Larry Schwartztol, who gave us invaluable assistance with research and cite-checking. Our greatest debts of gratitude are owed to Gail Abbey, for her skilled research, cite-checking, proofreading, and review of drafts, and Judy Hunt, who did everything imaginable to help us put the manuscript together. They worked tirelessly, selflessly, and with great spirit and good humor in support of our effort to complete this book. Their devotion to this project was quite extraordinary, and we are truly grateful.

*

Editorial Note

We have followed certain stylistic conventions which we hope will allow readers to digest the materials presented with relative ease. There are no footnotes – all case citations are included in the text. Most internal citations and quotation marks have been eliminated from quoted material, and this is not indicated in the text. If brackets appeared in the original of any quoted material, we removed them – brackets are shown only when we have modified a quotation.

We have also incorporated into the text the most recent amendments to the Federal Rules. Those amendments were forwarded to Congress by the Chief Justice of the United States in the Spring of 2007. *See* Orders of the Supreme Court of the United States Adopting and Amending Rules and Forms, Orders 30-33 (Apr. 30, 2007). Absent contrary congressional action, the amended rules will take effect on December 1, 2007. The Advisory Committee Notes make clear that the amendments affecting the rules cited in our text – which include both stylistic changes and, in some instances, the renumbering of subsections – are not intended to effect substantive changes in the law. On the assumption that Congress is unlikely to reject these uncontroversial amendments, the book references and quotes the rules in the form in which they will appear effective December 1, 2007. The Appendix contains a conversion chart which may be useful to those researching issues pertaining to the renumbered rules.

*

Table of Contents

PART ONE

REVIEW OF DISTRICT COURT DECISIONS

*

Table of Cases

References are to pages.

*

FEDERAL COURTS
STANDARDS OF REVIEW

Appellate Court Review of
District Court Decisions
and Agency Actions

*

Part One

REVIEW OF DISTRICT COURT DECISIONS

———————

*

Chapter I

THE FUNDAMENTALS: CONSTITUTIONAL CONSIDERATIONS; THE FOUR PRINCIPAL STANDARDS OF REVIEW; AND THE FACT/LAW PARADIGM

The four principal standards describing the degree of scrutiny with which federal appellate courts examine decisions emanating from district courts – generally characterized as *de novo*, clearly erroneous, abuse of discretion, and plain error review – are probably best understood as legislative and common-law allocations of decisional authority between trial and appellate judges. With respect to the first three standards, which one governs consideration of any particular appellate claim is, in the broadest sense, determined pursuant to the "fact/law" paradigm, a model of decisionmaking derived from the belief that trial judges are better positioned to decide questions of fact, while the appellate bench is better suited to resolve questions of law. The highly deferential plain error standard, which generally supplants the first three review standards when a party raises an issue for the first time on appeal, results from legislative and judicial mandates giving effect to notions of fair play in litigation and economy in the use of judicial resources.

Wholly apart from these considerations, however, constitutional mandates pertaining to the decisionmaking authority vested in juries, the guarantee of due process of law, and the bar against twice being tried for the same criminal offense, significantly define appellate scrutiny of certain claims of trial level error. Before discussing the four principal standards and the fact/law paradigm informing them, the effect of each of these constitutional provisions on appellate review is briefly summarized.

A. CONSTITUTIONAL CONSIDERATIONS

In the criminal context, appellate review of not guilty verdicts is altogether barred by the Double Jeopardy Clause. *See United States v. Martin Linen Supply Co.*, 430 U.S. 564, 571 (1977). And when a jury renders a guilty verdict, appellate review of the underlying factual findings, as well as the jury's application of the law to those facts, is largely defined by the Trial by Jury Clauses of the Sixth Amendment and Article III, Section 2 of the Constitution, as well as by the Constitution's due process guarantee. Thus, with very few exceptions, largely limited to guilty verdicts implicating First Amendment free speech issues, *see, e.g., Bose Corp. v. Consumers Union of U.S., Inc.*, 466 U.S. 485, 503–08 (1984) (citing precedent supporting independent appellate review of the portions of criminal verdicts implicating First Amendment free speech principles), a jury's finding of guilt is subject only to very limited review. Assuming no procedural or evidentiary error, a jury's findings of fact and its application of the governing law to those facts are reviewed only to ensure that a defendant's due process rights have not been violated by a verdict based on evidence from which no reasonable factfinder could infer guilt beyond a reasonable doubt. *See Jackson v. Virginia*, 443 U.S. 307 (1979); *see also* Part One, Chapter III.E, *infra*.

In civil cases, the Seventh Amendment's Trial by Jury and Re-examination Clauses generally protect the common-law authority of a jury to find the facts and to apply the law to those facts to reach a verdict. *See generally Markman v. Westview Instruments, Inc.*, 517 U.S. 370, 376–78 (1996); *Balt. & Carolina Line, Inc. v. Redman*, 295 U.S. 654 (1935). Pursuant to these constitutional strictures, judicial interference with a jury's decisionmaking authority is, with few exceptions, constrained to the legal question of whether "the facts are sufficiently clear that the law requires a particular result." *Weisgram v. Marley Co.*, 528 U.S. 440, 448 (2000). In other words, assuming no procedural or evidentiary error, challenges to a civil jury's authority to find the facts and apply the governing law to those facts generally are limited to the question of whether, giving the benefit of all reasonable inferences to the nonmoving party, any reasonable juror could find for that party on the basis of the properly admitted evidence. *See Reeves v. Sanderson Plumbing Prods., Inc.*, 530 U.S. 133, 149–51 (2000).

The scope of the Seventh Amendment's protection is largely, though not exclusively, determined by English common law at the time of its adoption. *See Gasperini v. Ctr. for Humanities, Inc.*, 518 U.S. 415, 432–36 (1996); *see also Balt. & Carolina Line*, 295 U.S. 654. And exceptions to the Seventh Amendment's prohibition on plenary review of jury findings falling within its scope are largely confined to verdicts implicating First Amendment free speech issues. *See, e.g., Bose*, 466 U.S. at 501, 508–09 & n.27; *Harte-Hanks Commc'ns, Inc. v. Connaughton*, 491 U.S. 657, 688–89 (1989) (actual malice); *see also Cooper Indus., Inc. v. Leatherman Tool Group, Inc.*, 532 U.S. 424 (2001) (holding that in the context of a due process challenge, a jury's punitive damage award is not a "fact" protected by the Seventh Amendment).

B. THE STANDARDS GOVERNING REVIEW OF PRESERVED CLAIMS OF ERROR; PLAIN ERROR REVIEW OF UNPRESERVED CLAIMS; AND REVIEW OF JURISDICTIONAL ISSUES

As noted, apart from the described constitutional mandates, appellate review standards are probably most appropriately analyzed as legislative and common-law allocations of decisionmaking authority between trial and appellate judges. In determining the degree to which circuit courts will defer to the decisions of district court judges, legislators and the judiciary routinely refer to four broad types of review, each of which entails a different degree of appellate scrutiny. Three, *de novo*, clearly erroneous, and abuse of discretion, apply to claims of error that were raised and properly preserved in the trial court. The fourth, the plain error standard (sometimes referred to as manifest injustice or miscarriage of justice review), governs unpreserved or "forfeited" claims of error.

Appellate courts review preserved challenges to conclusions of law *de novo*, affording no deference to the trial judge's decision. *See, e.g., First Options of Chi., Inc. v. Kaplan*, 514 U.S. 938, 947–48 (1995). In contrast, challenges to a trial judge's findings of fact, which often need not be preserved, are reviewed with great deference, subject only to review for clear error. *See, e.g., Anderson v. Bessemer City*, 470 U.S. 564, 574–75 (1985). And review of preserved challenges to a trial judge's discretionary decisions, though deferential, is variable. The actual degree of scrutiny with which any particular discretionary decision is reviewed depends upon the extent to which a judge's decisionmaking authority is circumscribed by the Constitution, statutes, rules, or case precedent. *See, e.g., United States v. Taylor*, 487 U.S. 326, 335–43 (1988) (considering the bounds of a trial judge's discretion to choose between dismissal with or without prejudice to remedy a violation of the Speedy Trial Act).

If error is found pursuant to one of these three standards, the availability of a remedy will, with few exceptions, be determined pursuant to the harmless error doctrine. This doctrine requires that appellate judgments be made "without regard to errors or defects which do not affect the substantial rights of the parties." 28 U.S.C. § 2111. Thus, while an appellate court presented with a properly preserved issue may determine that a legal, factual, or discretionary error was committed, the error must be disregarded if it is harmless.

The fourth principal standard, plain error review, often, but not always, supplants *de novo*, clearly erroneous, and abuse of discretion review when a party forfeits an issue by failing to preserve it properly before the trial court. The various rules codifying this standard allow appellate courts to consider plain errors affecting the substantial rights of a complaining party though they were not brought to the trial court's attention. *See, e.g.,* FED. R. CRIM. P. 52(b); FED. R. CIV. P. 51(d)(2); FED. R. EVID. 103(d). Plain error review thus "defines a single category of forfeited-but-reversible error," *United States v. Olano*, 507 U.S. 725, 732 (1993), which, while providing an avenue for the appeal of unpreserved claims, places a heavy burden on the appealing party to demonstrate not only that an error was "obvious" and "affect[ed]" his or her "substantial rights," but also that it "seriously affects the fairness, integrity, or public reputation of judicial proceedings," *Johnson v. United States*, 520 U.S. 461, 466–67 (1997).

With respect to guilty verdicts and pleas in criminal prosecutions, failure to preserve most legal, discretionary, and factual determinations by a judge means that review will be pursuant to the plain error standard. The principal exception to this rule involves sufficiency challenges to guilty verdicts rendered in bench trials, which, in all but a few circuits, are reviewed pursuant to the standard enunciated in *Jackson v. Virginia*, 443 U.S. 307, regardless of whether the defendant preserved the challenge by seeking a judgment of acquittal in the trial court. *See* Part One, Chapter III.E.2, *infra*.

In the civil context, plain error review is infrequently sought. There are several reasons for this. First, Federal Rule of Civil Procedure 52, which allows a party to challenge the sufficiency of the evidence supporting factual findings in bench trials regardless of whether that party "requested findings, objected to them, moved to amend them, or moved for partial findings," *see* FED. R. CIV. P. 52(a)(5), renders plain error review inapplicable to such challenges. Plain error review is also irrelevant when the sufficiency of the evidence supporting a civil jury verdict is challenged, since absent a properly filed and renewed motion for a judgment as a matter of law, *see* FED. R. CIV. P. 50, appellate courts are altogether barred from considering such challenges. *See Unitherm Food Sys., Inc. v. Swift–Eckrich, Inc.*, 546 U.S. 394, 407 (2006). Finally, with respect to many other unpreserved challenges to alleged error in civil cases, the slim possibility of reversal simply does not justify the cost of attempting to surmount the significant hurdles of plain error review.

With one exception, matters that are affirmatively waived before a trial court, meaning intentionally relinquished or abandoned rather than forfeited, *see Olano*, 507 U.S. at 733, are not subject to appellate review. The exception pertains to threshold jurisdictional issues implicating the subject matter, case or controversy, and standing requirements derived from Article III of the Constitution. These issues, which are subject to *de novo* review, cannot be forfeited or waived by the parties to a suit. Indeed, because federal courts are empowered to hear only those matters falling within the judicial power defined in Article III and entrusted to them by Congress, appellate courts normally are obliged to address such threshold jurisdictional issues regardless of whether they have been raised by the parties. *Bender v. Williamsport Area Sch. Dist.*, 475 U.S. 534, 541 (1986).

C. THE FACT/LAW PARADIGM AND ITS LIMITATIONS

The principal paradigm determining how closely an appellate court will scrutinize a trial judge's decision is easily stated: findings of fact are subject to very limited review and conclusions of law are subject to *de novo* review. This simple, two-part model derives from the well-established belief that given "the respective institutional advantages of trial and appellate courts," lawmaking is best performed at the appellate level and factfinding at the trial level. *Salve Regina Coll. v. Russell*, 499 U.S. 225, 231–33 (1991). To explain how this model operates in assigning *de novo* or deferential review to a particular appellate challenge, it is necessary, first, to define its components.

Laws are rules or modes of conduct that are prescribed or formally recognized as binding by a legislature, court, or some other controlling authority. They are the governing principles pursuant to which judges or juries determine the relevance and significance of historical facts, resolve subsidiary issues, and reach the ultimate judgment in a case. They may be articulated in great detail, or they may consist of no more than very generally described normative concepts such as "reasonableness."

Historical facts, sometimes referred to as "basic" or "primary" facts, *Thompson v. Keohane*, 516 U.S. 99, 109–10 (1995), are proved, at least to some significant degree of probability, by inferences from evidence. For the most part, laws are not implicated in inferring such facts. Rather, subject only to certain very loose decisional constraints, historical facts are derived from the application of logic and human experience to the received physical, documentary, and testimonial evidence. *See Bose*, 466 U.S. at 501 n.17; *see generally* ALDISERT, THE JUDICIAL PROCESS: TEXT, MATERIALS & CASES 678–79 (1996).

Many decisions by district court judges are readily identified pursuant to these definitions and consequently fit easily within the fact/law paradigm. Thus, for example, when a trial judge identifies the legal precepts pursuant to which a question will be decided, an appellate court will have no problem characterizing the trial judge's statement of those precepts as conclusions of "law" subject to *de novo* review. Similarly, when a judge articulates the historical facts to which he or she will apply the controlling law, those statements are readily identified as findings of "fact" subject to clearly erroneous review.

In addition, when a law is defined in significant detail, trial level conclusions achieved pursuant to that law generally are easily characterized by the fact/law paradigm. In such instances, a trial judge reaches a decision pursuant to a straightforward comparison of the historical facts found to the specifically articulated requirements of the law. On appeal, a party may claim that the judge applied the wrong law, inaccurately characterized the correct law, incorrectly measured the historical facts against the correct law, or made findings of historical fact that are not supported by the evidence. The first three of these challenged judicial determinations are easily characterized as "law," the last as "fact." The fact/law paradigm thus functions as an accurate proxy for determining whether the trial court or appellate bench is better suited to perform the decisionmaking task implicated on appeal.

When, however, a controlling law is defined pursuant only to abstract legal norms or principles, trial level decisionmaking necessarily involves more than a neat comparison of fact to law. It requires, instead, a nuanced assessment or characterization of the historical facts in light of the governing legal norms. In other words, when a legal principle is only abstractly defined, it serves not as a standard against which the historical facts can be measured, but rather as something more akin to a general guide for the exercise of considered judgment. The conclusions resulting from the exercise of this sort of judgment are referred to as "mixed finding[s] of law and fact," *Bose*, 466 U.S. at 501 & n.17, and, on appeal, are commonly characterized as "mixed question[s] of law and fact," *United States v. Gaudin*, 515 U.S. 506, 512 (1995); *accord Pullman–Standard v. Swint*, 456 U.S. 273, 289 & n.19 (1982). As the labels suggest, mixed findings or mixed questions generally defy ready categorization as either law or fact. Consequently, the fact/law paradigm falters as a method for determining whether appellate review should be *de novo* or deferential.

Some simple hypotheticals illustrate both how the fact/law paradigm operates to assign deferential or *de novo* review to many appellate issues and the limitations of the paradigm when it comes to appellate challenges to mixed findings.

HYPOTHETICAL EXAMPLES: THE "FMSS" CASES

Assume that the fictitious Federal Monthly Stipend Statute (the "FMSS") states:

> An indigent person will receive a monthly stipend from the Benefits Agency if he or she appears in person at the benefits office to receive the stipend no later than the tenth day of the month in which benefits are sought. This appearance requirement will be waived only in the event of compelling, extenuating circumstances.
>
> Pursuant to this title, a putative claimant will have a cause of action for any stipend improperly withheld by the agency. The district courts of the United States shall have jurisdiction over any civil action under this title, so long as a claimant files a complaint in district court within 180 days after being denied a benefit. The 180–day limitation is a mandatory jurisdictional requirement. In a civil action under this title, any party may demand a jury trial.

1. WITHIN THE PARADIGM: A SPECIFICALLY DEFINED LAW, HISTORICAL FACTS, AND THE COMPARISON OF THE LATTER TO THE FORMER

Mary Doe, who is indigent and otherwise qualifies for a benefit stipend under the FMSS, claims that she was denied what she was due in February. The agency rejects her claim because, according to agency officials, Ms. Doe did not appear in person at the benefits office to collect her stipend on or before the tenth of the month. Ms. Doe files a complaint in district court within the 180–day jurisdictional limitation.

Assume that Ms. Doe requests a bench trial. Assume, as well, that in their arguments to the district judge, both parties present their views regarding the proper interpretation of the FMSS's appearance requirement. At the conclusion of the trial, the district judge enters judgment for the agency and issues findings of fact and conclusions of law describing the appearance requirement of the FMSS and stating that Ms. Doe did not appear in the benefits office to collect her stipend until February 11.

Both of the judge's determinations are easily characterized pursuant to the fact/law paradigm and, consequently, the governing standards of appellate review are readily identifiable. If Ms. Doe raises the issue on appeal, the appellate court will review the judge's articulation of the FMSS's appearance requirement *de novo* as a statement of law and, if error is found, will apply the harmless error doctrine to determine whether reversal is appropriate. Given the parties' arguments, the issue was clearly preserved.

With respect to the judge's conclusion regarding the date of Ms. Doe's appearance, if Ms. Doe raises the issue on appeal, the appellate court will review this factual finding pursuant to the highly deferential clearly erroneous standard of Federal Rule of Civil Procedure 52 and, again, will apply the harmless error doctrine to any error found. Pursuant to Rule 52(a)(5), challenges to the sufficiency of the evidence supporting factual findings in bench trials are not subject to a preservation requirement.

Now assume that Ms. Doe demands a jury trial, the district judge instructs the jury on the appearance requirement of the FMSS, and the jury renders a general verdict for the agency, implicitly determining that Ms. Doe did not appear in the benefits office on or before February 10.

Again, each of the determinations that might be appealed is easily characterized. The appellate court will review *de novo* a preserved claim that the trial judge's instruction did not accurately characterize the law and will apply the harmless error doctrine to any error found. If Ms. Doe moved for a judgment as a matter of law before the case was sent to the jury and properly renewed that motion after the verdict, the appellate court would also review *de novo* an appellate challenge to the sufficiency of the evidence supporting the verdict. Such a motion effectively converts what would otherwise have been a factual question, reserved to the jury by the Seventh Amendment, into a legal question regarding the sufficiency of the evidence supporting the verdict for the agency. *See Neely v. Martin K. Eby Constr. Co.*, 386 U.S. 317, 320–23 (1967). In resolving the motion, the trial judge, giving the benefit of all reasonable inferences to the agency, would have decided only whether, as a matter of law, the properly admitted evidence would allow any reasonable juror to find for the agency. *See Reeves*, 530 U.S. at 149–51. The appellate court, giving no deference to the trial judge's legal conclusion, would review the matter *de novo*, examining the record evidence pursuant to the same standard applied by the trial judge. *See id.* at 151–54.

2. STILL WITHIN THE PARADIGM: ABSTRACT LAWS

Looking to the same hypothetical statute, assume that at trial Ms. Doe's son testifies, without contradiction, that on February 11 he delivered to the agency a note from Ms. Doe indicating that she was unable to pick up her stipend because she was hospitalized.

- If the judge rules in a bench trial or instructs a jury that illness cannot be a "compelling, extenuating circumstance" unless a claimant offers medical evidence to prove that she could not meet the appearance requirement, this is a statement of law.

- If the judge rules in a bench trial or instructs a jury that a claimant can preserve her right to receive a stipend if she gives "timely notice" of compelling, extenuating circumstances to the agency, this is also a statement of law.

- And, if the trial judge, relying on the normative standard of fairness, rules in a bench trial or instructs a jury that "timely notice" means notice that provides "fair warning in light of all of the circumstances," this, too, is a statement of law.

Each of these determinations constitutes a judicial gloss on the FMSS that easily falls on the law side of the fact/law paradigm. In contrast to the trial judge's articulations of the FMSS's appearance requirement referred to in the first two hypotheticals, these statements do not parrot the literal text of the statute. Nevertheless, they are statements of controlling legal principles defining the relevance of historical facts to the decisionmaking process by which Ms. Doe's claim will be resolved.

If challenges to these statements of law are properly preserved, they will be reviewed *de novo*. If the losing party in a jury trial failed to object before the trial court, Federal Rule of Civil Procedure 51(d)(2) would allow that party to seek plain error review of the instructions. If the losing party in a bench trial failed to preserve the issue, appellate review of the judge's characterizations of the law would also be for plain error. Pursuant to either *de novo* or plain error review, the appellate court will assess the accuracy of these statements by reference to the language and structure of the FMSS, the case law interpreting it and analogous statutes, and any compelling legislative history.

If review is *de novo* and the appellate court finds error, the error is unlikely to be harmless, since each of these statements of law is relevant to whether the agency acted improperly in failing to waive the appearance requirement. If the claim was not properly preserved, the multipart test for determining whether any potential error is plain and merits reversal will prove a more difficult hurdle.

3. THE LIMITS OF THE PARADIGM: A MIXED QUESTION RESULTING FROM THE APPLICATION OF AN ABSTRACT LAW TO HISTORICAL FACTS

As defined in the previous hypothetical, "timely notice" exemplifies the sort of abstract legal norm, application of which results in a mixed finding at the trial level and a mixed question of law and fact on appeal. To illustrate, assume again that Ms. Doe's son testifies, during a bench trial, that on February 11 he delivered a note to the agency indicating that his mother could not pick up her February stipend because she was hospitalized. But assume, also, that during this trial he testifies that he provided the agency with a copy of medical records demonstrating that Ms. Doe had indeed been hospitalized since before the first of February. Assume, as well, that copies of the medical records were properly admitted into evidence.

During the trial, the judge describes his view of the FMSS and relevant common-law precedent, stating:

- Hospitalization is always a compelling, extenuating circumstance.

- A claimant can preserve her right to receive a stipend if she gives "timely notice" of hospitalization.

- "Timely notice" means notice that gives "fair warning in light of all the circumstances."

At the conclusion of the trial, the judge renders judgment for Ms. Doe and issues findings of fact and conclusions of law incorporating his originally expressed views of the FMSS and, in addition, finds:

- Ms. Doe was hospitalized during the first 10 days of February.

- Ms. Doe's son delivered the note and medical records on February 11.

- In light of the fact that Ms. Doe's note and supporting medical records were delivered to the agency only one day after the tenth-of-the-month appearance deadline, Ms. Doe gave "fair warning" to the agency that was "timely."

The standards of review applicable to all but the last of the trial judge's six determinations are easily identified pursuant to the fact/law paradigm. The first three statements are conclusions of law describing principles governing resolution of Ms. Doe's case. Challenges to these statements will be reviewed *de novo* if properly preserved. The fourth and fifth statements are findings of historical fact based on documentary evidence, as well as the trial judge's assessment of the credibility of Ms. Doe's son. As such, they are subject to clearly erroneous review under Federal Rule of Civil Procedure 52.

The proper characterization of the last conclusion is more difficult, however. This is a classic mixed finding arising from the application of an abstractly defined legal standard, timely notice, to the facts of a particular case. It is not intuitively obvious whether the trial court's conclusion that the actions of Ms. Doe's son gave fair warning to the agency, and thus amounted to timely notice, is a finding of fact or a conclusion of law. In other words, this conclusion cannot be readily characterized pursuant to the fact/law paradigm. With respect to such mixed questions of law and fact, courts must explicitly address the functional considerations from which the fact/law paradigm is derived in order to determine whether the question is best left largely to the trial court through deferential review or is more appropriately decided by the appellate bench pursuant to *de novo* review.

D. THE FUNCTIONAL APPROACH: THE THEORY INFORMING THE PARADIGM

Legal principles that result in mixed findings at the trial level and mixed questions on appeal are generally broad, often fluid, sometimes common sense concepts that cannot be "reduced to a neat set of legal rules." *Ornelas v. United States*, 517 U.S. 690, 695–96 (1996); *see also Harte-Hanks*, 491 U.S. at 686. The content of these principles is not revealed by simple reference to a literal text. Rather, these rules acquire meaning only through application to the circumstances of particular cases. *See Harte–Hanks*, 491 U.S. at 686; *see also, e.g., City of Monterey v. Del Monte Dunes at Monterey, Ltd.*, 526 U.S. 687, 720–21 (1999) (substantial advancement of legitimate public interests as defined by regulatory takings doctrine); *Ornelas*, 517 U.S. at 697 ("reasonable suspicion" to stop and "probable cause" to conduct a warrantless car search); *Cooter & Gell v. Hartmarx Corp.*, 496 U.S. 384, 401–02 (1990) (sanctions under Federal Rule of Civil Procedure 11); *Thornburg v. Gingles*, 478 U.S. 30, 77–79 (1986) (vote dilution under § 2 of the Voting Rights Act); *Bose*, 466 U.S. at 501–03 (actual malice).

Such fluid principles can be more precisely defined through legislative enactment and, as noted, may gain meaning through repeated judicial interpretation, *see, e.g., Pierce v. Underwood*, 487 U.S. 552, 562 (1988) (quoting Professor Rosenberg's description of how, over the years, judicial decisions may allow "a formless problem to take shape ... and the contours of a guiding principle to emerge"). Thus, for example, a series of judicial decisions might establish that under the hypothetical FMSS, notice almost always constitutes fair warning (and is therefore timely) if it is given on or before the statute's tenth-of-the-month appearance deadline, but rarely constitutes fair warning if it is given after that deadline. Such precedent would create a particularly defined, binding legal standard. Application of the timeliness norm would thereby be reduced to the same type of straightforward comparison of fact to law required by application of the FMSS's tenth-of-the-month appearance requirement.

When, however, fluid principles have not been or cannot be specifically defined, the Supreme Court often looks to the functional considerations from which the fact/law paradigm is derived to determine the appropriate standard of review. In other words, the Court looks to which judicial actor is better suited, "as a matter of the sound administration of justice," to decide the matter. *Miller v. Fenton*, 474 U.S. 104, 114 (1985).

Pursuant to this functional analysis, the Court favors deferential review when "it appears that the district court is 'better positioned' than the appellate court to decide the issue in question." *Salve Regina Coll.*, 499 U.S. at 233 (quoting *Miller*, 474 U.S. at 114). "When, for example, the issue involves the credibility of witnesses and therefore turns largely on an evaluation of demeanor," deferential review is favored. *Miller*, 474 U.S. at 114; *see also id.* at 116–17. In such situations, "there are compelling ... [reasons] for leaving the process of applying law to fact to the trial court and according its determinations presumptive weight." *Id.* at 114. The Court also favors deferential review when "probing appellate scrutiny will not contribute to the clarity of legal doctrine." *Salve Regina Coll.*, 499 U.S. at 233.

De novo review is favored when there is a perceived need for the appellate courts "to maintain control of, and to clarify ... legal principles." *Ornelas*, 517 U.S. at 697. And such a need is often recognized when the interests at issue are deemed too important to trust to the judgment of a single district judge constrained by "the logistical burdens" of the trial process, *Salve Regina Coll.*, 499 U.S. at 231–32, but rather are thought better addressed through the "reflective dialogue" and "collective judgment" characteristic of appellate courts, *id.* at 232. As the Supreme Court explained in *Bose Corp. v. Consumers Union of United States, Inc.*:

> A finding of fact in some cases is inseparable from the principles through which it was deduced. At some point, the reasoning by which a fact is "found" crosses the line between application of those ordinary principles of logic and common experience which are ordinarily entrusted to the finder of fact into the realm of a legal rule upon which the reviewing court must exercise its own independent judgment. Where the line is drawn varies according to the nature of the substantive law at issue. *Regarding certain largely factual questions in some areas of the law, the stakes – in terms of impact on future cases and future conduct – are too great to entrust them finally to the judgment of the trier of fact.*

466 U.S. at 501 n.17 (emphasis added).

The issue in *Bose* was whether a district judge's finding of "actual malice" pursuant to *New York Times Co. v. Sullivan*, 376 U.S. 254 (1964), should have been reviewed for clear error, as a finding of fact, or *de novo*, as a conclusion of law. The district judge found that the testimony of the defendant's key witness regarding the truthfulness of the disparaging statement at issue was not credible and that the plaintiff, Bose Corporation, had proved by clear and convincing evidence that the defendant had published the statement with knowledge that it was false, or with reckless disregard of its falsity. *Bose*, 466 U.S. at 490–91, 497–98.

On review, the Supreme Court first stated that the court of appeals had correctly declined to second-guess the trial judge's credibility findings. *Id.* at 500. "[C]redibility determinations are reviewed under the clearly-erroneous standard because the trier of fact has had the 'opportunity to observe the demeanor of the witnesses.'" *Harte-Hanks*, 491 U.S. at 688 (quoting *Bose*, 466 U.S. at 499–500).

With respect to the determination of "actual malice," however, the Court concluded that review should be *de novo*. *See Bose*, 466 U.S. at 514. The Court pointed to the common-law heritage of the actual malice rule, which assigned judges "an especially broad role ... in applying it to specific factual situations." *Id.* at 502. The Court also emphasized that the content of the rule is "not revealed simply by its literal text, but rather is given meaning through the evolutionary process of common-law adjudication." *Id.* However, the linchpin of the Court's analysis was a detailed review of the case law demonstrating that "the constitutional values protected by the rule make it imperative that judges – and in some cases judges of [the Supreme] Court – make sure that it is correctly applied." *Id.; see also id.* at 503–11. As the opinion explained, the "Court's role in marking out the limits of ... [constitutional] standard[s] through the process of case-by-case adjudication ... has been vitally important in cases involving restrictions on the freedom of speech protected by the First Amendment, particularly in those cases in which it is contended that the communication in issue is within one of the few classes of 'unprotected' speech," *id.* at 503, including "[l]ibelous speech," "fighting words," "incitement to riot," "obscenity," and "child pornography," *id.* at 504.

In *Miller v. Fenton*, 474 U.S. 104, the Court, citing *Bose*, again made clear that the perceived importance of the interests at issue can be a critical factor in determining that *de novo* review of a mixed question is appropriate. The question before the *Miller* Court was whether a state court determination that a criminal defendant's confession was voluntary was an issue of fact, and thus entitled to a presumption of correctness under the then-controlling federal habeas statute, or a question of law subject to *de novo* review. *Id.* at 105–06. In resolving the issue, the Court first stated that "an unbroken line of cases, coming to [it] both on direct appeal and on review of applications to lower federal courts for a writ of habeas corpus, forecloses the ... conclusion that the 'voluntariness' of a confession merits something less than independent federal consideration." *Id.* at 112.

The Court then turned to functional considerations to explain why, contrary to the circuit court's conclusion, recent Supreme Court decisions characterizing various issues as matters of fact for purposes of habeas review had not undermined the force of the cited precedent. *Id.* It explained:

> At least in those instances in which Congress has not spoken and in which the issue falls somewhere between a pristine legal standard and a simple historical fact, the fact/law distinction at times has turned on a determination that, as a matter of the sound administration of justice, one judicial actor is better positioned than another to decide the issue in question. Where, for example, as with proof of actual malice in First Amendment libel cases, the relevant legal principle can be given meaning only through its application to the particular circumstances of a case, the Court has been reluctant to give the trier of fact's conclusions presumptive force and, in so doing, strip a federal appellate court of its primary function as an expositor of law.

Id. at 114. Describing how such functional considerations supported its decision not "to abandon the ... longstanding position that the ultimate question of the admissibility of a confession merits treatment as a legal inquiry requiring plenary federal review," *id.* at 115, the Court emphasized that, with respect to confessions coming from the states, it had "consistently looked to the Due Process Clause of the Fourteenth Amendment to test admissibility," *id.* at 116. As the Court explained, "[t]he locus of the right is significant because it reflects the ... consistently held view that the admissibility of a confession turns as much on whether the techniques for extracting the statements, as applied to *this* suspect, are compatible with a system that presumes innocence and assures that a conviction will not be secured by inquisitorial means as on whether the defendant's will was in fact overborne." *Id.* "This hybrid quality of the voluntariness inquiry, subsuming, as it does, a complex of values, itself militates against treating the question as one of simple historical fact." *Id.* In conclusion, the Court emphasized the role that *de novo* federal review plays in protecting constitutional rights when the prosecution secures a conviction through a defendant's own confession. *Id.* at 117–18.

Although the decision in *Miller* gave significant weight to the constitutionally protected status of the right against self-incrimination, the Court also made clear that *de novo* review of a mixed question is not inevitable merely because a constitutional right is at issue. When "the issue involves the credibility of witnesses and therefore turns largely on an evaluation of demeanor, there are compelling and familiar justifications for leaving the process of applying law to fact to the trial court." *Id.* at 114. It is "[p]rincipally for that reason," the Court observed, that "juror bias merits treatment as a 'factual issue' ... notwithstanding the intimate connection between such determinations and the constitutional guarantee of an impartial jury." *Id.* at 114–15; *see also Keohane*, 516 U.S. at 111 (explaining that the trial court's superior capacity to resolve credibility issues had prompted the Court to type questions of juror bias and competency as factual issues under the then-controlling federal habeas statute).

In sum, the label "mixed question of law and fact" does not imply a particular standard of review. It is descriptive, not normative. It simply alerts a reviewing court that the level of deference owed a trial judge's decision cannot be identified pursuant to the fact/law paradigm. Thus, in addressing mixed questions, a reviewing court may have to consider the nature of the decisional process implicated in light of the respective institutional strengths of the trial and appellate courts in order to determine whether the trial or appellate bench is better suited to make the decision and, consequently, whether *de novo* or deferential review would better serve the fair administration of justice.

E. DISCRETIONARY DECISIONS: MIXED QUESTIONS OF LAW AND FACT AND THE ABUSE OF DISCRETION STANDARD OF REVIEW

A decision committed to a trial judge's discretion is a decision with respect to which Congress or the courts have decided that there is no single right or wrong answer, but rather a range of acceptable choices. *See Zervos v. Verizon N.Y., Inc.*, 252 F.3d 163, 168–69 (2d Cir. 2001); *see also Wheat v. United States*, 486 U.S. 153, 164 (1988). Consequently, the legal rules governing discretionary decisions are, almost by definition, broadly defined, fluid concepts that achieve meaning through application to particular factual scenarios. The appeal of a discretionary decision thus can fairly be characterized as raising a mixed question, albeit one with respect to which review pursuant to the abuse of discretion standard is required.

If neither statutory directive nor existing judicial precedent clearly indicates that the application of an abstract legal precept is committed to a trial court's discretion, an appellate court will be required to decide, as with many mixed questions, which court is better suited to resolve the issue. In such a case, if a court declines to review *de novo*, it will apply either the clearly erroneous or abuse of discretion standard. Both of the latter standards are deferential, but, as explained in subsequent chapters, the degree of appellate scrutiny allowed pursuant to abuse of discretion review is more variable than that permitted pursuant to clearly erroneous review.

Cooter & Gell v. Hartmarx Corp. is a good example of a case in which the Supreme Court undertook a mixed question analysis to determine whether abuse of discretion review was appropriate. In that case, the Court addressed several challenges to a district judge's decision to impose sanctions under the then-existing version of Rule 11 of the Federal Rules of Civil Procedure. *Cooter & Gell*, 496 U.S. at 388, 390. Under the Rule, an attorney's signature on a pleading constituted a certificate that she had read it and, based on "reasonable inquiry," believed it to be well-grounded in fact and legally tenable. *Id.* at 391–92. The district court found that the allegations in petitioner's complaint were "completely baseless" and imposed sanctions. *Id.* at 389–90.

The Supreme Court affirmed in relevant part, rejecting the claim "that the Court of Appeals did not apply a sufficiently rigorous standard in reviewing the District Court's imposition of Rule 11 sanctions." *Id.* at

399; *see also id.* at 405. In reaching this decision, the Court first noted that Rule 11 determinations involve the consideration of three types of issues:

> The court must consider factual questions regarding the nature of the attorney's prefiling inquiry and the factual basis of the pleading or other paper. Legal issues are raised in considering whether a pleading is warranted by existing law or a good faith argument for changing the law and whether the attorney's conduct violated Rule 11. Finally, the district court must exercise its discretion to tailor an appropriate sanction.

Id. at 399. The Court then explained that while a majority of circuits applied the deferential abuse of discretion standard to all of these issues, two circuits reviewed *de novo* a "district court's legal conclusions in Rule 11 proceedings." *Id.* at 399–401.

In determining that the deferential abuse of discretion standard should be applied to all aspects of a Rule 11 determination, the Court found that, "as a matter of the sound administration of justice, deference [is] owed to the judicial actor ... better positioned ... to decide the issue in question." *Id.* at 403. It noted that "[a] district court's ruling that a litigant's position is factually well grounded and legally tenable for Rule 11 purposes is ... fact specific," *id.*, and requires the trial court to make "some assessment of the signer's credibility," *id.* at 402. It also observed that Rule 11's policy goals highlight the district court's unique competence to resolve Rule 11 issues: "The district court is best acquainted with the local bar's litigation practices and thus best situated to determine when a sanction is warranted to serve Rule 11's goal of specific and general deterrence." *Id.* at 404. Consequently, the Court concluded, district courts are best suited to make these determinations.

The *Cooter* Court acknowledged that "some variation in the application of a standard based on reasonableness is inevitable." *Id.* at 405. But it concluded that *de novo* review of such issues can serve little purpose, since "[f]act-bound resolutions cannot be made uniform through appellate review, de novo or otherwise. An appellate court's review of whether a legal position was reasonable or plausible enough under the circumstances is unlikely to establish clear guidelines for lower courts; nor will it clarify the underlying principles of law." *Id.* Accordingly, the Court found abuse of discretion review appropriate. *Id.* at 404; *see also Pierce,* 487 U.S. at 559–63 (weighing similar considerations in determining that the abuse of discretion standard, rather than *de novo* review, governs the appeal of attorneys' fee awards).

F. THE MIXED QUESTION IN THE FINAL "FMSS" HYPOTHETICAL

Returning to the final FMSS hypothetical, it should now be easier to determine whether *de novo* or deferential review appropriately governs the trial judge's conclusion that Ms. Doe gave fair warning to the agency and that her notice was thus timely. Although a determination of what constitutes timely notice does not rest primarily on evaluations of witness demeanor or other courtroom events that a trial judge is better positioned than an appellate court to assess, it also does not involve interests or principles necessitating appellate control over the development of the law. No constitutional rights are implicated, and the impact of any particular determination of timeliness on future cases and conduct appears minimal given the almost unlimited range of potential factual scenarios that could give rise to the question. Consequently, deferential review, whether for clear error or abuse of discretion, seems most appropriate.

G. A FINAL QUALIFYING COMMENT ON REVIEW OF MIXED QUESTIONS

Although the mixed question concept is critical to a complete understanding of the fact/law paradigm and the functional analysis underlying it, in practice there is often little debate about the standard of appellate review applicable to a particular mixed question. This is in part because review of many mixed questions is controlled by constitutional constraints that are largely independent of the fact/law paradigm. Thus, as noted in Part One, Chapter I.A, *supra*, appellate review of not guilty verdicts, which often result from a judge's or jury's application of only generally or abstractly defined laws to historical facts, is altogether barred by the Constitution's Double Jeopardy Clause. *See Martin Linen Supply*, 430 U.S. at 571. In addition, review of guilty verdicts is significantly defined by the Trial by Jury Clauses of the Sixth Amendment and Article III, Section 2 of the Constitution, as well as by the Constitution's due process guarantee. *See generally Jackson*, 443 U.S. 307; *see also* Part One, Chapter III.E, *infra*. And in civil cases, where again the governing laws may be only abstractly defined, the Seventh Amendment often limits appellate consideration of a jury's findings of fact and the conclusions resulting from its application of law to those facts to the legal question of whether there was sufficient evidence to send the case to the jury in the first place. *See Weisgram*, 528 U.S. at 448. Moreover, mixed questions that are assigned by statute, rule, or common law to a trial judge for the exercise of her discretion are, by definition, subject to the variable, though generally deferential, abuse of discretion standard of review.

Finally, with respect to many of the remaining mixed findings, which court is better suited to decide the issue (and therefore which standard of review controls) has often been resolved by settled precedent. *See, e.g., Ornelas*, 517 U.S. at 697 (holding that "reasonable suspicion" to stop and "probable cause" to perform a warrantless car search, two mixed questions, are reviewed *de novo*). Of course, until a particular mixed question is typed a question of law, a question of fact, or a discretionary matter by Congress or the Supreme Court, different standards may apply in different circuits. *See, e.g., Pierce*, 487 U.S. at 558 (describing the predecision, intercircuit conflict regarding the standard of review applicable to "substantial justification" determinations for purposes of Equal Access to Justice Act fee awards). Consequently, circuit- and subject-specific research may prove critical when a mixed question is raised on appeal.

Chapter II

CLEARLY ERRONEOUS REVIEW OF JUDICIAL FACTFINDING

It is well settled that, as between district court judges and the appellate bench, "[f]actfinding is the basic responsibility of [the] district courts." *Pullman-Standard v. Swint*, 456 U.S. 273, 291–92 (1982). Consequently, most findings of fact that are not reserved to civil juries by the Seventh Amendment, or criminal juries by the Trial by Jury Clauses of the Sixth Amendment and Article III, Section 2 of the Constitution, are subject to the deferential "clearly erroneous" standard of review. The exception of note pertains to judge-made factual findings supporting criminal verdicts in bench trials. Those supporting not guilty verdicts are shielded from review by the Double Jeopardy Clause, *see United States v. Martin Linen Supply* Co., 430 U.S. 564, 571 (1977), while those supporting guilty verdicts generally are reviewed pursuant to the standard articulated in *Jackson v. Virginia*, 443 U.S. 307 (1979); *see* Part One, Chapter III.E.2, *infra*.

The clearly erroneous standard is codified in Federal Rule of Civil Procedure 52, which provides:

> Findings of fact, whether based on oral or other evidence, must not be set aside unless clearly erroneous, and the reviewing court must give due regard to the trial court's opportunity to judge the witnesses' credibility.

FED. R. CIV. P. 52(a)(6). By its terms, this standard applies only to civil judgments issued in actions "tried on the facts without a jury or with an advisory jury" and to "findings and conclusions" issued in support of actions "granting or refusing an interlocutory injunction." FED. R. CIV. P. 52(a)(1), (2). However, the standard is understood to apply to "any other form of factfinding" performed by judges in civil proceedings. *Maine v. Taylor*, 477 U.S. 131, 144–45 (1986). Moreover, the Supreme Court has noted that, although "[t]he Federal Rules of Criminal Procedure contain no counterpart to [Rule 52(a)(6)] ... the considerations underlying [the Rule] – the demands of judicial efficiency, the expertise developed by trial judges, and the importance of first-hand observation – all apply with full force in the criminal context, at least with respect to factual questions having nothing to do with [the ultimate conclusion of] guilt. Accordingly, the 'clearly erroneous' standard of review long has been applied to nonguilt findings of fact by district courts in criminal cases."

Id. at 145; *see also Hernandez v. New York*, 500 U.S. 352, 365–66 (1991) (plurality opinion).

Pursuant to the clearly erroneous standard, a trial judge's findings of fact are presumptively correct. *See Bose Corp. v. Consumers Union of U.S., Inc.*, 466 U.S. 485, 500 (1984). This presumption "recognizes and rests upon the unique opportunity afforded the trial court judge to evaluate the credibility of witnesses and to weigh the evidence." *Inwood Labs., Inc. v. Ives Labs., Inc.*, 456 U.S. 844, 855 (1982). But "[t]he rationale for deference to the original finder of fact is not limited to the superiority of the trial judge's position to make determinations of credibility." *Anderson v. Bessemer City*, 470 U.S. 564, 574 (1985). The comparative expertise of district court and appellate judges, as well as the cost of duplicative appellate decisionmaking are also important considerations. As the Supreme Court has explained:

> The trial judge's major role is the determination of fact, and with experience in fulfilling that role comes expertise. Duplication of the trial judge's efforts in the court of appeals would very likely contribute only negligibly to the accuracy of fact determination at a huge cost in diversion of judicial resources. In addition, the parties to a case on appeal have already been forced to concentrate their energies and resources on persuading the trial judge that their account of the facts is the correct one; requiring them to persuade three more judges at the appellate level is requiring too much. As the Court has stated in a different context, the trial on the merits should be the "main event" . . . rather than a "tryout on the road."

Id. at 574–75. Judge Traynor rather succinctly made a similar point when he observed:

> The problem is that the facts are forever gone and no scientific method of inquiry can ever be devised to produce facsimiles that bring the past to life. The judicial process deals with probabilities, not facts, and we must therefore be on guard against making fact skepticism our main preoccupation.

Traynor, *Fact Skepticism and the Judicial Process*, 106 U. Pa. L. Rev. 635, 636 (1958). The clearly erroneous standard ensures that the task of fact approximation does not become the main preoccupation of the appellate bench.

"Although the meaning of the phrase 'clearly erroneous' is not immediately apparent," the Supreme Court has established certain principles governing its application. *Bessemer City*, 470 U.S. at 573. "[F]oremost" among these is the rule, articulated in *United States v. U.S. Gypsum Co.*, 333 U.S. 364 (1948), that "a finding is 'clearly erroneous' when although there is evidence to support it, the reviewing court on the entire evidence is left with the definite and firm conviction that a mistake has been committed." *Bessemer City*, 470 U.S. at 573. In applying the *Gypsum* standard, a reviewing court should "not reverse a lower court's finding of fact simply because [it] would have decided the case differently." *Easley v. Cromartie*, 532 U.S. 234, 242 (2001). "The reviewing court oversteps the bounds of its duty under [Rule 52(a)(6)] if it undertakes to duplicate the role of the lower court." *Bessemer City*, 470 U.S. at 573. Consequently, "[w]here there are two permissible views of the evidence, the factfinder's choice between them cannot be clearly erroneous." *Id.* at 574.

The Court also instructs that "the presumption of correctness that attaches to factual findings is stronger in some cases than in others." *Bose*, 466 U.S. at 500. "The conclusiveness of a finding of fact depends on the nature of the materials on which the finding is based." *Id.* at 500 n.16. Thus, as the Court describes it, the standard of review "does not change" regardless of whether a trial was long and complex or short and straightforward, "but the likelihood that the appellate court will rely on the presumption tends to increase when trial judges have lived with the controversy for weeks or months instead of just a few hours." *Id.* at 500; *see also Easley*, 532 U.S. at 243.

Similarly, though "[t]he same 'clearly erroneous' standard applies to findings based on documentary evidence as to those based entirely on oral testimony, ... the presumption [of correctness] has lesser force in the former situation than in the latter." *Bose*, 466 U.S. at 500. This is so because "only the trial judge can be aware of the variations in demeanor and tone of voice that bear so heavily on the listener's understanding of and belief in what is said." *Bessemer City*, 470 U.S. at 575. Consequently, if "a trial judge's finding is based on his decision to credit the testimony of one of two or more witnesses, each of whom has told a coherent and facially plausible story that is not contradicted by extrinsic evidence, that finding, if not internally inconsistent, can virtually never be clear error." *Id.* However, because "factors other than demeanor and inflection go into the decision whether or not to believe a witness," credibility determinations are not entirely insulated from appellate review. *Id.* Thus, for example, if "[d]ocuments or objective evidence ... contradict the witness' story" or if testimony is so "internally inconsistent or implausible on its face that a reasonable factfinder would not credit it[,] ... the court of appeals may well find clear error even in a finding purportedly based on a credibility determination." *Id.*

Finally, the Supreme Court has repeatedly stated that the clearly erroneous standard " 'does not inhibit an appellate court's power to correct ... a finding of fact that is predicated on a misunderstanding of the governing rule of law.' " *Thornburg v. Gingles*, 478 U.S. 30, 79 (1986) (quoting *Bose*, 466 U.S. at 501); *see also Pullman–Standard*, 456 U.S. at 287; *United States v. Miss. Valley Generating Co.*, 364 U.S. 520, 526 (1961). "[I]f the trial court bases its findings upon a mistaken impression of applicable legal principles, the reviewing court is not bound by the clearly erroneous standard." *Inwood Labs.*, 456 U.S. at 855 n.15. Rather, appellate courts exercise plenary review in determining whether a trial judge evaluated the evidence pursuant to an inapplicable or incorrectly articulated legal standard.

Thus, for example, factual findings based on an incorrect burden or standard of proof are not protected by clear error review. As the Court has explained, clearly erroneous review does not describe "a degree of certainty" to which some fact must be proven in the first instance. *Concrete Pipe & Prods. of Cal., Inc. v. Constr. Laborers Pension Trust for S. Cal.*, 508 U.S. 602, 622–23 (1993). Rather, that first instance degree of certainty, pursuant to which "the factfinder must evaluate the raw evidence," is prescribed by various standards of proof, including "preponderance of the evidence," "clear and convincing," and "beyond a reasonable doubt." *Id.* Clearly erroneous review, in contrast, describes the degree of certainty with which the appellate court must be able to conclude that the "factfinder in the first instance made a mistake in concluding that a fact had been proven *under the applicable standard of proof.*" *Id.* (emphasis added); *cf. Anderson v. Liberty Lobby, Inc.*, 477 U.S. 242, 252 (1986) (appellate review of summary judgment and directed verdict rulings incorporates controlling standard of proof).

Given the considerations informing the clearly erroneous standard's presumption of correctness, when an appellate court determines that a finding of fact is based on an incorrect legal principle or standard of proof, a remand to allow the district judge to find the facts under the correct legal standard is the typical remedy. *See Pullman–Standard*, 456 U.S. at 291–92. An appellate court will be justified in finding facts itself only when the record, viewed in light of the correct legal standard, admits of a single resolution of the factual issue. *See id.* The same considerations counsel remand when a trial court fails to make findings on a material issue. *See id.* at 291–92 & n.22.

Chapter III

DE NOVO REVIEW OF CONCLUSIONS OF LAW: A SAMPLING OF SUBSTANTIVE STANDARDS

In contrast to district courts, courts of appeals "are structurally suited to the collaborative judicial process that promotes decisional accuracy." *Salve Regina Coll. v. Russell*, 499 U.S. 225, 232 (1991). "District judges preside alone over fast-paced trials," *id.* at 231, whereas "courts of appeals employ multijudge panels that permit [the] reflective dialogue and collective judgment" that is critical to the thoughtful development of the law, *id.* at 232. Consequently, as the Supreme Court has explained, "[i]ndependent appellate review of legal issues best serves the dual goals of doctrinal coherence and economy of judicial administration." *Id.* at 231.

While "an efficient and sensitive appellate court ... will ... consider" the trial judge's legal analysis, *id.* at 232, it is not bound by it. This is true whether the issue under review involves federal, state, or foreign law. *See id.* at 231–35 (district judge's federal and state law determinations reviewed *de novo*); FED. R. CIV. P. 44.1 (district judge's foreign law determinations reviewed as questions of law). Plenary review allows federal appellate courts to achieve their principal functions of dispute resolution (through error correction in individual cases) and lawmaking (through declaration of legal principles). Trial judges contribute to the development of the law when appellate courts endorse the reasoning of their decisions, but appellate judges owe no deference to that reasoning.

The authority of the federal courts of appeals to decide legal issues is not absolute, however. The intermediate appellate courts are bound to follow the precedent of the Supreme Court, *see Thurston Motor Lines, Inc. v. Jordan K. Rand, Ltd.*, 460 U.S. 533, 535 (1983) (per curiam), and, with respect to matters of state law, the interpretations of the highest court of the state, *see Comm'r of Internal Revenue v. Estate of Bosch*, 387 U.S. 456, 465 (1967). Moreover, "[i]f a court, employing traditional tools of statutory construction [to interpret federal legislation], ascertains that Congress had an intention on the precise question at issue, that intention is the law and must be given effect." *Chevron U.S.A., Inc. v. Natural Res. Def. Council, Inc.*, 467 U.S. 837, 843 n.9 (1984). Appellate decision-making is also constrained by various doctrines of judicial restraint, including *stare decisis, see, e.g., Flood v. Kuhn*, 407 U.S. 258 (1972), law-of-the-circuit and law-of-the-case, *see, e.g., LaShawn A. v. Barry*, 87 F.3d 1389 (D.C. Cir. 1996) (en banc), and collateral estoppel, *see, e.g., Allen v. McCurry*, 449 U.S. 90 (1980). Finally, the courts of appeals obviously are bound to decide cases within constitutional limits.

The essence of *de novo* review is easily understood: presented with a legal issue, an appellate court decides the question anew, according no deference to the trial court's resolution of the matter. This explains little, however, about how *de novo* review works in practice. This is because *de novo* review requires nothing more of an appellate court than that it decide legal issues as would the first level decisionmaker. In other words, as a standard, *de novo* review is without unique content. It adds nothing of its own to the appellate process, but rather simply mandates that an appellate court apply the substantive standards governing resolution of the legal question at issue. Obviously, these substantive standards are as varied as the law itself. *De novo* review is thus endlessly plastic.

This does not mean, however, that a practical sense of the standard is impossible to convey. The discussion that follows clarifies the *de novo* standard by highlighting how appellate courts apply certain important substantive and procedural legal principles underpinning trial level dispute resolution. Subsection A addresses subject matter jurisdiction and Article III standing, two critical prerequisites to federal court action. Subsection B reviews the law governing motions to dismiss for failure to state a claim. And, subsections C through E describe the primary procedural mechanisms – summary judgment, judgment as a matter of law, and judgment of acquittal – that facilitate judicial resolution of claims, civil and criminal, with respect to which there are no material issues of fact appropriate for resolution by a factfinder. The discussion obviously does not cover all of the substantive principles that inform *de novo* review, and it is weighted more toward civil than criminal litigation. But the areas reviewed are important in federal jurisprudence and offer a good sense of the breadth of analysis encompassed by *de novo* review.

A. SUBJECT MATTER JURISDICTION AND CONSTITUTIONAL STANDING IN CIVIL CASES: THE UNWAIVABLE ARTICLE III PREREQUISITES TO FEDERAL JUDICIAL REVIEW

The inferior "[f]ederal courts are not courts of general jurisdiction; they have only the power that is authorized by Article III of the Constitution and the statutes enacted by Congress pursuant thereto." *Bender v. Williamsport Area Sch. Dist.*, 475 U.S. 534, 541 (1986); *see also Exxon Mobil Corp. v. Allapattah Servs., Inc.*, 545 U.S. 546, 552 (2005). Subject matter jurisdiction, which is defined by Article III and the various authorizing provisions enacted by Congress, and constitutional standing, which is derived directly from the "case or controversy" requirement of Article III, Section 2, Clause 1, are the essential, unwaivable prerequisites to the exercise of federal judicial power. *See Ins. Corp. of Ireland, Ltd. v. Compagnie des Bauxites de Guinee*, 456 U.S. 694, 701–02 (1982) (subject matter jurisdiction); *United States v. Hays*, 515 U.S. 737, 742–43 (1995) (standing). Unless the record affirmatively demonstrates subject matter jurisdiction and standing, the presumption is that a federal court lacks jurisdiction. *See DaimlerChrysler Corp. v. Cuno*, ___ U.S. ___, ___, 126 S. Ct. 1854, 1861 n.3 (2006); *Bender*, 475 U.S. at 546. This inviolate rule ensures the "separation and equilibration of powers, restraining the courts from acting at certain times, and even restraining them from acting permanently regarding certain subjects." *Steel Co. v. Citizens for a Better Env't*, 523 U.S. 83, 101 (1998).

Although Article III standing is often characterized as an issue of subject matter jurisdiction, *see, e.g., DaimlerChrysler*, ___ U.S. at ___ , 126 S. Ct. at 1861 n.3; *Bender*, 475 U.S. at 541–42; *Young Am. Corp. v. Affiliated Computer Servs., (ACS) Inc.*, 424 F.3d 840, 843 (8th Cir. 2005); *Ctr. for Reprod. Law & Policy v. Bush*, 304 F.3d 183, 193 (2d Cir. 2002), the two doctrines involve different inquiries and serve distinct purposes. A party may be able to show that a court has subject matter jurisdiction, but be unable to demonstrate Article III standing, and vice versa. Nevertheless, the shared role that subject matter jurisdiction and Article III standing play in defining and restricting federal judicial power gives rise to several procedural practices common to the resolution of both types of issues.

First, separation of powers concerns generally require federal courts to resolve questions regarding subject matter jurisdiction and Article III standing before ruling on the merits of a claim. *See Steel Co.*, 523 U.S. at 98–101. As the Court in *Steel Co. v. Citizens for a Better Environment* explained, for a "court to pronounce upon the meaning or the constitutionality of a state or federal law when it has no jurisdiction to do so is, by very definition, for [that] court to act ultra vires." *Id.* at 101–02.

This is not to say that federal courts need always resolve questions of subject matter jurisdiction or Article III standing before addressing other threshold non-merits issues. District courts do not, for example, "overstep Article III limits when they decline jurisdiction of state-law claims on discretionary grounds without determining whether those claims fall within their pendent jurisdiction or abstain under *Younger v. Harris*, 401 U.S. 37 (1971), without deciding whether the parties present a case or controversy." *Ruhrgas AG v. Marathon Oil Co.*, 526 U.S. 574, 585 (1999). Nor are courts barred from pretermitting a challenge to constitutional standing to dismiss on mootness grounds, *see Arizonans for Official English v. Arizona*, 520 U.S. 43, 66–67 (1997), or, in certain circumstances, from resolving questions of personal jurisdiction prior to finding subject matter jurisdiction, *Ruhrgas*, 526 U.S. at 584–85, or from responding to *forum non conveniens* pleas before determining subject matter jurisdiction, *Sinochem Int'l Co. Ltd. v. Malaysia Int'l Shipping Corp.*, ___ U.S. ___, ___, 127 S. Ct. 1184, 1188 (2007). A court that dismisses on the basis of such "non-merits grounds . . . before finding subject-matter jurisdiction, makes no assumption of law-declaring power that violates the separation of powers principles underlying ... *Steel Company*." *Ruhrgas*, 526 U.S. at 584–85; *see also Tenet v. Doe*, 544 U.S. 1, 6 n.4 (2005) (such rules of dismissal "represent[] the sort of threshold question[s that the Court has] recognized may be resolved before addressing jurisdiction"); *Kowalski v. Tesmer*, 543 U.S. 125, 128–29 (2004) (assuming Article III standing in order to "address the alternative threshold question" of whether the plaintiffs had prudential standing to assert the rights of others).

Second, because subject matter jurisdiction and Article III standing ensure that federal courts do not exceed their constitutional authority, they cannot be forfeited or waived. *See Ins. Corp. of Ireland*, 456 U.S. at 702 (subject matter jurisdiction); *Hays*, 515 U.S. at 742 (standing). Thus, a party may challenge a court's subject matter jurisdiction or a plaintiff's Article III standing anytime after the filing of the complaint up through an appeal to the Supreme Court. *See, e.g., Ins. Corp. of Ireland*, 456 U.S. at 702 (subject matter jurisdiction); *Nat'l Org. for Women, Inc. v. Scheidler*, 510 U.S. 249, 255 (1994) (standing). Indeed, it does not matter whether the parties raise a jurisdictional challenge, for the courts are obligated to "police" the existence of subject matter jurisdiction and Article III standing on their own initiative. *Ruhrgas*, 526 U.S. at 583 (subject matter jurisdiction); *DaimlerChrysler*, ___ U.S. at ___, 126 S. Ct. at 1860 (standing).

Finally, it should be noted that litigants frequently challenge subject matter jurisdiction and Article III standing pursuant to Federal Rule of Civil Procedure 12(b)(1), which allows a party to seek dismissal on jurisdictional grounds prior to answering a complaint. Although Rule 12(b)(1) refers only to "lack of subject-matter jurisdiction," it is commonly used to raise Article III standing defects, as well as claims of sovereign immunity. *See* 5B Wright & Miller, Federal Practice & Procedure § 1350 & nn.7–8 (2004). However, because parties may raise jurisdictional challenges at any point during litigation and because courts are obligated to address such issues *sua sponte*, Rule 12(b)(1) provides the first, but not the only, opportunity for the courts to consider these matters. *See also* Fed. R. Civ. P. 12(h)(3) ("If the court determines at any time that it lacks subject-matter jurisdiction, the court must dismiss the action.").

1. SUBJECT MATTER JURISDICTION

Subject matter jurisdiction, which is a central and defining concept in federal jurisprudence, encompasses the Article III and statutory "prescriptions delineating the classes of cases" that federal courts are authorized to hear. *Kontrick v. Ryan*, 540 U.S. 443, 455 (2004). As noted, it serves "institutional interests[,] ... keep[ing] the federal courts within the bounds the Constitution and Congress have prescribed," and, therefore, cannot be waived and must be raised by the courts, including the Supreme Court, on their own initiative. *Ruhrgas*, 526 U.S. at 583.

Subject matter jurisdiction is distinct from personal jurisdiction, which delineates "the persons . . . falling within a court's adjudicatory authority." *Kontrick*, 540 U.S. at 455. Derived from the Due Process Clause, personal jurisdiction restricts judicial power primarily as a matter of individual liberty, rather than as a matter of sovereignty, and, thus, unlike subject matter jurisdiction, may be waived. *Ins. Corp. of Ireland*, 456 U.S. at 702–03; *see also* FED. R. CIV. P. 12(h)(1). Subject matter jurisdiction is also distinct from "the essential ingredients of a federal claim for relief" – a pleading requirement with which it is sometimes "confused or conflated." *Arbaugh v. Y & H Corp.*, 546 U.S. 500, 503 (2006). Although a party pursuing a federal claim must plead all of the elements of the asserted cause of action, failure to do so does not deprive a court of jurisdiction. Rather, it results in a dismissal on the merits pursuant to Federal Rule of Civil Procedure 12(b)(6). *See* Part One, Chapter III.B, *infra* (discussing the standards governing motions to dismiss for failure to state a claim).

Congress may authorize the district courts to resolve claims encompassed within any of the subjects of jurisdiction described in Article III, Section 2, Clause 1 of the Constitution. *See Ins. Corp. of Ireland*, 456 U.S. at 701–02. The "basic" statutory authorizations of "federal-court subject-matter jurisdiction are contained in 28 U.S.C. §§ 1331 and 1332." *Arbaugh*, 546 U.S. at 513. Section 1332 implements Article III's diversity and alienage provisions but restricts judicial authority over such controversies to claims exceeding $75,000. 28 U.S.C. § 1332. Section 1331, which mirrors but is not coextensive with the "arising under" provision of Article III, *Verlinden B. V. v. Cent. Bank of Nig.*, 461 U.S. 480, 494–95 (1983), defines general federal question jurisdiction: "The district courts shall have original jurisdiction of all civil actions arising under the Constitution, laws, or treaties of the United States." 28 U.S.C. § 1331.

Pursuant to Article III's "arising under" language, Congress also authorizes the courts to exercise jurisdiction over more particularized federal question claims. The statutory provisions defining special federal question jurisdiction – some of which are contained in substantive statutes and others of which are found in the Judicial Code – restrict the authority of the courts on the basis of a wide variety of factors, including, among others, the type of claim at issue, the identity of the plaintiff or defendant, and the amount in controversy. *See Arbaugh*, 546 U.S. at 515 n.11 (citing examples).

The burden is on a party seeking federal court review to demonstrate the existence of the statutory prerequisites to jurisdiction. *See McNutt v. Gen. Motors Acceptance Corp.*, 298 U.S. 178, 189 (1936). With respect to the amount-in-controversy requirement applicable to diversity suits originating in district court, "the sum claimed by the plaintiff controls if the claim is apparently made in good faith. It must appear to a legal certainty that the claim is really for less than the jurisdictional amount to justify dismissal." *St. Paul Mercury Indem. Co. v. Red Cab Co.*, 303 U.S. 283, 288–89 (1938). What a party must otherwise show to

demonstrate subject matter jurisdiction depends upon whether a challenge pertains to the "arising under" element of general or special
federal question jurisdiction, a non-"arising under" factor restricting
judicial authority over special federal question claims, or the diversity
requirement of § 1332.

Whether asserted pursuant to § 1331 or one of the special federal
question statutes, "[a] district court's federal-question jurisdiction . . .
extends over only those cases in which a well-pleaded complaint establishes either that federal law creates the cause of action or that the
plaintiff's right to relief necessarily depends on resolution of a substantial question of federal law in that federal law is a necessary element of
one of the well-pleaded . . . claims." *Christianson v. Colt Indus. Operating Corp.*, 486 U.S. 800, 808 (1988). An anticipated defense cannot
provide a basis for "arising under" jurisdiction, even if it is alleged in a
complaint and even if all parties agree that the federal question raised by
the anticipated defense presents the only genuine matter at issue. *Id.* at
809. The same principles apply to federal removal jurisdiction defined in
28 U.S.C. § 1441. *Beneficial Nat'l Bank v. Anderson*, 539 U.S. 1, 6
(2003). "As a general rule, absent diversity jurisdiction," a state court
action cannot be removed to federal court "if the complaint does not
affirmatively allege a federal claim." *Id.* Thus, assuming supplemental
jurisdiction is not available under 28 U.S.C. § 1367(a), "a state claim
may be removed . . . only . . . when Congress expressly so provides . . . or
when a federal statute wholly displaces the state-law cause of action
through complete pre-emption." *Id.* at 8.

A plaintiff properly invokes general federal question jurisdiction
under § 1331 when the complaint asserts "a colorable claim 'arising
under' the Constitution or laws of the United States." *Arbaugh*, 546 U.S.
at 513. Plaintiffs invoking special federal question jurisdiction carry the
same minimal burden with respect to the "arising under" element of the
particularized jurisdictional provision. *See Christianson*, 486 U.S. at
807–08. The complaint need only contain a "colorable" or "nonfrivolous" assertion that the cause of action arises under the statutorily
specified law or laws. *See, e.g., Rosselló-González v. Calderón-Serra*, 398
F.3d 1, 15 (1st Cir. 2004) (finding jurisdiction under 28 U.S.C. § 1343(3)
because complaint asserted a "colorable" claim under 42 U.S.C. § 1983);
Sea-Land Serv., Inc. v. Lozen Int'l, LLC, 285 F.3d 808, 814 (9th Cir.
2002) (finding jurisdiction over state law counterclaim under 28 U.S.C.
§ 1337(a) because Interstate Commerce Act counterclaim was not "obviously frivolous").

Pursuant to the standard enunciated by the Supreme Court in *Bell
v. Hood*, dismissal for failure to demonstrate the "arising under" element of federal question jurisdiction is appropriate in only two situations: where a federal claim "clearly appears to be immaterial and made
solely for the purpose of obtaining jurisdiction or where [it] is wholly
insubstantial and frivolous," meaning "patently without merit." 327
U.S. 678, 682–83 (1946); *see also Arbaugh*, 546 U.S. at 513 & n.10; *Steel
Co.*, 523 U.S. at 89. In other words, a nonfrivolous assertion that a claim

arises under federal law cannot be "defeated ... by the possibility that the averments might fail to state a cause of action on which petitioners could actually recover." *Bell v. Hood*, 327 U.S. at 682. Neither can it be defeated by the mere possibility that the petitioner may be unable to make out the facts supporting the asserted cause of action. "The reason for this is that the court must assume jurisdiction to decide whether the allegations state a cause of action on which the court can grant relief as well as to determine issues of fact arising in the controversy." *Id.* at 682.

Under *Bell v. Hood*, the "arising under" element of federal question jurisdiction is satisfied if a complaint, on its face, states an "arguable" federal claim. *Steel Co.*, 523 U.S. at 89; *see also Hagans v. Lavine*, 415 U.S. 528, 542 & n.10 (1974) ("Once a federal court has ascertained that a plaintiff's jurisdiction-conferring claims are not insubstantial on their face, no further consideration of the merits of the claims is relevant...."). More precisely, it is satisfied if the asserted claim is sustainable under one construction of the federal laws at issue, though it may be defeated under another. *Hagans*, 415 U.S. at 542 & n.10 (citing *Bell v. Hood*, 327 U.S. at 682); *see also Oneida Indian Nation v. County of Oneida, N.Y.*, 414 U.S. 661, 666–67 (1974) ("arising under" element of both § 1331 and § 1362 satisfied by tribe's "assertion that [it] had a federal right to possession governed wholly by federal law [which] cannot be said to be so insubstantial, implausible, foreclosed by prior decisions of [the Supreme] Court, or otherwise completely devoid of merit as not to involve a federal controversy within the jurisdiction of the District Court, whatever may be the ultimate resolution of the federal issues on the merits").

If a purported challenge to the "arising under" element of federal question jurisdiction, in substance, seeks dismissal for failure to state all of the elements of the asserted cause of action, a district court may, if the jurisdictional claim is colorable, convert the Rule 12(b)(1) motion to a Rule 12(b)(6) motion to dismiss for failure to state a claim upon which relief can be granted. *See, e.g., Fraternal Order of Police Dep't of Corr. Labor Comm. v. Williams*, 375 F.3d 1141, 1144 (D.C. Cir. 2004); *Health Cost Controls v. Skinner*, 44 F.3d 535, 537–38 (7th Cir. 1995); *see also* Part One, Chapter III.B, *infra* (discussing the standards governing the resolution of Rule 12(b)(6) motions). By the same token, if the parties litigating such a motion submit, and the court considers, extra pleading materials, the trial court may convert the purported Rule 12(b)(1) motion to one for summary judgment pursuant to Federal Rule of Civil Procedure 56. *See Fraternal Order of Police*, 375 F.3d at 1144; *Boyle v. Governor's Veterans Outreach & Assistance Ctr.*, 925 F.2d 71, 74–75 (3d Cir. 1991); *see also* Part One, Chapter III.C, *infra* (discussing the standards governing the resolution of Rule 56 summary judgment motions). If the trial court fails to convert the motion, but rather dismisses for lack of subject matter jurisdiction, the appellate court may recharacterize the district court's ruling and review it, as appropriate, pursuant to Rule 12(b)(6) or Rule 56. *See, e.g., Fraternal Order of Police*, 375 F.3d at 1144; *Nowak v. Ironworkers Local 6 Pension Fund*, 81 F.3d 1182, 1187 (2d Cir. 1996).

When a jurisdictional question pertains to a non-"arising under" restriction on special federal question jurisdiction, or the diversity requirement of § 1332, the complainant's burden is different. Assuming there is no overlap between the jurisdictional restriction and the cause of action, the plaintiff must be prepared to demonstrate not only that the complaint, on its face, meets the specified threshold jurisdictional requirement, but also that the facts asserted in support of the jurisdictional restriction are true. *See Gibbs v. Buck*, 307 U.S. 66, 71–72 (1939); *McNutt*, 298 U.S. at 189; *see also Land v. Dollar*, 330 U.S. 731, 735 & n.4 (1947). The procedures followed by the district courts and the standards of review applied by the courts of appeals differ depending upon whether a jurisdictional challenge is facial or factual.

In resolving a facial challenge (sometimes referred to as a sufficiency challenge) to a non-"arising under" restriction, the district court accepts as true all allegations in the complaint, as well as any uncontested facts contained in the record, giving the complainant the benefit of any reasonable inferences that can be drawn from them. *See, e.g., Valentin v. Hosp. Bella Vista*, 254 F.3d 358, 363 (1st Cir. 2001); *Herbert v. Nat'l Acad. of Scis.*, 974 F.2d 192, 197 (D.C. Cir. 1992). Consequently, the only questions on appeal are "whether the district court's application of the law [to the asserted facts] is correct and, if the decision is based on undisputed facts, whether those facts are indeed undisputed." *Harris v. P.A.M. Transp., Inc.*, 339 F.3d 635, 637 (8th Cir. 2003); *see also Herbert*, 974 F.2d at 197. The standard of review is *de novo*. *See, e.g., Gabriel v. Preble*, 396 F.3d 10, 12–13 (1st Cir. 2005).

When the accuracy of the facts supporting a jurisdictional requirement is questioned, the complainant must prove the facts by a preponderance of the evidence. *See McNutt*, 298 U.S. at 189. The complainant's "averments are entitled to no presumptive weight" and "the [district] court enjoys broad authority to order discovery, consider extrinsic evidence, and hold evidentiary hearings in order to determine its own jurisdiction." *Valentin*, 254 F.3d at 363; *see also Paper, Allied–Indus., Chem. & Energy Workers Int'l Union v. Cont'l Carbon Co.*, 428 F.3d 1285, 1292 (10th Cir. 2005); Fed. R. Civ. P. 12(i) (district courts have discretion to hold pretrial hearings to resolve Rule 12(b) and (c) motions). On review, the trial court's articulation of the controlling law and its ultimate conclusion regarding jurisdiction are reviewed *de novo*, but its underlying findings of fact are reviewed only for clear error. *See, e.g., Golden v. Gorno Bros., Inc.*, 410 F.3d 879, 881 (6th Cir. 2005); *Gualandi v. Adams*, 385 F.3d 236, 240 (2d Cir. 2004). Discovery rulings are reviewed for abuse of discretion. *See, e.g., Macharia v. United States*, 334 F.3d 61, 64 (D.C. Cir. 2003).

There are two instances when courts do not apply the facial/factual model in resolving challenges to non-"arising under" requirements of special federal question claims: when the challenged requirement is also an element of the asserted cause of action, *see, e.g., Garcia v. Copenhaver, Bell & Assocs., M.D.'s, P.A.*, 104 F.3d 1256, 1261 (11th Cir. 1997); *Clark v. Tarrant County, Tex.*, 798 F.2d 736, 741 (5th Cir. 1986), and when resolution of the challenge to the non-"arising under" requirement demands resolution of an aspect of the substantive claim, *see, e.g., Sizova v. Nat'l Inst. of Standards & Tech.*, 282 F.3d 1320, 1324 (10th Cir. 2002); *Roberts v. Corrothers*, 812 F.2d 1173, 1177 (9th Cir. 1987). *See also Arbaugh*, 546 U.S. at 515 n.11 ("Congress has exercised its prerogative to restrict the subject-matter jurisdiction of federal district courts based on a wide variety of factors, some of them also relevant to the merits of a case."). In such cases, most circuits, applying the rationale of *Bell v. Hood*, find jurisdiction unless the federal claim is " 'immaterial,' 'made solely for the purpose of obtaining federal jurisdiction,' or 'wholly insubstantial and frivolous.' " *Safe Air for Everyone v. Meyer*, 373 F.3d 1035, 1040 (9th Cir. 2004) (quoting *Bell v. Hood*, 327 U.S. at 683–83). Because, in these instances, "the defendant's challenge to the court's jurisdiction is also a challenge to the existence of a federal cause of action, the proper course of action for the district court (assuming that the plaintiff's federal claim is not immaterial and made solely for the purpose of obtaining federal jurisdiction and is not insubstantial and frivolous) is to find that jurisdiction exists and deal with the objection as a direct attack on the merits of the plaintiff's case." *Williamson v. Tucker*, 645 F.2d 404, 415 (5th Cir. 1981); *see also United States v. North Carolina*, 180 F.3d 574, 580 (4th Cir. 1999) (same); *Garcia*, 104 F.3d at 1261 (same); *Clark*, 798 F.2d at 741–42 (same).

In other words, when a non-"arising under" restriction is intertwined with the merits of a claim, a court may, if it is satisfied that it has jurisdiction under *Bell v. Hood*, convert the Rule 12(b)(1) motion to a Rule 12(b)(6) motion to dismiss for failure to state a claim or, if the challenge is factual, to a Rule 56 motion for summary judgment. *See, e.g., Paper, Allied–Indus.*, 428 F.3d at 1292; *Safe Air for Everyone*, 373 F.3d at 1039–40; *Morrison v. Amway Corp.*, 323 F.3d 920, 925 (11th Cir. 2003); *Sierra Club v. Shell Oil Co.*, 817 F.2d 1169, 1172 (5th Cir. 1987). The greater procedural protections afforded by Rule 56 appropriately protect plaintiffs who, in truth, are facing challenges to the merits of their complaints. *See Garcia*, 104 F.3d at 1261. Moreover, in a jury trial, when the jurisdictional question is inextricably intertwined with the merits, reliance on Rule 56 ensures that the trial judge does not violate a plaintiff's Seventh Amendment rights. *See Morrison*, 323 F.3d at 930.

Until the Supreme Court's 2006 decision in *Arbaugh*, courts sometimes struggled to discern whether Congress intended that a threshold limitation in a special federal question statute restrict the district court's subject matter jurisdiction, define an element of the cause of action, or both. *See Arbaugh*, 546 U.S. at 510–13. *Arbaugh* should eliminate much of the confusion, establishing, as it does, a "bright line" rule that unless Congress "clearly states that a threshold limitation on a statute's scope shall count as jurisdictional," "courts should treat the restriction as nonjurisdictional." *Id.* at 515–16.

2. ARTICLE III STANDING

The doctrine of standing derives from Article III's case or controversy requirement. *See Allen v. Wright*, 468 U.S. 737, 750–51 (1984). The standing inquiry "focuses on the party seeking to get his complaint before a federal court and not on the issues he wishes to have adjudicated." *Flast v. Cohen*, 392 U.S. 83, 99 (1968). The question for the court is whether the plaintiff is "the proper party" to have brought suit. *Raines v. Byrd*, 521 U.S. 811, 818 (1997). To answer this question, the court must look to whether the plaintiff has "alleged such a personal stake in the outcome of the controversy as to assure that concrete adverseness which sharpens the presentation of issues upon which the court so largely depends for illumination of difficult" legal questions. *Baker v. Carr*, 369 U.S. 186, 204 (1962). This requisite "stake in the outcome" ensures that the suit is one that is amenable to judicial resolution in that "the legal questions presented ... will be resolved, not in the rarified atmosphere of a debating society, but in a concrete factual context conducive to a realistic appreciation of the consequences of judicial action." *Valley Forge Christian Coll. v. Ams. United for Separation of Church & State, Inc.*, 454 U.S. 464, 472 (1982).

Article III standing, like subject matter jurisdiction, is a threshold jurisdictional requirement that can be neither forfeited nor waived. *See Lewis v. Casey*, 518 U.S. 343, 349 n.1 (1996); *Hays*, 515 U.S. at 742; *Nat'l Org. for Women*, 510 U.S. at 255. "The federal courts are under an independent obligation to examine their own jurisdiction, and standing is perhaps the most important of the jurisdictional doctrines." *Hays*, 515 U.S. at 742. If a plaintiff lacks standing, the courts are prohibited from resolving the merits of the complaint. *See Steel Co.*, 523 U.S. at 101–02.

A party invoking federal jurisdiction bears the burden of proving the three elements making up the "irreducible constitutional minimum" necessary to demonstrate standing. *Lujan v. Defenders of Wildlife*, 504 U.S. 555, 560–61 (1992); *accord Bennett v. Spear*, 520 U.S. 154, 167–68 (1997). "First and foremost, there must be alleged (and ultimately proved) an 'injury in fact' – a harm suffered by the plaintiff that is concrete and actual or imminent, not conjectural or hypothetical. Second, there must be causation – a fairly traceable connection between the plaintiff's injury and the complained-of conduct of the defendant. And third, there must be redressability – a likelihood that the requested relief will redress the alleged injury." *Steel Co.*, 523 U.S. at 103; *see also DaimlerChrysler*, ___ U.S. at ___, 126 S. Ct. at 1861. Failure to establish any one of these elements deprives the federal courts of jurisdiction to hear the suit. *Steel Co.*, 523 U.S. at 103–04.

The elements of standing "are not mere pleading requirements[,] but rather an indispensable part of the plaintiff's case." *Lujan v. Defenders of Wildlife*, 504 U.S. at 561. Therefore, "each element must be supported in the same way as any other matter on which the plaintiff bears the burden of proof, *i.e.*, with the manner and degree of evidence required at the successive stages of the litigation." *Id.*

Pretrial, a "challenge to a plaintiff's standing can take two forms: a motion to dismiss ... based exclusively on [the] plaintiff's pleadings, [or] a motion for summary judgment, in which evidence ... pertinent to standing [is] evaluated by the district court." *Bischoff v. Osceola County, Fla.*, 222 F.3d 874, 878 (11th Cir. 2000); *see also Haase v. Sessions*, 835 F.2d 902, 904 (D.C. Cir. 1987). In addition, the court, on its own initiative, may undertake pretrial evidentiary hearings for the purpose of ascertaining whether a plaintiff has standing. *Haase*, 835 F.2d at 903.

In ruling on a motion to dismiss for lack of standing at the pleading stage, the district court (and the court of appeals reviewing *de novo*) must accept as true all material allegations in the complaint, construing them in the light most favorable to the plaintiff. *Jenkins v. McKeithen*, 395 U.S. 411, 421–22 (1969) (plurality opinion); *see also Haase*, 835 F.2d at 906. "[G]eneral factual allegations of injury resulting from the defendant's conduct may suffice [to demonstrate standing], for on a motion to dismiss [on the pleadings it is] presum[ed] that general allegations embrace those specific facts that are necessary to support the claim." *Lujan v. Defenders of Wildlife*, 504 U.S. at 561; *see also Steel Co.*, 523 U.S. at 104 (same); *Nat'l Org. for Women*, 510 U.S. at 256 (same). If the case is dismissed for lack of standing, the dismissal is without preclusive or *res judicata* effect. *See, e.g., Media Techs. Licensing, LLC v. Upper Deck Co.*, 334 F.3d 1366, 1369–70 (Fed. Cir. 2003); *St. Pierre v. Dyer*, 208 F.3d 394, 399–400 (2d Cir. 2000). Consequently, at the pleading stage, Rule 12(b)(1), not 12(b)(6), is the proper procedural mechanism for seeking dismissal for lack of standing. *See, e.g., Alliance for Envtl. Renewal, Inc. v. Pyramid Crossgates Co.*, 436 F.3d 82, 88 n.6 (2d Cir. 2006); *Rent Stabilization Ass'n of N.Y. v. Dinkins*, 5 F.3d 591, 594 (2d Cir. 1993).

"[T]he purpose of Rule 56 is to enable a party who believes there is no genuine dispute as to a specific fact essential to the other side's case to demand at least one sworn averment of that fact before the lengthy process of litigation continues." *Lujan v. Nat'l Wildlife Fed'n*, 497 U.S. 871, 888–89 (1990). Because it is the plaintiff's burden to demonstrate standing, a plaintiff whose standing is challenged at the summary judgment stage "can no longer rest on ... 'mere allegations,' but must 'set forth' by affidavit or other evidence 'specific facts'" establishing that there are genuine issues pertaining to injury, causation, and redressability. *Lujan v. Defenders of Wildlife*, 504 U.S. at 561 (quoting the then-controlling version of Fed. R. Civ. P. 56). "In ruling upon a Rule 56 motion, a District Court must resolve any factual issues of controversy in favor of the non-moving party...." *Lujan v. Nat'l Wildlife Fed'n*, 497 U.S. at 888. Thus, if a party seeking dismissal avers material facts suggesting that the plaintiff has no standing and the plaintiff avers material facts supporting standing, the court must deny the motion to dismiss. If, however, the plaintiff fails to demonstrate that there are genuine issues of fact with respect to injury, causation, or redressability, the district court should grant summary judgment and dismiss the case. *See generally* Part One, Chapter III.C, *infra* (discussing the standards applicable to Rule 56 motions).

Pretrial standing questions need not always be resolved on the face of the pleadings or on the basis of affidavits submitted in connection with a motion for summary judgment. District courts have discretion to order discovery and conduct pretrial evidentiary hearings regarding standing. *See, e.g., Duke Power Co. v. Carolina Envtl. Study Group, Inc.*, 438 U.S. 59, 67–68, 72 (1978); *Haase*, 835 F.2d at 907; *see also* FED. R. CIV. P. 12(i). In fact, several circuits explicitly prohibit district courts from resolving disputed factual questions or making credibility determinations essential to the question of standing on the basis of affidavits alone. *See, e.g., Bischoff*, 222 F.3d at 880–81 (following First and Fifth Circuit cases). Once a district court initiates a fact-based standing inquiry, discovery by the parties should be allowed, "subject to whatever defenses and privileges a party can properly assert in response to the discovery process." *Haase*, 835 F.2d at 907. Factual findings made by the court in support of a standing determination are subject to clearly erroneous review. *See Duke Power*, 438 U.S. at 77; *see also Rivera v. Wyeth–Ayerst Labs.*, 283 F.3d 315, 319 (5th Cir. 2002). *But see Steir v. Girl Scouts of the USA*, 383 F.3d 7, 15 n.9 (1st Cir. 2004) (acknowledging the prevailing rule but declining to decide whether *de novo* or clearly erroneous review applies to factual findings supporting standing determinations).

If a plaintiff survives a standing challenge in a motion to dismiss or a motion for summary judgment, the issue nevertheless may be raised anew at trial. In such cases, the burden of establishing standing remains on the plaintiff, who must "adequately" support the elements with "the evidence adduced at trial." *Lujan v. Defenders of Wildlife*, 504 U.S. at 561.

Even when standing has not been challenged in the district court, it may be raised on appeal by a party or *sua sponte* by the circuit court. *See, e.g., Steffan v. Perry*, 41 F.3d 677, 697 n.20 (D.C. Cir. 1994) (en banc). How a court of appeals resolves a standing issue that was not addressed below depends upon the posture of the case. Thus, in some instances, an appellate court will itself determine whether the trial court record demonstrates the plaintiff's standing. *See, e.g., Wilderness Soc'y v. Norton*, 434 F.3d 584, 589–94 (D.C. Cir. 2006); *Clajon Prod. Corp. v. Petera*, 70 F.3d 1566, 1571–74 (10th Cir. 1995). But if "the factual record compiled in the district court is inadequate to the task," the court of appeals must remand the case to the district court for appropriate factual findings. *Democratic Senatorial Campaign Comm. v. Fed. Election Comm'n*, 139 F.3d 951, 952 (D.C. Cir. 1998) (per curiam). If an appellate court finds that the standing inquiry overlaps with the merits but concludes that the elements of standing have not been satisfied, vacatur of the district court's judgment and a remand for dismissal of the case for want of jurisdiction is a frequent remedy. *See, e.g., Taylor v. FDIC*, 132 F.3d 753, 767 (D.C. Cir. 1997); *Clajon Prod. Corp.*, 70 F.3d at

1574 (dismissing case for lack of jurisdiction despite identity of the injury-in-fact requirement and the substantive claim). This makes sense, because a federal court may not rule on the merits of a claim after concluding that the party bringing the claim lacks standing. *See Steel Co.*, 523 U.S. at 101–02.

A last cautionary observation: Perhaps because the Article III case or controversy limitation on federal judicial authority underpins both standing and mootness, the two doctrines are sometimes erroneously conflated. In *Friends of the Earth, Inc. v. Laidlaw Environmental Services (TOC), Inc.*, the Supreme Court noted that the "confusion is understandable, given this Court's repeated statements that the doctrine of mootness can be described as 'the doctrine of standing set in a time frame.'" 528 U.S. 167, 189 (2000) (quoting *Arizonans for Official English*, 520 U.S. at 68 n.22). Under this misguided formulation, the Court explained, judges sometimes erroneously assumed that "[t]he requisite personal interest that must exist at the commencement of the litigation (standing) must continue throughout its existence (mootness)." *Id.*

The *Friends of the Earth* Court went on to demonstrate that the inquiries pertaining to standing and mootness are discernibly different. *Id.* at 190–92. First, it noted that in a lawsuit brought to force compliance with a legal obligation, "it is the plaintiff's burden to establish standing by demonstrating that, if unchecked by the litigation, the defendant's allegedly wrongful behavior will likely occur or continue, and that the threatened injury [is] certainly impending." *Id.* at 190. By contrast, a defendant to such a suit who claims that its voluntary actions have mooted the case "bears the formidable burden of showing that it is absolutely clear the allegedly wrongful behavior could not reasonably be expected to recur." *Id.* "The plain lesson . . . is that there are circumstances in which . . . harmful conduct may be too speculative to support standing, but not too speculative to overcome mootness." *Id.*

The Court next observed that "if mootness were simply 'standing set in a time frame,' the exception to mootness that arises when the defendant's allegedly unlawful activity is 'capable of repetition, yet evading review,' could not exist." *Id.* This is because "[s]tanding admits of no similar exception; if a plaintiff lacks standing at the time the action commences, the fact that the dispute is capable of repetition yet evading review will not entitle the complainant to a federal judicial forum." *Id.* at 191.

Finally, highlighting one of the important functions served by the standing doctrine, the Court explained that standing ensures, "among other things, that the scarce resources of the federal courts are devoted to those disputes in which the parties have a concrete stake." *Id.* Because mootness issues often arise after the courts have invested considerable resources in the resolution of the dispute, abandonment of the case at that advanced stage "may prove more wasteful than frugal," thus undermining rather than serving the goals of standing. *See id.* at 191–92.

In light of these distinctions, the Court found that, in the case under review, "[t]he appellate court erred in concluding that a citizen suitor's claim for civil penalties must be dismissed as moot when the defendant, albeit after commencement of the litigation, has come into compliance." *Id.* at 173–74. The Court explained: "In directing dismissal of the suit on grounds of mootness, the Court of Appeals incorrectly conflated our case law on initial standing to bring suit, *see, e.g., Steel Co. v. Citizens for a Better Environment*, 523 U.S. 83 (1998), with our case law on postcommencement mootness, *see, e.g., City of Mesquite v. Aladdin's Castle, Inc.*, 455 U.S. 283 (1982)." *Friends of the Earth*, 528 U.S. at 174.

The plaintiffs in *Friends of the Earth* would not have had standing had they commenced their lawsuit after the defendant had complied with the disputed statute. At that juncture, the plaintiffs could not have shown any cognizable injury, nor could they have claimed injunctive relief for the defendant's past violations of the statute. Moreover, the plaintiffs could not have sought a declaration against potential future violations of the statute, because such a claim would have been too speculative. *See City of Los Angeles v. Lyons*, 461 U.S. 95, 107 n.7 (1983) (holding that a plaintiff lacked standing to seek an injunction against the enforcement of police choke hold policy because he could not credibly allege that the policy posed a realistic threat to him). However, because the plaintiffs in *Friends of the Earth* filed their lawsuit before the defendant acted to comply with the statute, the plaintiffs had standing and their claim for civil penalties was not moot. *See also Super Tire Eng'g Co. v. McCorkle*, 416 U.S. 115 (1974) (in suit for declaratory and injunctive relief brought by employers whose operations had been subject to an economic strike and who alleged that state regulations giving benefits to striking workers were invalid under federal labor policy, the strike's termination did not moot the claim for declaratory relief).

B. DISMISSALS BASED ON A COMPLAINANT'S FAILURE TO STATE A CLAIM: FEDERAL RULE OF CIVIL PROCEDURE 12(b)(6)

Pursuant to Federal Rule of Civil Procedure 12(b)(6), a defendant, before filing a responsive pleading, may seek dismissal of a complaint for failure to state a claim. Rule 12(b)(6) motions enable district courts to "streamline[] litigation by dispensing with needless discovery and fact-finding." *Neitzke v. Williams*, 490 U.S. 319, 326–27 (1989). The rule allows courts "to eliminate actions that are fatally flawed in their legal premises and destined to fail, and thus to spare litigants the burdens of unnecessary pretrial and trial activity." *Advanced Cardiovascular Sys., Inc. v. SciMed Life Sys., Inc.*, 988 F.2d 1157, 1160 (Fed. Cir. 1993) (citing *Neitzke*, 490 U.S. at 326–27). Pursuant to Rule 12(b)(6), a court must "assess[] the legal feasibility of the complaint, but [may] not weigh the evidence that might be offered to support it." *Global Network Commc'ns,*

Inc. v. City of New York, 458 F.3d 150, 155 (2d Cir. 2006). Dismissals for failure to state a claim under Rule 12(b)(6) are reviewed *de novo* – meaning that appellate courts apply the same decisional principles as the district courts. *See, e.g., Kottmyer v. Maas*, 436 F.3d 684, 688 (6th Cir. 2006); *Kingman Park Civic Ass'n v. Williams*, 348 F.3d 1033, 1039–40 (D.C. Cir. 2003).

"When a federal court reviews the sufficiency of a complaint, before the reception of any evidence either by affidavit or admissions, its task is necessarily a limited one. The issue is not whether a plaintiff will ultimately prevail but whether the claimant is entitled to offer evidence to support the claims." *Swierkiewicz v. Sorema N.A.*, 534 U.S. 506, 511 (2002). Whether a complaint entitles a plaintiff to offer evidence is necessarily informed by the pleading rules described in Federal Rules of Civil Procedure 8 and 9. *See id.* at 512–14.

Rule 8(a), which with "limited exceptions" applies to all civil actions, *id.* at 513, requires that a complaint include "a short and plain statement of the claim showing that the pleader is entitled to relief," FED. R. CIV. P. 8(a)(2). Such a statement need only "give the defendant fair notice of what the plaintiff's claim is and the grounds upon which it rests." *Swierkiewicz*, 534 U.S. at 512; *see also Dura Pharms., Inc. v. Broudo*, 544 U.S. 336, 346 (2005). "This simplified notice pleading standard relies on liberal discovery rules and summary judgment motions to define disputed facts and issues and to dispose of unmeritorious claims." *Swierkiewicz*, 534 U.S. at 512. Relatedly, Rule 8(d)(1) provides that "[n]o technical form" of pleading is required, while Rule 8(e) states that "[p]leadings must be construed so as to do justice."

In light of Rule 8's liberal pleading standards, the likelihood of success on the merits is not the proper measure of a Rule 12(b)(6) motion. *See Swierkiewicz*, 534 U.S. at 515. "Indeed it may appear on the face of the pleadings that a recovery is very remote and unlikely but that is not the test." *Id.* Rather, dismissal is proper " 'only if it is clear that no relief could be granted under any set of facts that could be proved consistent with the allegations.' " *Id.* at 514 (quoting *Hishon v. King & Spalding*, 467 U.S. 69, 73 (1984)). A plaintiff is "not required on the face of [the] complaint to allege every legal element or fact that must be proven" to support a particular claim. *Kingman Park*, 348 F.3d at 1040; *see also Bennett v. Schmidt*, 153 F.3d 516, 518 (7th Cir.1998). In fact, it is generally accepted that "a complaint sufficiently raises a claim even if it points to no legal theory or even if it points to the wrong legal theory as a basis for that claim, as long as relief is possible under any set of facts that could be established consistent with the allegations." *Tolle v. Carroll Touch, Inc.*, 977 F.2d 1129, 1134 (7th Cir. 1992); *see also Morales–Vallellanes v. Potter*, 339 F.3d 9, 14 (1st Cir. 2003); *Simonton v. Runyon*, 232 F.3d 33, 36–37 (2d Cir. 2000). Thus, for example, "[b]ecause racial discrimination in employment is 'a claim upon which relief can be granted,' ... 'I was turned down for a job because of my race' is all a complaint has to say." *Bennett v. Schmidt*, 153 F.3d at 518. It should be noted, however, that a complaint may be subject to dismissal for failure to state a claim if it alleges facts supporting an affirmative defense. *See Jones v. Bock*, ___ U.S. ___, ___, 127 S. Ct. 910, 921 (2007). Pro se complaints, "however inartfully pleaded," are held to even less stringent standards and may be dismissed for failure to state a claim only if "it appears beyond doubt that the plaintiff can prove no set of facts in support of his claim which would entitle him to relief." *Hughes v. Rowe*, 449 U.S. 5, 10 & n.7 (1980) (per curiam).

The two most notable of the limited exceptions to Rule 8's liberal pleading requirements are described in Federal Rule of Civil Procedure 9(b), which "provides for greater particularity in all averments of fraud or mistake," *Swierkiewicz*, 534 U.S. at 513, and the pleading provision of the Private Securities Litigation Reform Act of 1995 ("PSLRA"), which "insists that securities fraud complaints 'specify' each misleading statement; that they set forth the facts 'on which a belief' that a statement is misleading was 'formed'; and that they 'state with particularity facts giving rise to a strong inference that the defendant acted with the required state of mind,'" *Dura Pharms.*, 544 U.S. at 345 (quoting 15 U.S.C. §§ 78u–4(b)(1), (2)). As noted, however, the Supreme Court "has declined to extend such exceptions to other contexts," *Swierkiewicz*, 534 U.S. at 513, absent a clear statutory indication that greater particularity is required. *See Jones v. Bock*, ___ U.S. at ___, 127 S. Ct. at 919–22 ("Given that the [Prison Litigation Reform Act] does not itself require plaintiffs to plead exhaustion, such a result must be obtained by the process of amending the Federal Rules, and not by judicial interpretation.").

In reviewing a Rule 12(b)(6) motion, a court must accept as true all factual allegations contained in the complaint, *Leatherman v. Tarrant County Narcotics Intelligence & Coordination Unit*, 507 U.S. 163, 164 (1993), and assume all reasonable factual inferences that can be drawn from those facts in the plaintiff's favor. *See, e.g., Garfield v. NDC Health Corp.*, 466 F.3d 1255, 1261 (11th Cir. 2006); *E. Food Servs. v. Pontifical Catholic Univ. Servs. Ass'n*, 357 F.3d 1, 3 (1st Cir. 2004); *Pinker v. Roche Holdings Ltd.*, 292 F.3d 361, 374 n.7 (3d Cir. 2002). However, a court "need not ... accept as true legal conclusions or unwarranted factual inferences." *Kottmyer*, 436 F.3d at 688; *see also Garfield*, 466 F.3d at 1264 (noting that the PSLRA's requirement that a complaint "state with particularity facts giving rise to a strong inference that the defendant acted with the required state of mind" "alters the usual contours of a Rule 12(b)(6) ruling because, while a court continues to give all reasonable inferences to plaintiffs, those inferences supporting scienter must be strong ones"). A court may consider all exhibits attached to the complaint, documents incorporated into the complaint by reference, and documents on which the plaintiff relied in drafting the complaint, as well as matters with respect to which judicial notice may be taken. *See Kaempe v. Myers*, 367 F.3d 958, 965 (D.C. Cir. 2004) (collecting cases); *Chambers v. Time Warner, Inc.*, 282 F.3d 147, 153 & n.3 (2d Cir. 2002) (collecting cases); *Collins v. Morgan Stanley Dean Witter*, 224 F.3d 496, 498–99 & n.1 (5th Cir. 2000) (collecting cases).

Rule 12(d) provides that if, on a motion to dismiss for failure to state a claim, "matters outside the pleadings are presented to and not excluded by the court, the motion must be treated as one for summary judgment under Rule 56 [and a]ll parties must be given a reasonable opportunity to present all the material that is pertinent to the motion." The district court retains discretion to decide whether to review unincorporated materials, but if it does, the Rule 12(b)(6) motion normally must be converted to one for summary judgment. *See, e.g., Fagin v. Gilmartin*, 432 F.3d 276, 284–86 (3d Cir. 2005); *Courtenay Commc'ns Corp. v. Hall*, 334 F.3d 210, 213 (2d Cir. 2003); *see also Garfield*, 466 F.3d at 1260 n.2 (stating the general rule, but noting that "in the context of securities fraud, SEC documents [may be treated] as public records capable of being judicially noticed at the motion to dismiss stage").

If a district court considers unincorporated materials that are not capable of being judicially noticed, but fails to treat the Rule 12(b)(6) motion as one for summary judgment, the appellate court may reverse and remand the case so that the motion can be properly considered under Rule 56. *See, e.g., Global Network Commc'ns*, 458 F.3d 150; *County of Santa Fe v. Pub. Serv. Co. of N.M.*, 311 F.3d 1031, 1045, 1050 (10th Cir. 2002). Alternatively, if the appellate court satisfies itself that dismissal would have been justified on the basis of the complaint alone, it may affirm. *See, e.g., Jacobs v. City of Chicago*, 215 F.3d 758, 766 (7th Cir. 2000); *GFF Corp. v. Associated Wholesale Grocers, Inc.*, 130 F.3d 1381, 1384 (10th Cir. 1997). Finally, the court of appeals may characterize the district court's Rule 12(b)(6) dismissal as a grant of summary judgment under Rule 56 and affirm, so long as both sides had a reasonable opportunity to present evidence and there are no genuine issues of material fact. *See, e.g., Ctr. for Auto Safety v. Nat'l Highway Traffic Safety Admin.*, 452 F.3d 798, 805 (D.C. Cir. 2006); *Boateng v. InterAmerican Univ., Inc.*, 210 F.3d 56, 60–61 (1st Cir. 2000); *see also Romero v. Int'l Terminal Operating* Co., 358 U.S. 354, 357 n.4 (1959). "[V]igorous enforcement of the conversion requirement helps ensure that courts will refrain from engaging in fact-finding when considering a motion to dismiss, and also that plaintiffs are given a fair chance to contest defendants' evidentiary assertions where a court nonetheless does consider evidence extrinsic to the complaint...." *Courtenay Commc'ns*, 334 F.3d at 213.

C. SUMMARY JUDGMENT: FEDERAL RULE OF CIVIL PROCEDURE 56

Summary judgment practice is predicated on the goal of conserving "public and private resources." *Celotex Corp. v. Catrett*, 477 U.S. 317, 327 (1986). A "principal purpose[] of the ... rule is to isolate and dispose of factually unsupported claims or defenses." *Id.* at 323–24. In resolving motions for summary judgment, district judges "pierce the pleadings and ... assess the proof in order to see whether there is a genuine need for trial." *Matsushita Elec. Indus. Co. v. Zenith Radio*

Corp., 475 U.S. 574, 587 (1986). The question is whether "there are any genuine factual issues that properly can be resolved only by a finder of fact because they may reasonably be resolved in favor of either party." *Anderson v. Liberty Lobby, Inc.*, 477 U.S. 242, 250 (1986).

Appellate courts review a decision to grant summary judgment *de novo*, applying the same standards as the district courts. *See, e.g., Wolfe v. Barnhart*, 446 F.3d 1096, 1100 (10th Cir. 2006); *Bowlin v. Montanez*, 446 F.3d 817, 819 (8th Cir. 2006). Those standards are largely derived from Federal Rule of Civil Procedure 56 and the Supreme Court's seminal decisions in *Anderson v. Liberty Lobby, Inc.*, 477 U.S. 242, and *Celotex Corp. v. Catrett*, 477 U.S. 317.

Under Rule 56, a "party claiming relief," as well as a "party against whom relief is sought," may move, "with or without supporting affidavits, for summary judgment on all or part of the claim." FED. R. CIV. P. 56(a), (b). "A supporting or opposing affidavit must be made on personal knowledge, set out facts that would be admissible in evidence, and show that the affiant is competent to testify on the matters stated. . . . The court may permit an affidavit to be supplemented or opposed by depositions, answers to interrogatories, or additional affidavits." FED. R. CIV. P. 56(e)(1).

As required by Rule 56(c):

> The judgment sought should be rendered if the pleadings, the discovery and disclosure materials on file, and any affidavits show that there is no genuine issue as to any material fact and that the movant is entitled to judgment as a matter of law.

In applying this rule, "the mere existence of *some* alleged factual dispute between the parties will not defeat an otherwise properly supported motion for summary judgment; the requirement is that there be no *genuine* issue of *material* fact." *Liberty Lobby*, 477 U.S. at 247–48.

"Materiality" is determined by the applicable substantive law. "Only disputes over facts that might affect the outcome of the suit under the governing law will properly preclude the entry of summary judgment. Factual disputes that are irrelevant or unnecessary will not be counted." *Id.* at 248.

Determining whether a dispute is "genuine" is a somewhat more complicated task. Simply stated, a dispute over a material fact is genuine if the "caliber" and "quantity" of evidence would "allow a rational finder of fact," *id.* at 254, to "return a verdict for the nonmoving party," *id.* at 248. Thus, as the Court has explained, "the 'genuine issue' summary judgment standard is very close to the 'reasonable jury' directed verdict standard" of Federal Rule of Civil Procedure 50(a). *Id.* at 251. The primary difference between the two is that the former is applied to documentary evidence submitted before trial, while the latter is applied to the evidence admitted at trial. *Id.* "In essence, though, the inquiry . . . is the same: whether the evidence presents a sufficient disagreement to require submission to a jury or whether it is so one-sided that one party must prevail as a matter of law." *Id.* at 251–52.

In undertaking the "genuine issue" inquiry, a court "must view the evidence presented through the prism of the [controlling] substantive evidentiary burden." *Id.* at 254. "If the defendant in a run-of-the-mill civil case moves for summary judgment . . . based on the lack of proof of a material fact, the judge must ask himself not whether he thinks the evidence unmistakably favors one side or the other," but rather whether there is evidence of a quantity and quality that would allow "reasonable jurors [to] find by a preponderance of the evidence that the plaintiff is entitled to a verdict." *Id.* at 252. By the same token, if the standard of proof at trial is, for example, "clear and convincing evidence," a court must find "no genuine issue if the evidence presented in the opposing affidavits is of insufficient caliber or quantity to allow a rational finder of fact to find [the fact in dispute] by clear and convincing evidence." *Id.* at 254.

To avoid usurping the role of the factfinder, a court deciding a summary judgment issue must accept as true the opposing party's evidence and assume all justifiable inferences that can be drawn therefrom. *See id.* at 255; *see also Beck v. Prupis*, 529 U.S. 494, 497 n.3 (2000). The court may not weigh the evidence to determine the "truth of the matter" as a factfinder would, and it may not make credibility determinations. *See Liberty Lobby*, 477 U.S. at 249, 255. Thus, the Supreme Court has explained that while a court must "give credence to the evidence favoring the nonmovant," it may only credit the "evidence supporting the moving party that is uncontradicted and unimpeached, at least to the extent that [it] comes from disinterested witnesses." *Reeves v. Sanderson Plumbing Prods., Inc.*, 530 U.S. 133, 149–51 (2000) (describing the standards governing judgments as a matter of law, but noting that the summary judgment and judgment as a matter of law standards mirror each other).

What is not entirely clear is the significance of the reference in *Reeves* to "disinterested witnesses." A literal reading would preclude consideration of uncontradicted and unimpeached testimony submitted by a moving party, simply because it comes from a witness with an interest in the outcome of the case. However, circuit courts that have addressed the issue generally refuse to so interpret the phrase. *See, e.g., Lauren W. ex rel. Jean W. v. Deflaminis*, 480 F.3d 259, 271–72 (3d Cir. 2007) ("[T]he court should believe uncontradicted testimony [submitted by a moving party] unless it is inherently implausible even if the testimony is that of an interested witness."); *Stratienko v. Cordis Corp.*, 429 F.3d 592, 597–98 (6th Cir. 2005) (to interpret *Reeves* as a blanket prohibition on consideration of affidavits of interested persons when the affidavits are submitted by a moving party would "lead[] to absurd consequences"). *But see Med. Care Am., Inc. v. Nat'l Union Fire Ins. Co.*, 341 F.3d 415, 420–22 & n.18 (5th Cir. 2003) (in resolving a motion for judgment as a matter of law, uncontradicted and unimpeached testimony supporting the moving party could not be considered because the moving party was one of the testifying witness's principal clients).

Rule 56(e)(2) provides that "[w]hen a motion for summary judgment is properly made and supported, an opposing party may not rely merely on allegations or denials in its own pleading; rather, its response must – by affidavits or as otherwise provided in this rule – set out specific facts showing a genuine issue for trial." In *Celotex*, the Court made clear that it is the burden of proof at trial that defines what a movant must show in order to require such a response from the adverse party. *See* 477 U.S. at 322–24. When the nonmoving party bears the burden of proof at trial on a dispositive issue, the moving party's burden of production "may be discharged by 'showing' – that is, pointing out to the district court – that there is an absence of evidence to support the nonmoving party's case." *Id.* at 325. Whether or not accompanied by affidavits, such a motion will be considered to have been "properly made and supported" as required by Rule 56(e) and will thus obligate the adverse party to "go beyond the pleadings and by her own affidavits, or by the 'depositions, answers to interrogatories, and admissions on file,' designate 'specific facts showing that there is a genuine issue for trial.' " *Id.* at 324 (quoting the pre–2007 version of FED. R. CIV. P. 56(e)). If "after adequate time for discovery," the adverse party "fails to make a showing sufficient to establish the existence of an element essential to that party's case," summary judgment must be granted. *Id.* at 322. In such a situation, "[t]he moving party is entitled to a judgment as a matter of law because the nonmoving party has failed to make a sufficient showing on an essential element of her case with respect to which she has the burden of proof." *Id.* at 323.

In contrast, when the moving party bears the burden of proof with respect to a dispositive issue, it must, using the materials specified in Rule 56(c), point to credible evidence that, if not controverted at trial, would entitle it to a judgment as a matter of law. *See id.* at 331, 334 (Brennan, J., dissenting) (describing the principles with respect to which he and the majority agreed). "Such an affirmative showing shifts the burden of production to the party opposing the motion and requires that party either to produce evidentiary materials that demonstrate the existence of a 'genuine issue' for trial" or to seek additional time for discovery. *Id.* (citing FED. R. CIV. P. 56(e), (f)); *see also Matsushita Elec. Indus. Co.*, 475 U.S. at 586–87.

As noted, Rule 56(e)(1) requires that "[a] supporting or opposing affidavit," supplemented by depositions or answers to interrogatories, "set out facts that would be admissible in evidence." This does not require that evidence be produced "in a form that would be admissible at trial." *Celotex*, 477 U.S. at 324. Rather, Rule 56(e) permits a summary judgment motion to be supported or opposed "by any of the kinds of evidentiary materials listed in Rule 56(c)." *Id.*; *see also Pietrowski v. Town of Dibble*, 134 F.3d 1006, 1008 (10th Cir. 1998); *Duplantis v. Shell Offshore, Inc.*, 948 F.2d 187, 192 (5th Cir. 1991). *But see Bushman v. Halm*, 798 F.2d 651, 655 n.5 (3d Cir.1986) (interpreting *Celotex* to permit consideration of a document that "was not in affidavit form nor authenticated as required by Rule 56(e)"). "Occasional statements . . . that the party opposing summary judgment must present admissible evidence should be understood in this light, as referring to the content or substance, rather than the form, of the submission." *Winskunas v. Birnbaum*, 23 F.3d 1264, 1268 (7th Cir. 1994); *see also Bailey v. Floyd County Bd. of Educ.*, 106 F.3d 135, 145 (6th Cir. 1997). If a district court declines to consider proffered evidence on the grounds that it will be inadmissible at trial, that determination will be reviewed only for abuse of discretion. *Gen. Elec. Co. v. Joiner*, 522 U.S. 136, 143 (1997).

Most denials of summary judgment motions are interlocutory in nature and thus not subject to immediate review. *See, e.g., Easter v. Am. W. Fin.*, 381 F.3d 948, 956 n.4 (9th Cir. 2004); *Empire Fire & Marine Ins. Co. v. Brantley Trucking, Inc.*, 220 F.3d 679, 681 n.5 (5th Cir. 2000). *But see, e.g., Mitchell v. Forsyth*, 472 U.S. 511 (1985) (holding that a district court's denial of a defendant's summary judgment motion was immediately appealable because the defendant was a public official asserting the defense of "qualified immunity" and his claim of immunity turned on whether certain uncontested facts showed a violation of clearly established law). If, however, the denial of a summary judgment motion is part of or accompanied by a final order otherwise disposing of a case before trial on the merits is complete, the appellate court, at its discretion, may consider the order denying summary judgment. *See, e.g., Max Arnold & Sons, LLC v. W.L. Hailey & Co.*, 452 F.3d 494, 505 (6th Cir. 2006) (on appeal of an order granting summary judgment to plaintiff, judicial economy favors consideration of the partial denial of defendant's cross motion for summary judgment); *Am. Motorists Ins. Co. v. United Furnace Co.*, 876 F.2d 293, 302 (2d Cir. 1989) (on appeal of an order granting defendant's motion to dismiss on ripeness grounds, judicial economy favors consideration of plaintiff's denied cross motion for summary judgment).

After a trial on the merits, the general rule is that an appeal of the denial of a summary judgment motion will not be considered. *See Chemetall GMBH v. ZR Energy, Inc.*, 320 F.3d 714, 718 (7th Cir. 2003) (citing cases). This is because " 'a denial of summary judgment based on a genuine dispute of material facts becomes moot and [therefore] unreviewable after trial since the dispute as to the facts has been resolved.' " *Becker v. Poling Transp. Corp.*, 356 F.3d 381, 391 (2d Cir. 2004) (quoting 19 MOORE, MOORE'S FEDERAL PRACTICE § 205.08[2] (1997)). However, a majority of circuits recognize an exception to this rule in the infrequent case in which the denial of summary judgment turned on a question of law rather than the presence of disputed facts. *See Chemetall*, 320 F.3d at 719 (citing cases). In these circuits, "when the material facts [were] not in dispute and the denial of summary judgment [was] based on the interpretation of a purely legal question, such a decision is appealable after final judgment." *White Consol. Indus., Inc. v. McGill Mfg. Co.*, 165 F.3d 1185, 1190 (8th Cir. 1999). *But see Varghese v. Honeywell Int'l, Inc.*, 424 F.3d 411, 423 (4th Cir. 2005) (upholding general rule of nonappealability regardless of basis of summary judgment order).

As noted above, *de novo* review of an entry of summary judgment is the norm. *See, e.g., United Paperworkers Int'l Union, Local 14 v. Int'l Paper Co.*, 64 F.3d 28, 31 (1st Cir. 1995); *Jurcev v. Cent. Cmty. Hosp.*, 7 F.3d 618, 623 (7th Cir. 1993). Without deference to the decision below, the appellate court examines the record to determine whether the district judge incorrectly identified the controlling substantive law, incorrectly applied the correct substantive law, or "overlooked or impermissibly resolved any disputed material facts." *Connors v. Incoal, Inc.*, 995 F.2d 245, 252 (D.C. Cir. 1993); *see also White v. ABCO Eng'g Corp.*, 221 F.3d 293, 300 (2d Cir. 2000). Courts of appeals rarely review true summary judgment rulings pursuant to the deferential "clearly erroneous" standard governing review of judicial findings of fact. *See, e.g., Brennan v. Twp. of Northville*, 78 F.3d 1152, 1156 (6th Cir. 1996) (standard of review applicable to judge's "erroneous factual assumption" made in the course of resolving summary judgment motion "is the same as that on summary judgment in general – de novo"); *Bowers v. Dep't of Justice*, 930 F.2d 350, 353 (4th Cir. 1991) ("[A]ny findings of fact made on a summary judgment motion are not entitled to the clearly erroneous protection on review."). Indeed, some circuits hold that "clear error review is *never* appropriate in the procedural context of a summary judgment motion when all facts are taken in the light most favorable to the nonmoving party." *Teamsters Indus. Employees Welfare Fund v. Rolls–Royce Motor Cars, Inc.*, 989 F.2d 132, 135 n.2 (3d Cir. 1993) (emphasis added); *see also Connors*, 995 F.2d at 251 n.9.

Occasionally, however, parties using the vehicle of a summary judgment motion will "submit[] their dispute to the court as a 'case stated,' " *United Paperworkers*, 64 F.3d at 31, or, in other words, as a case ready for decision on the merits. In these "somewhat unusual cases," "[t]he district court is . . . freed from the usual constraints that attend the adjudication of [such] motions." *Id*. The trial judge need not limit her consideration to the strictly legal question of whether the evidence viewed in the light most favorable to the nonmoving party is of a quality and quantity that would allow a reasonable juror to find for that party. Rather, deciding the case as she would in a bench trial, the trial judge "may engage in a certain amount of factfinding, including the drawing of inferences" regarding the "legal significance [that] should be ascribed to [the undisputed basic] facts." *Id*. In such instances, review of the resulting "summary judgment order" is sometimes for clear error, *see, e.g., García-Ayala v. Lederle Parenterals, Inc.*, 212 F.3d 638, 643–45 (1st Cir. 2000) (collecting cases); *Jurcev*, 7 F.3d at 623 (describing Seventh Circuit practice), though the conclusions of law supporting it will be reviewed *de novo, see, e.g., United Paperworkers*, 64 F.3d at 32 (reviewing *de novo* the district court's decision that a particular Supreme Court case was not controlling).

D. TESTING THE LEGAL SUFFICIENCY OF THE EVIDENCE IN CIVIL JURY TRIALS: FEDERAL RULE OF CIVIL PROCEDURE 50

Federal Rule of Civil Procedure 50 provides:

If a party has been fully heard on an issue during a jury trial and the court finds that a reasonable jury would not have a legally sufficient evidentiary basis to find for the party on that issue, the court may: (A) resolve the issue against the party; and (B) grant a motion for judgment as a matter of law against the party on a claim or defense that, under the controlling law, can be maintained or defeated only with a favorable finding on that issue.

FED. R. CIV. P. 50(a)(1). A motion for a judgment as a matter of law converts what would otherwise be a question of fact, reserved to the jury and generally protected from review by the Seventh Amendment, into a legal question. *See Galloway v. United States*, 319 U.S. 372, 388–89 (1943) (directed verdicts do not violate the Seventh Amendment); *Balt. & Carolina Line, Inc. v. Redman*, 295 U.S. 654, 656–59 (1935) (judgment notwithstanding the verdict does not violate the Seventh Amendment when issue was submitted to jury subject to reserved motion for directed verdict); *see also Weisgram v. Marley Co.*, 528 U.S. 440, 454 n.10 (2000); *Neely v. Martin K. Eby Constr. Co.*, 386 U.S. 317, 322 (1967). Such motions allow trial judges and, on review, appellate courts "to remove cases or issues from [a] jury's consideration when the facts are sufficiently clear that the law requires a particular result." *Weisgram*, 528 U.S. at 448; *see also id.* at 450. A properly granted judgment as a matter of law thus serves "the purpose of Rule 50 to speed litigation and to avoid unnecessary retrials." *Neely*, 386 U.S. at 326. However, because improperly granted judgments intrude upon the province of the jury, the standard is demanding and must be applied with caution. *See, e.g., Smith v. District of Columbia*, 413 F.3d 86, 97 (D.C. Cir. 2005); *Billingsley v. City of Omaha*, 277 F.3d 990, 993 (8th Cir. 2002).

Appellate courts review properly preserved sufficiency challenges *de novo*, applying the same standard as a trial judge resolving motions for judgments as a matter of law in the first instance. *See, e.g., Reeves*, 530 U.S. at 149–51; *see also* 9A WRIGHT & MILLER, FEDERAL PRACTICE & PROCEDURE §§ 2524 & n.3, 2540 & nn.10.1–.2 (1995 & Supp. 2006). Giving the benefit of all reasonable inferences to the party opposing the motion, both courts ask whether the properly admitted evidence would allow any reasonable juror to find for the nonmoving party. *See Reeves*, 530 U.S. at 149–51. Stated another way, the question is whether, "under the governing law, there can be but one reasonable conclusion as to the verdict." *Liberty Lobby*, 477 U.S. at 250. "If reasonable minds could differ as to the import of the evidence," a judgment as a matter of law may not be granted. *Id.* at 250–51. As the Supreme Court has explained, this "reasonable jury" standard is "very close" to the "genuine issue" summary judgment standard. *Id.* at 251.

The primary difference between the two motions is procedural; summary judgment motions are usually made before trial and decided on documentary evidence, while directed verdict motions are made at trial and decided on the evidence that has been admitted. In essence, though, the inquiry under each is the same: whether the evidence presents a sufficient disagreement to require submission to a jury or whether it is so one-sided that one party must prevail as a matter of law.

Id. at 251–52; *see also* Part One, Chapter III.C, *supra*.

While judgments as a matter of law are most often sought against the proponent of a claim, federal courts are free to grant judgment for the party bearing the burden of proof at trial. *See Slocum v. N.Y. Life Ins. Co.*, 228 U.S. 364, 369 (1913). The overarching question is the same: whether reasonable minds could differ with respect to what the evidence shows. *See, e.g., Marrero v. Goya of P.R., Inc.*, 304 F.3d 7, 22 (1st Cir. 2002); *EEOC v. Clear Lake Dodge*, 60 F.3d 1146, 1152 n.6 (5th Cir. 1995) (per curiam). Nevertheless, in practice, the standard for granting judgment in favor of a party bearing the burden of proof at trial is, "in critical respects[,] different from and more demanding than that applicable to the grant of [a] directed verdict *against* the proponent" of a claim. *Allen v. Zurich Ins. Co.*, 667 F.2d 1162, 1164 (4th Cir. 1982) (emphasis added); *see also Marrero*, 304 F.3d at 22. The evidence supporting the party bearing the burden of proof must be "so overwhelming that the jury could rationally reach no other result." *Broadnax v. City of New Haven*, 415 F.3d 265, 270 (2d Cir. 2005); *see also Marrero*, 304 F.3d at 22. "The ultimate conclusion that there is no genuine issue of fact depends not on [the nonmoving party's] failure to prove at least enough so that the controverted fact can be inferred, but rather ... on [the moving party having made] impossible any other equally strong inferences once the fact in issue is at least inferable." *Allen v. Zurich Ins. Co.*, 667 F.2d at 1164. Thus, before granting judgment, the trial judge or reviewing court "must be able to say not only that there is sufficient evidence to support the finding, even though other evidence could support as well a contrary finding, but additionally that there is insufficient evidence for permitting any different finding." *Massarsky v. Gen. Motors Corp.*, 706 F.2d 111, 119 (3d Cir. 1983). In general, instances in which a judgment as a matter of law is proper when the movant bears the burden of proof are "rare." *Broadnax*, 415 F.3d at 270; *see also EEOC v. Massey Yardley Chrysler Plymouth, Inc.*, 117 F.3d 1244, 1250 (11th Cir. 1997) (characterizing a judgment as a matter of law in favor of the party bearing the burden of proof as an "extreme step").

Like the tests for granting summary judgment in civil cases and judgments of acquittal in criminal cases, the standard for granting judgment as a matter of law "necessarily implicates the substantive evidentiary standard of proof that would apply at the trial on the merits." *Liberty Lobby*, 477 U.S. at 252; *see also id.* at 255. Consequently, in most civil cases, when a defendant seeks a judgment as a matter of law, the court "asks whether reasonable jurors could find by a preponderance of the evidence that the plaintiff is entitled to a verdict." *Id.* at 252. However, if the governing standard of proof is "clear and convincing evidence," then the courts must apply the reasonable juror standard in light of this greater evidentiary burden. *Id.* at 253–54.

Rule 50 provides that a motion for judgment as a matter of law may be granted only if the party opposing the motion has been "fully heard on an issue." FED. R. CIV. P. 50(a)(1). And, because "[c]redibility determinations, the weighing of the evidence, and the drawing of legitimate inferences from the facts are jury functions," a court "must disregard all evidence favorable to the moving party that the jury is not required to believe." *Reeves*, 530 U.S. at 150–51. As the Supreme Court has explained, this means that a court "should give credence to the evidence favoring the nonmovant as well as that evidence supporting the moving party that is uncontradicted and unimpeached, at least to the extent that that evidence comes from disinterested witnesses." *Id.* at 151; *see* Part One, Chapter III.C, *infra* (discussing the import of the phrase "disinterested witnesses"). In addition, courts of appeals reviewing sufficiency challenges must disregard all erroneously admitted evidence. *See Weisgram*, 528 U.S. at 453–56.

Rule 50 sets forth a two-step process for challenging the sufficiency of the evidence before the trial court. *See* FED. R. CIV. P. 50(a), (b). Rule 50(a) prescribes the first step, specifying that "[a] motion for judgment as a matter of law may be made at any time before the case is submitted to the jury." FED. R. CIV. P. 50(a)(2). It also provides that "the court *may* . . . resolve the issue against" a moving party when the "court finds that a reasonable jury would not have a legally sufficient evidentiary basis to find for the party on that issue." FED. R. CIV. P. 50(a)(1) (emphasis added). Thus, while a district court may enter a preverdict judgment (formerly known as a directed verdict) when it concludes that the evidence is legally insufficient, "it is not required to do so." *See Unitherm Food Sys., Inc. v. Swift–Eckrich, Inc.*, 546 U.S. 394, 405 (2006) (interpreting similar language in the pre–2006 version of the rule). In fact, as the Supreme Court has noted, efficiency concerns often counsel in favor of submitting to the jury issues with respect to which a trial judge thinks judgment is appropriate.

> If the jury agrees with the [trial] court's appraisal of the evidence, and returns a verdict for the party who moved for judgment as a matter of law, the case is at an end. If the jury brings in a different verdict, the trial court can grant a renewed motion for judgment as a matter of law. Then if the appellate court holds that the trial court was in error in its appraisal of the evidence, it can reverse and order judgment on the verdict of the jury, without any need for a new trial.

Id. at 406. Rule 50 makes no provision for seeking a new trial based on the insufficiency of the evidence prior to submission of a case to the jury, and the Court has held that trial courts are without authority to order such preverdict relief. *Id.* at 404–05.

Rule 50(b) prescribes the second step necessary to obtain appellate review of a sufficiency challenge, providing that "[i]f the court does not grant a motion ... made under Rule 50(a), the court is considered to have submitted the action to the jury subject to [it] later deciding the legal questions raised by the motion." However, Rule 50(b) does not obligate a district court to revisit the issue on its own motion, but rather provides that "[n]o later than 10 days after the entry of judgment ... the movant may file a renewed motion for judgment as a matter of law." A Rule 50(b) motion to renew (formerly known as a motion for judgment notwithstanding the verdict) can only advance grounds that were raised in a Rule 50(a) motion made prior to submission of the case to the jury. *See* FED. R. CIV. P. 50 advisory committee notes, 1963, 1991 & 2006 amendments. *Compare* FED. R. CRIM. P. 29(c) (explicitly stating that "[a] defendant is not required to move for a judgment of acquittal before the court submits the case to the jury as a prerequisite for making such a motion after jury discharge").

Rule 50(b) additionally provides that a party renewing a motion for judgment as a matter of law "may include an alternative or joint request for a new trial under Rule 59." In ruling on a renewed motion, a district court may allow a judgment to stand, order a new trial, or enter a judgment as a matter of law. FED. R. CIV. P. 50(b)(1), (2), (3). Pursuant to Rule 50(c), if a court grants judgment, it must conditionally rule on any joined or alternative new trial motion filed by the movant. FED. R. CIV. P. 50(c)(1).

In *Unitherm Food Systems, Inc. v. Swift–Eckrich, Inc.*, 546 U.S. 394, the Supreme Court established that the procedural requirements of Rule 50 are inviolate. The defendant in *Unitherm* had filed a preverdict Rule 50(a) motion for judgment as a matter of law. *Id.* at 398. The district court denied the motion and the jury returned a verdict for the plaintiff. *Id.* The defendant neither renewed its motion for judgment as a matter of law nor asked the trial court for a new trial based on the insufficiency of the evidence. On appeal, the Federal Circuit, interpreting Tenth Circuit law, ruled that a party who fails to file a postverdict sufficiency-of-the-evidence challenge can nonetheless seek a new trial on appeal, so long as the party filed a Rule 50(a) motion before submission of the case to the jury. *Id.* at 398–99.

Considering a challenge to this ruling, the Supreme Court first summarized precedent establishing "that an appellate court may not order judgment [following a verdict] where the verdict loser has failed strictly to comply with the procedural requirements of Rule 50(b)." *Id.* at 402 n.4. As the Court explained, these earlier cases established that "[a] postverdict motion is necessary because determination of whether a new trial should be granted or a judgment entered under Rule 50(b) calls for the judgment in the first instance of the judge who saw and heard the witnesses and has the feel of the case which no appellate printed transcript can impart. Moreover, the requirement of a timely application for judgment after verdict is not an idle motion because it is ... an essential part of the rule, firmly grounded in principles of fairness." *Id.* at 401.

The Court then noted that its "observations about the necessity of a postverdict motion under Rule 50(b), and the benefits of the district court's input at that stage, apply with equal force whether a party [claiming that the evidence is insufficient to support the verdict] is seeking judgment as a matter of law or simply a new trial." *Id.* at 402. It thus held that, because the defendant had failed to make "an appropriate postverdict motion in the district court," the court of appeals was powerless to order a new trial on the grounds that the evidence was insufficient to support the verdict. *Id.* at 404–07.

Assuming a sufficiency challenge is properly preserved, if an appellate court determines that the trial judge erroneously resolved a motion for judgment as a matter of law, the remedy is committed to that court's "informed discretion." *Neely*, 386 U.S. at 329. The Supreme Court made this clear in *Neely v. Martin K. Eby Construction Co.*, and, in 2007, Rule 50 was amended to describe this authority, *see* FED. R. CIV. P. 50(e); FED. R. CIV. P. 50 advisory committee notes, 2007 amendment. The question in *Neely* was whether a court of appeals, "after reversing the denial of a defendant's Rule 50(b) motion for judgment [as a matter of law], may itself order dismissal or direct entry of judgment for defendant." 386 U.S. at 321–22. Citing the language of Rule 50(c), as well as the accompanying Advisory Committee Notes, the Court first explained that if a district judge has improperly *granted* a motion for judgment as a matter of law, a court of appeals is free to (1) reverse and reinstate the jury's verdict or (2) reverse and grant a new trial. *Id.* at 323 & n.4. In choosing between these alternatives, an appellate court is not bound by the district judge's conditional ruling on any new trial motion filed by the party against whom judgment as a matter of law was granted. *Id.*

Turning to Rule 50(d) (amended and renumbered in 2007 as Rule 50(e)) and the available remedies when a district court judge has improperly *denied* a motion for judgment as a matter of law, the Court held that an appellate court may (1) reverse and direct the entry of a judgment for the party prevailing on appeal, (2) remand for the trial court to determine whether to grant a new trial or enter a judgment for the prevailing party, or (3) remand for a new trial. *Id.* at 323–29; *see also Weisgram*, 528 U.S. at 451–52. The Court explained that in exercising its discretion to select among these options, a court of appeals must give "due consideration [to] the rights of the verdict winner and the closeness of the trial court to the case." *Weisgram*, 528 U.S. at 451 (characterizing *Neely*). The appellate court "should be constantly alert" "to protect the rights of the party whose jury verdict has been set aside on appeal and who may have valid grounds for a new trial, some or all of which should be passed upon by the district court, rather than the court of appeals, because of the trial judge's first-hand knowledge of witnesses, testimony, and issues." *Neely*, 386 U.S. at 325; *Weisgram*, 528 U.S. at 451.

The Court concluded, however, that "these considerations do not justify an ironclad rule that the court of appeals should never order dismissal or judgment for defendant when the plaintiff's verdict has been set aside on appeal. Such a rule would not serve the purpose of Rule 50 to speed litigation and to avoid unnecessary retrials." *Neely*, 386 U.S. at 326. There are, it noted, "situations where the defendant's grounds for setting aside the jury's verdict raise questions of subject matter jurisdiction or dispositive issues of law which, if resolved in defendant's favor, must necessarily terminate the litigation." *Id.* at 327. "In such situations, and others like them, there can be no reason whatsoever to prevent the court of appeals from ordering dismissal of the action or the entry of judgment for the defendant." *Id.* Moreover, the Court reasoned that even with respect to cases in which the basis of a defendant's motion for judgment as a matter of law was the insufficiency of the plaintiff's evidence, the appellate court may be in as good a position as the trial judge to determine whether "fairness" dictates that the plaintiff should have an opportunity to retry the case. *Id.* Thus, for example, when a plaintiff who won the verdict argues that she is entitled to a new trial because the insufficiency of the evidence in her case was caused by the trial court's erroneous exclusion of evidence, the appellate court is as well suited as the trial court to address the issue. "[I]ssues like these are issues of law with which the courts of appeals regularly and characteristically must deal. The district court in all likelihood has already ruled on these questions in the course of the trial and, in any event, has no special advantage or competence in dealing with them." *Id.*

In sum, *Neely* makes clear that an appellate court must decide appropriate appellate remedies on a case-by-case basis, looking to the factors argued by the parties and identified by the court, as well as to whether the trial judge or the appellate bench is better suited to weigh those factors.

E. TESTING THE LEGAL SUFFICIENCY OF CRIMINAL TRIAL EVIDENCE

1. TAKING THE DECISION FROM A JURY: FEDERAL RULE OF CRIMINAL PROCEDURE 29 AND THE *JACKSON* STANDARD

In *Jackson v. Virginia*, 443 U.S. 307 (1979), the Supreme Court noted that the long-settled practice of allowing federal courts to enter judgments of acquittal when evidence is insufficient to sustain a conviction "only ... highlight[s] the traditional understanding in our system that the application of the beyond-a-reasonable-doubt standard to the evidence is not irretrievably committed to jury discretion." *Id.* at 317 n.10. A judgment of acquittal enables a federal court to protect a defendant's fundamental due process rights by removing from jury consideration a charge with respect to which no rational trier of fact could find guilt beyond a reasonable doubt. *Id.* at 317–19 & n.10.

The issue presented is a legal one. *United States v. Gaudin*, 515 U.S. 506, 517 (1995). Thus, a district court judge considering a motion for acquittal in the first instance and an appellate court reviewing the district court's decision apply the same standard. *Burks v. United States*, 437 U.S. 1, 16–17 & n.10 (1978). Neither court is to weigh the evidence or assess the credibility of witnesses. *Id.* at 16–17. And each must assume the inferences that are most favorable to the government. *Id.* The question, as articulated in *Jackson*, "is whether, after viewing the evidence in the light most favorable to the prosecution, *any* rational trier of fact could have found the essential elements of the crime beyond a reasonable doubt." 443 U.S. at 319; *see also id.* at 319 n.12 (noting that the often applied "substantial evidence" test of *Glasser v. United States*, 315 U.S. 60, 80 (1942), has "universally been understood" to encompass the same criterion).

Entry of a judgment of acquittal is thus "confined to cases where the prosecution's failure is clear." *Burks*, 437 U.S. at 17. But this does not mean that a sufficiency challenge can be resolved "through rote incantation" of the *Jackson* standard. *United States v. Collins*, 56 F.3d 1416, 1420 (D.C. Cir. 1995) (per curiam). Rather, a court must examine the record to ensure that a guilty verdict rests on inferences reasonably drawn from the evidence and not on mere speculation. *See, e.g., United States v. Long*, 905 F.2d 1572, 1576 (D.C. Cir. 1990); *see also United States v. Howard*, 179 F.3d 539, 542 (7th Cir. 1999); *United States v. Schuchmann*, 84 F.3d 752, 753 (5th Cir. 1996).

The *Jackson* standard "gives full play to the responsibility of the trier of fact fairly to resolve conflicts in the testimony, to weigh the evidence, and to draw reasonable inferences from basic facts to ultimate facts." *Jackson*, 443 U.S. at 319. "[T]he factfinder's role as weigher of the evidence is preserved through a legal conclusion that upon judicial review *all of the evidence* is to be considered in the light most favorable to the prosecution. The criterion thus impinges upon 'jury' discretion only to the extent necessary to guarantee the fundamental protection of due process of law." *Id.*

Federal Rule of Criminal Procedure 29 and the case law interpreting it prescribe the procedures for seeking a judgment of acquittal during a jury trial and the effect on appellate review of the procedures followed. The rule permits a defendant to seek a judgment of acquittal at the close of the government's case-in-chief and after both sides rest. FED. R. CRIM. P. 29(a). In addition, the rule states that a defendant "may move for a judgment of acquittal, or renew such a motion," within seven days of a guilty verdict or jury discharge. FED. R. CRIM. P. 29(c). If a defendant fails to seek a postverdict acquittal within the specified time, the trial court "may nonetheless consider that untimely motion if the court determines that the failure to file it on time was the result of excusable neglect." FED. R. CRIM. P. 29 advisory committee notes, 2005 amendments; *see also* FED. R. CRIM. P. 45(b)(1)(B). Rule 29 also specifies that a trial court may "on its own consider whether the evidence is insufficient," but it must do so before it submits the case to the jury. FED. R. CRIM. P. 29(a); *see also Carlisle v. United States*, 517 U.S. 416, 421–23 (1996).

A motion for judgment of acquittal at the close of the government's case-in-chief is said to "implement[] the requirement that the prosecution must establish a prima facie case by its own evidence before the defendant may be put to his defense." 2A WRIGHT, FEDERAL PRACTICE & PROCEDURE § 462 & n.5 (2000) (citing cases). In reality, however, there is no mechanism to enforce this "requirement" since, pursuant to Rule 29(b), a district judge can reserve a motion made at the close of the government's case, "proceed with the trial ..., and decide the motion either before the jury returns a verdict or after it returns a verdict of guilty or is discharged without having returned a verdict."

Rule 29 does provide that when a trial court reserves decision, "it must decide the motion on the basis of the evidence at the time the ruling was reserved." FED. R. CRIM. P. 29(b). The Advisory Committee Notes state that appellate review should be similarly limited. FED. R. CRIM. P. 29 advisory committee notes, 1994 amendments. In contrast, if a district judge, following the government's case-in-chief, *denies* a motion for acquittal, any evidence subsequently submitted by the defendant will be considered on appellate review. *United States v. Calderon*, 348 U.S. 160, 164 & n.1 (1954). Thus, a defendant who believes that critical defense evidence will fill the gaps in the prosecution's case, must either stand on her motion and test the sufficiency of the government's prima facie case on appeal or present a complete defense to the jury and risk bolstering the case against her.

Rule 29 explicitly states that "[a] defendant is not required to move for a judgment of acquittal before the court submits the case to the jury as a prerequisite for making such a motion after jury discharge." FED. R. CRIM. P. 29(c). *Compare* FED. R. CIV. P. 50 (making clear that while motions for judgment as a matter of law may be "renewed" postverdict, they may not be initiated postverdict). However, a defendant gains an undisputed advantage from a preverdict judgment, since " '[s]ubject[ion] ... to postacquittal factfinding proceedings going to guilt or innocence violates the Double Jeopardy Clause.' " *Smith v. Massachusetts*, 543 U.S. 462, 467 (2005) (quoting *Smalis v. Pennsylvania*, 476 U.S. 140, 145 (1986)). Consequently, appeal and retrial are prohibited when a defendant secures a judgment of acquittal before a jury returns a verdict. *Id.* If a judgment of acquittal is entered after a jury has deadlocked, appeal and retrial are similarly prohibited. *See id.*; *see also United States v. Martin Linen Supply Co.*, 430 U.S. 564, 571 (1977). If, however, a judgment of acquittal is entered after a guilty verdict is returned, "the Double Jeopardy Clause *does not* preclude a prosecution appeal to reinstate the jury verdict of guilty." *Smith v. Massachusetts*, 543 U.S. at 467 (citing *United States v. Wilson*, 420 U.S. 332, 352–53 (1975)) (emphasis added); *see also* 18 U.S.C. § 3731 (providing for appeal by the United States except where barred by the Double Jeopardy Clause).

If a district court grants a motion for a judgment of acquittal after a guilty verdict, it must conditionally resolve any defense motion seeking a new trial pursuant to Federal Rule of Criminal Procedure 33. FED. R.

Crim. P. 29(D)(1). IF A TRIAL COURT CONDITIONALLY GRANTS A NEW TRIAL MOTION AND THE APPELLATE COURT REVERSES THE JUDGMENT OF ACQUITTAL, "THE TRIAL COURT MUST PROCEED WITH THE NEW TRIAL UNLESS THE APPELLATE COURT ORDERS OTHERWISE." Fed. R. Crim. P. 29(D)(3)(A). IF THE DISTRICT COURT CONDITIONALLY DENIES A NEW TRIAL MOTION, THE DEFENDANT MAY, ON APPEAL, ARGUE THAT THE CONDITIONAL DENIAL OF THE NEW TRIAL MOTION WAS ERROR. Fed. R. Crim. P. 29(D)(3)(B). IF THE APPELLATE COURT REVERSES THE JUDGMENT OF ACQUITTAL, IT MAY DIRECT THE DISTRICT COURT TO UNDERTAKE A NEW TRIAL. *SEE ID.* A DEFENDANT'S REQUEST FOR A NEW TRIAL DOES NOT WAIVE HIS RIGHT TO AN ACQUITTAL IF THE EVIDENCE IS INSUFFICIENT TO SUPPORT HIS CONVICTION. *BURKS*, 437 U.S. AT 17–18. ON APPEAL, CONDITIONAL RULINGS ON NEW TRIAL MOTIONS ARE REVIEWED FOR ABUSE OF DISCRETION. *SEE, E.G., UNITED STATES V. ESPAILLET*, 380 F.3D 713, 720 (2D CIR. 2004); *UNITED STATES V. WARD*, 274 F.3D 1320, 1322–23 (11TH CIR. 2001) (PER CURIAM).

If a defendant fails to request a judgment of acquittal or fails to follow the procedures of Rule 29, appellate review of any subsequent sufficiency challenge is for plain error. *See Clyatt v. United States*, 197 U.S. 207, 221–22 (1905) (citing *Wiborg v. United States*, 163 U.S. 632, 658 (1896)); *see also Carlisle*, 517 U.S. at 436 (Ginsburg, J., concurring) (relying on the government's concession that a defendant who files an untimely motion for acquittal is entitled to plain error review). With respect to the vast majority of appellate challenges, reversal pursuant to the plain error standard is more difficult to secure than reversal based on preserved error subject to the harmless error doctrine. *See* Part One, Chapters VI–VIII, *infra* (describing review under the harmless error and plain error standards). Reversal for plain error is only possible when an appellate court finds an error that is "plain" (meaning clear or obvious) and that "affects" a defendant's "substantial rights." *United States v. Olano*, 507 U.S. 725, 732–34 (1993). When these first three requirements are met, "an appellate court must then determine whether the forfeited error seriously affects the fairness, integrity or public reputation of judicial proceedings before it may exercise its discretion to correct the error." *Johnson v. United States*, 520 U.S. 461, 469–70 (1997) (citing *Olano*, 507 U.S. at 736).

In the sufficiency context, however, there is a question as to whether plain error review is really any different than *de novo* review. As noted by the D.C. Circuit, review under the plain error standard should "[p]resumably . . . be more deferential than under the usual [*Jackson*] standard." *United States v. White*, 1 F.3d 13, 17 (D.C. Cir. 1993). But because "[t]he *Jackson* standard already suggests that [a court] would only reverse for an error that was 'plain' (in the sense of 'obvious') and requires, by definition, that the error prejudice substantial rights," it is "hard to imagine" what that more deferential standard would be. *Id.*; *see also United States v. Spinner*, 152 F.3d 950, 956 (D.C. Cir. 1998) (acknowledging the circuit's previously expressed uncertainty regarding how plain error review of sufficiency claims might differ from *de novo* review under *Jackson*). The Ninth Circuit has similarly noted the difficulty of distinguishing "manifest miscarriage of justice" or "plain error" review from the review applicable when a "defendant has made all the proper motions." *United States v. Alvarez–Valenzuela*, 231 F.3d 1198, 1200–01 (9th Cir. 2000); *see also United States v. Vizcarra–Martinez*, 66 F.3d 1006, 1010 (9th Cir. 1995).

Although the Supreme Court has never explicitly addressed the question, its analysis of unpreserved sufficiency challenges suggests that there may be little difference between review of preserved and unpreserved claims. Applying a plain error standard to an unpreserved sufficiency claim in *Clyatt*, the Court declared it "the imperative duty of a court to see that all the elements of [the charged] crime are proved, or at least that testimony is offered which justifies a jury in finding those elements." 197 U.S. at 222. Similarly in *Wiborg v. United States*, the Court, assessing the record under the plain error standard, examined the evidence to determine whether the jury's inferences were "unreasonabl[e]" and whether there was "adequate proof" to sustain them. 163 U.S. at 658–60. With respect to one defendant, it found that the jury's verdict was not unreasonable given the record evidence. *Id.* at 659. With respect to two others, it reversed after concluding that there was "nothing sufficiently justifying" the jury's presumption of knowledge, a necessary prerequisite to guilt in that case. *Id.* at 660. Although these cases predate *Jackson*, their analysis essentially tracks the reasonable inferences test articulated in it.

A number of circuits apply the *Jackson* standard to unpreserved or improperly preserved sufficiency claims, essentially equating *de novo* and plain error sufficiency review. The Third Circuit, for example, holds that a failure of proof, as measured by the *Jackson* standard, constitutes reversible plain error since the affirmance of "a conviction where the government has failed to prove each essential element of the crime beyond a reasonable doubt 'affects substantial rights,' and seriously impugns 'the fairness, integrity and public reputation of judicial proceedings.' " *United States v. Gaydos*, 108 F.3d 505, 509 (3d Cir. 1997) (quoting *Olano*, 507 U.S. at 732); *see also United States v. Mornan*, 413 F.3d 372, 381–82 (3d Cir. 2005); *United States v. Wolfe*, 245 F.3d 257, 260–61 (3d Cir. 2001). Although noting that it has "stated the plain error standard in different words," including, "palpably wrong" and "miscarriage of justice," *United States v. Bowie*, 892 F.2d 1494, 1496–97 (10th Cir. 1990), the Tenth Circuit also concludes that plain error review and *de novo* review of preserved sufficiency claims "usually amount to largely the same exercise," *United States v. Kimler*, 335 F.3d 1132, 1141 n.10 (10th Cir. 2003), because "a conviction in the absence of sufficient evidence of guilt is plainly an error, clearly prejudice[s] the defendant, and almost always creates manifest injustice," *United States v. Goode*, 483 F.3d 676, 681 n.1 (10th Cir. 2007). The First and Eighth Circuits also assess improperly preserved sufficiency challenges pursuant to the *Jackson* reasonable inferences standard, though the former court describes its review as one requiring a defendant to "demonstrate clear and gross injustice." *See, e.g., United States v. Van Horn*, 277 F.3d 48, 54–56 (1st Cir. 2002); *United States v. Stein*, 233 F.3d 6, 20–21 (1st Cir.

2000); *United States v. Londondio*, 420 F.3d 777, 786 (8th Cir. 2005); *United States v. Cole*, 262 F.3d 704, 708 (8th Cir. 2001).

In contrast, other courts have explicitly declined to apply the *Jackson* standard to unpreserved or improperly preserved sufficiency challenges. *See, e.g., United States v. Herrera*, 313 F.3d 882, 884–85 & n.* (5th Cir. 2002) (en banc) (per curiam); *United States v. Owens*, 301 F.3d 521, 527–28 (7th Cir. 2002); *United States v. Thompson*, 279 F.3d 1043, 1050–51 (D.C. Cir. 2002); *United States v. Hernandez*, 227 F.3d 686, 694 (6th Cir. 2000). Some of these courts will grant unpreserved or improperly preserved sufficiency challenges only if "the record is devoid of evidence pointing to guilt." *Herrera*, 313 F.3d at 885; *see also Thompson*, 279 F.3d at 1051; *Hernandez*, 227 F.3d at 694. Others, applying a slightly less demanding standard, will also reverse when evidence was presented if the evidence "was so tenuous that a conviction would be shocking." *United States v. Whitlow*, 381 F.3d 679, 685 (7th Cir. 2004); *see also United States v. Wright*, 63 F.3d 1067, 1072 (11th Cir. 1995).

Whether the "devoid of evidence" standard (or anything close to it) survives *Jackson* is questionable. In *Jackson*, the Court "granted certiorari to consider the . . . claim that . . . a federal habeas corpus court must consider not whether there was *any* evidence to support a state-court conviction, but whether there was sufficient evidence to justify a rational trier of the facts to find guilt beyond a reasonable doubt." *Jackson*, 443 U.S. at 312–13. Stated another way, the question was whether the "no-evidence doctrine" of *Thompson v. City of Louisville*, 362 U.S. 199 (1960), then regularly applied by federal courts of appeals resolving sufficiency challenges under the controlling habeas statute, satisfied the due process guarantee "that no person shall be made to suffer the onus of a criminal conviction except upon sufficient proof." *Jackson*, 443 U.S. at 316. Pursuant to the no-evidence doctrine, as long as a jury was given a proper reasonable doubt instruction, a state conviction would be reversed as unconstitutional only if the record was devoid of evidence supporting the conviction. *Id.* (citing, as an example, *Cunha v. Brewer*, 511 F.2d 894 (8th Cir. 1975)). The *Jackson* Court explicitly rejected that doctrine. *Id.* Explaining that a properly instructed jury, or trial judge sitting as jury, "may occasionally convict even when it can be said that no rational trier of fact could find guilt beyond a reasonable doubt," *id.* at 317, the Court held that under the Due Process Clause "the critical inquiry on review of the sufficiency of the evidence to support a criminal conviction must be . . . *whether the record evidence could reasonably support a finding of guilt beyond a reasonable doubt*," *id.* at 318 (emphasis added).

One semantic matter that sometimes causes particular confusion with respect to review of unpreserved or improperly preserved sufficiency challenges is worth noting. In many circuits, the term "waiver" is used to describe the effect of a defendant's failure properly to preserve a sufficiency challenge. Thus, for example, some opinions state that a defendant who puts on a defense after a motion to acquit has been denied at the close of the government's case-in-chief, will be considered to have "waived" his right to appeal the sufficiency of the evidence if he fails to renew the initial motion at the close of all of the evidence or as specified in Rule 29(c). *See, e.g., United States v. Maldonado–García*, 446 F.3d 227, 230 (1st Cir. 2006); *United States v. Booker*, 436 F.3d 238, 241 (D.C. Cir. 2006); *United States v. Wagner*, 382 F.3d 598, 611 n.2 (6th Cir. 2004); *United States v. Delgado*, 256 F.3d 264, 274 (5th Cir. 2001); *Cole*, 262 F.3d at 708; *United States v. Taylor*, 226 F.3d 593, 596 (7th Cir. 2000); *Bowie*, 892 F.2d at 1496. Similarly, various opinions state that a defendant who altogether fails to seek a judgment of acquittal "waives" any sufficiency challenge on appeal. *See, e.g., United States v. DeGeorge*, 380 F.3d 1203, 1216 (9th Cir. 2004); *United States v. Lopez*, 380 F.3d 538, 547 (1st Cir. 2004); *United States v. Gooding*, 351 F.3d 738, 741 (6th Cir. 2003); *United States v. Buchmeier*, 255 F.3d 415, 419 (7th Cir. 2001). In addition, while a defendant seeking a judgment of acquittal need not articulate a particular basis for challenging the sufficiency of the evidence, when a defendant does cite specific grounds without making it clear that he is also challenging the sufficiency of the evidence generally, grounds that are not argued are often said to be "waived." *See, e.g., United States v. Moore*, 363 F.3d 631, 637 (7th Cir. 2004), *vacated*, 543 U.S. 1100 (2005); *Kimler*, 335 F.3d at 1141; *Herrera*, 313 F.3d at 884–85; *United States v. Chance*, 306 F.3d 356, 369 (6th Cir. 2002); *United States v. Belardo–Quiñones*, 71 F.3d 941, 945 (1st Cir. 1995).

Given the broadly accepted meaning of the term "waiver" in the appellate context, its application in these situations is a misnomer. A waiver is generally understood to involve an " 'intentional relinquishment or abandonment of a known right.' " *Olano*, 507 U.S. at 733 (quoting *Johnson v. Zerbst*, 304 U.S. 458, 464 (1938)). When a right is waived, any "error" on the part of the district court with respect to that right is "extinguish[ed]" and appeal is prohibited. *Id.* at 733–34. While, as noted, there may be some disagreement regarding the meaning of plain error review in the sufficiency context, virtually all circuits will review unpreserved or improperly preserved sufficiency challenges if the error is "bad enough." *See* 2A WRIGHT, FEDERAL PRACTICE & PROCEDURE § 469 (2000); *see also id.* at § 469 nn. 19–24 (citing cases). Thus, despite the frequently applied waiver label, review of unpreserved or improperly preserved sufficiency claims is more accurately described as taking place within the forfeiture framework. *See also Goode*, 483 F.3d at 681 ("Although we have described the failure to raise a challenge in district court as a 'waiver,' it is more precisely termed a forfeiture when there is no suggestion of a knowing, voluntary failure to raise the matter."); *Van Horn*, 277 F.3d at 54 (absent renewal, a defendant's "objection is deemed forfeited"); *Alvarez-Valenzuela*, 231 F.3d at 1200 ("After reviewing the cases cited by both parties, we interpret Rule 29(a) to suggest that failure to renew the motion at the end of trial does not mean that it has been waived, but only that a higher standard of review is to be imposed.").

2. REVERSING GUILTY VERDICTS IN BENCH TRIALS FOR INSUFFICIENT EVIDENCE: *JACKSON* PLUS

The constitutional right to trial by jury, *see* U.S. CONST. art. III, § 2; U.S. CONST. amend. VI, does not extend to all criminal proceedings. *See Cheff v. Schnackenberg*, 384 U.S. 373, 379 (1966) (plurality opinion) (prosecution of "petty offenses" does not require a jury trial). Moreover, pursuant to Federal Rule of Criminal Procedure 23(a), a defendant may waive the right to a jury trial.

When a criminal case is tried without a jury, Rule 23(c) provides that "the court must find the defendant guilty or not guilty." The rule also states that "[i]f a party requests before the finding of guilty or not guilty, the court must state its specific findings of fact in open court or in a written decision or opinion." FED. R. CRIM. P. 23(c).

In *Jackson*, the Supreme Court held that "the critical inquiry on review of the sufficiency of the evidence to support a criminal conviction must be ... to determine whether the record evidence could reasonably support a finding of guilt beyond a reasonable doubt." 443 U.S. at 318. In reaching this conclusion, the Court drew no distinction between judge and jury verdicts. *See id.* at 318 n.11 (referring to the "fact finder in a criminal case"). And while circuit opinions resolving sufficiency challenges to convictions rendered in bench trials frequently cite the "substantial evidence" test of *Glasser*, 315 U.S. at 80, most modern decisions track the *de novo*, but highly deferential standard enunciated in *Jackson*. Thus, when the sufficiency of the evidence to support a bench conviction is challenged on appeal, the governing standard is the same as if the challenged conviction had been rendered by a jury. The question is whether, " 'after viewing the evidence in the light most favorable to the prosecution, any rational trier of fact could have found the essential elements of the crime beyond a reasonable doubt.' " *United States v. Baldwin*, 414 F.3d 791, 796 (7th Cir. 2005) (quoting *Jackson*, 443 U.S. at 319); *see also United States v. Meléndez-Torres*, 420 F.3d 45, 49 (1st Cir. 2005); *United States v. Shambry*, 392 F.3d 631, 634 (3d Cir. 2004); *United States v. Turner*, 319 F.3d 716, 720 (5th Cir. 2003); *United States v. Magallon–Jimenez*, 219 F.3d 1109, 1112 (9th Cir. 2000); *United States v. Norman T.*, 129 F.3d 1099, 1103 (10th Cir. 1997); *United States v. Bryant*, 117 F.3d 1464, 1467–68 (D.C. Cir. 1997).

If a defendant fails to request special findings, as permitted by Rule 23(c), and the district judge makes none, the court of appeals will infer the findings necessary to support any theory of guilt presented to the district judge, provided the inferred findings are supported by the evidence viewed in the light most favorable to the prosecution. *See, e.g., United States v. Farrell*, 126 F.3d 484, 491 (3d Cir. 1997); *United States v. Powell*, 973 F.2d 885, 889 (10th Cir. 1992); *United States v. Musser*, 873 F.2d 1513, 1519 (D.C. Cir. 1989).

When a trial judge does state "specific findings of fact" pursuant to Rule 23(c), some courts of appeals hold that although the ultimate inference of guilt is subject to *de novo* review pursuant to *Jackson*, underlying findings of historical fact are subject to the clearly erroneous standard of Federal Rule of Civil Procedure 52(a)(6). *See, e.g., United States v. Caseer*, 399 F.3d 828, 839–44 (6th Cir. 2005); *United States v. Lockhart*, 382 F.3d 447, 450–51 (4th Cir. 2004); *United States v. DeCorte*, 851 F.2d 948, 951–54 (7th Cir. 1988). Although the Supreme Court has made it plain that Rule 52(a)(6)'s clearly erroneous standard applies in the criminal context "with respect to factual questions having nothing to do with guilt," *Maine v. Taylor*, 477 U.S. 131, 145 (1986), the Court has yet to say whether clearly erroneous review is appropriate when the challenged findings pertain to an element of the offense. In any event, it may be that there is no real difference between *de novo* review under *Jackson* and review under the clearly erroneous standard, given the highly deferential nature of the former and the fact that clearly erroneous review, when applied in the criminal context, must necessarily take account of the government's burden to prove each element of an offense beyond a reasonable doubt. *See generally Concrete Pipe & Prods. of Cal., Inc. v. Constr. Laborers Pension Trust for S. Cal.*, 508 U.S. 602, 622–23 (1993) (Clearly erroneous review describes the degree of certainty with which the appellate court must be able to find that the factfinder "made a mistake in concluding that a fact had been proven *under the applicable standard of proof.*") (emphasis added); *see also United States v. Delerme*, 457 F.2d 156, 160 (3d Cir. 1972) (concluding that, in so far as a trial judge's findings of historical facts are subject to a sufficiency challenge, "there is no practical difference" between the *Jackson* standard and clearly erroneous review).

There is no suggestion in Rule 23(c) that a motion for a judgment of acquittal must be made before the trial court in order to preserve a sufficiency challenge to a bench conviction. And by its language, Federal Rule of Criminal Procedure 29, governing motions for judgments of acquittal, applies only to jury trials. Moreover, Rule 29 arguably "has no real application when a case is tried by the court since" the trial judge "must conduct the same analysis of the law and the evidence whether [she] evaluates a motion for acquittal under Rule 29 or adjudicates a not guilty plea." *United States v. Grace*, 367 F.3d 29, 34 (1st Cir. 2004). Consequently, most circuits that have addressed the issue hold that the failure to seek a judgment of acquittal in a bench trial does not affect review of an appellate challenge to the sufficiency of the evidence supporting a trial judge's guilty verdict. *See United States v. Hurn*, 368 F.3d 1359, 1368 n.5 (11th Cir. 2004); *Grace*, 367 F.3d at 34; *United States v. Ceballos–Torres*, 218 F.3d 409, 411 n.3 (5th Cir. 2000); *United States v. Hogan*, 89 F.3d 403, 404 (7th Cir. 1996); *United States v. Atkinson*, 990 F.2d 501, 502–03 (9th Cir. 1993) (en banc); *United States v. Cox*, 929 F.2d 1511, 1514 (10th Cir. 1991); *United States v. Besase*, 373 F.2d 120, 121 (6th Cir. 1967); *see also United States v. Khan*, 461 F.3d 477, 487–88 (4th Cir. 2006) (reviewing *de novo* without explicitly addressing the issue); *United States v. Whitlock*, 663 F.2d 1094, 1097 n.24 (D.C. Cir. 1980) (opinion of Robinson, J.). *But see United States v.*

Schier, 438 F.3d 1104, 1107 (11th Cir. 2006) (when a defendant in a bench trial moves for a judgment of acquittal at the close of the government's case but fails to renew the motion at the close of all of the evidence, the appellate court will affirm the conviction against a sufficiency challenge unless to do so would amount to a manifest miscarriage of justice).

Chapter IV

REVIEW OF FINDINGS AND CONCLUSIONS SUPPORTING RULE 52 JUDGMENTS IN CIVIL BENCH TRIALS: CLEARLY ERRONEOUS REVIEW, *DE NOVO* REVIEW, AND THE "MIXED QUESTION" CONUNDRUM

The Trial by Jury and Re-examination Clauses of the Seventh Amendment protect the common law authority of a jury to find the facts and apply the law to those facts to reach a verdict. *See generally Markman v. Westview Instruments, Inc.*, 517 U.S. 370, 376–78 (1996); *Balt. & Carolina Line, Inc. v. Redman*, 295 U.S. 654 (1935). Pursuant to these constitutional strictures, judicial interference with a jury's decisionmaking authority is, absent procedural or evidentiary error, generally constrained to the legal question of whether "the facts are sufficiently clear that the law requires a particular result." *Weisgram v. Marley Co.*, 528 U.S. 440, 448 (2000). Whether raised before a trial judge pursuant to a motion for judgment as a matter of law or challenged on appeal after properly preserving the issue below, the test is the same: giving the benefit of all reasonable inferences to the nonmoving party, the court asks whether any reasonable juror could find for that party on the basis of the properly admitted evidence. *See Reeves v. Sanderson Plumbing Prods., Inc.*, 530 U.S. 133, 149–51 (2000); *see also* Part One, Chapter III.D, *supra*.

No similar constitutional limitations constrain judicial action in cases tried without a jury or with an advisory jury. In such cases, Federal Rule of Civil Procedure 52, and the case law interpreting it, largely prescribe when and how district judges may find facts and reach conclusions of law in support of judgments and, to a lesser degree, how closely appellate courts may scrutinize those findings and conclusions.

Rule 52 states:

> In an action tried on the facts without a jury or with an advisory jury, the court must find the facts specially and state its conclusions of law separately. The findings and conclusions may be stated on the record after the close of the evidence or may appear in an opinion or a memorandum of decision filed by the court.

FED. R. CIV. P. 52(a)(1). The requirement that the facts be found specially encourages care on the part of trial judges, makes possible meaningful appellate review of those facts, and promotes the application of *res judicata* and estoppel by judgment. *See* FED. R. CIV. P. 52 advisory committee notes, 1946 amendment. And it applies whether a district judge issues a judgment following submission of all of the evidence or exercises her discretion to enter a judgment on partial findings. *See* FED. R. CIV. P. 52(c). A judge may issue a judgment on partial findings with respect to a "claim or defense that, under the controlling law, can be maintained or defeated only with a favorable finding on that issue" "[i]f a party has been fully heard on an issue" and "the court finds against the party on that issue." FED. R. CIV. P. 52(c). (In 2007, the language of Rule 52(c) was amended to clarify that the standards governing Rule 50 motions for judgment as a matter of law in jury cases and their review on appeal are inapplicable to review of judgments on partial findings in bench trials. *See* FED. R. CIV. P. 52 advisory committee notes, 2007 amendment.)

Rule 52 also specifies the standard of appellate review applicable to factual findings supporting judgments and partial judgments. Subsection (a)(6), titled Setting Aside the Findings, provides:

> Findings of fact, whether based on oral or other evidence, must not be set aside unless clearly erroneous, and the reviewing court must give due regard to the trial court's opportunity to judge the witnesses' credibility.

Pursuant to the clearly erroneous standard, judicial findings of fact are presumptively correct. *See Bose Corp. v. Consumers Union of U.S., Inc.,* 466 U.S. 485, 500 (1984). This presumption "recognizes and rests upon the unique opportunity afforded the trial court judge to evaluate the credibility of witnesses and to weigh the evidence," *Inwood Labs., Inc. v. Ives Labs., Inc.,* 456 U.S. 844, 855 (1982), the comparative expertise of trial and appellate judges, and the cost of duplicative appellate decision-making, *Anderson v. Bessemer City,* 470 U.S. 564, 574–75 (1985). Pursuant to this presumption, a finding of fact will not be overturned as "clearly erroneous" unless, "although there is evidence to support it, the reviewing court on the entire evidence is left with the definite and firm conviction that a mistake has been committed." *Id.* at 573; *see also* Part One, Chapter II, *supra* (discussing Supreme Court precedent giving meaning to the clearly erroneous standard).

In addition, Rule 52 makes clear that, in contrast to most questions raised on appeal, an appellate challenge to the sufficiency of the evidence supporting the factual findings on which a judgment or judgment on partial findings rests is not affected by a party's failure to preserve the issue. Rule 52(a)(5) states:

> A party may later question the sufficiency of the evidence supporting the findings, whether or not the party requested findings, objected to them, moved to amend them, or moved for partial findings.

Plain error review is, consequently, inapplicable to review of such challenges. However, when a district judge altogether fails to make findings or fails to make findings with respect to a material issue, appellate courts normally vacate the judgment and remand for the judge to make those findings. *See Pullman–Standard v. Swint*, 456 U.S. 273, 291–92 & n.22 (1982).

Rule 52 does not describe how conclusions of law are to be reviewed. It is well understood, however, that they are not subject to clearly erroneous review. *See id.* at 287. Appellate courts are consequently free to correct a trial judge's "errors of law, including those that may infect a so-called mixed finding of law and fact, or a finding of fact that is predicated on a misunderstanding of the governing rule of law." *Bose*, 466 U.S. at 501. Thus, just as when a jury verdict is based on an erroneous instruction, if a trial judge's finding of "ultimate" fact – so characterized because it is the finding that determines the outcome of litigation – is a result of the application of an improper standard to the subsidiary facts, it may be corrected as a matter of law. *Id.* at 500 n.16 & 501. Similarly, if a trial court's findings of subsidiary or historical facts are predicated "upon a mistaken impression of applicable legal principles, the reviewing court is not bound by the clearly erroneous standard." *Inwood Labs.*, 456 U.S. at 855 & n.15. When faced with the latter situation, appellate courts either will state that the error committed by the trial court is legal and subject the trial court's factual finding to *de novo* review, *see, e.g., Houston Exploration Co. v. Halliburton Energy Servs., Inc.*, 359 F.3d 777, 779 (5th Cir. 2004); *Harrison v. United States*, 284 F.3d 293, 297–98 (1st Cir. 2002), or will conclude that the findings of fact predicated on the incorrect articulation of the law are clearly erroneous, *see, e.g., United States v. Capital Sand Co.*, 466 F.3d 655, 658 (8th Cir. 2006); *Red Lake Band of Chippewa Indians v. United States*, 936 F.2d 1320, 1324–25 (D.C. Cir. 1991).

Unlike challenges to the sufficiency of the evidence supporting factual findings, Rule 52 does not exempt challenges to a trial judge's legal conclusions from the preservation requirement of *de novo* review. Legal issues that are first presented on appeal are typically subject to plain error review, *see, e.g., Crawford v. Falcon Drilling Co.*, 131 F.3d 1120, 1123–29 (5th Cir. 1997), or one of the closely related doctrines allowing appellate review only to avoid a "miscarriage of justice" or a "manifest injustice," *see, e.g, Tho Dinh Tran v. Alphonse Hotel Corp.*, 281 F.3d 23, 32–33 (2d Cir. 2002), *overruled on other grounds by Slayton v. Am. Express Co.*, 460 F.3d 215 (2d Cir. 2006) (manifest injustice); *DiMarco-Zappa v. Cabanillas*, 238 F.3d 25, 34–35 (1st Cir. 2001) (miscarriage of justice).

Although the standards of review applicable to findings of fact and conclusions of law supporting judgments in civil bench trials are thus fairly easily stated, Rule 52 does not "furnish particular guidance with respect to distinguishing law from fact." *Bose*, 466 U.S. at 501. The rule "broadly requires that findings of fact not be set aside unless clearly erroneous. It does not make exceptions or purport to exclude certain categories of factual findings from the obligation of a court of appeals to accept a district court's findings unless clearly erroneous. It does not divide facts into categories; in particular, it does not divide findings of fact into those that deal with 'ultimate' and those that deal with 'subsidiary' facts." *Pullman-Standard*, 456 U.S. at 287. Rather, the clearly erroneous standard has been held to apply to all findings of fact supporting a judgment "including those described as 'ultimate facts' because they may determine the outcome of litigation." *Bose*, 466 U.S. at 501.

The broad applicability of the clearly erroneous standard to ultimate facts, as well as to subsidiary facts, can, at times, make it difficult to determine whether a particular challenge is subject to clear error or *de novo* review. Judgments either consist of or rest on conclusions derived from the application of law to historical or subsidiary facts. If the relevant law sets forth a specifically defined factual test – *e.g.*, "a claim must be filed within ten days" – the applicable standards of review are easy to discern. The governing law against which the facts are measured (the 10–day limitation) is reviewed *de novo*, and the historical facts (including the date when the claimant acted) are reviewed for clear error. In contrast, when the governing law admits of no specific factual test, but rather consists of more generally defined principles – *e.g.*, whether a person acted "reasonably" or "in good faith" – the conclusion resulting from that law's application to the pertinent subsidiary or historical facts will necessarily be "inseparable from the principles through which it was deduced." *Bose*, 466 U.S. at 501 n.17. The appropriate standard of review applicable to these "mixed findings of law and fact" is not readily discernible. *See generally* Part One, Chapter I.C and D, *supra* (describing in greater detail the analytical framework defining mixed questions).

In determining which standard of review governs mixed findings supporting Rule 52 judgments, the Supreme Court generally applies a functional approach assessing, as a matter of the sound administration of justice, which judicial actor, the trial judge or the court of appeals, is better suited to decide a particular issue. *See, e.g.*, *Thornburg v. Gingles*, 478 U.S. 30, 77–79 (1986); *Bose*, 466 U.S. at 498–511; *Comm'r of Internal Revenue v. Duberstein*, 363 U.S. 278, 289 (1960); *see also* Part One, Chapter I.D, *supra*. In contrast, practice among the courts of appeals is far less uniform. Indeed, "[t]he question of the appropriate standard of review for mixed issues of fact and law has long bedeviled appellate courts." *Reich v. Lancaster*, 55 F.3d 1034, 1044 (5th Cir. 1995).

Some appellate decisions, following the Supreme Court's functional approach, look to the nature of the inquiry that is required when a governing rule of law is applied to established facts in order to determine whether the trial judge or the appellate court is better suited to decide a particular mixed question. *See, e.g.*, *Koirala v. Thai Airways Int'l, Ltd.*, 126 F.3d 1205, 1210 (9th Cir. 1997); *Nodaway Valley Bank v. Cont'l Cas. Co.*, 916 F.2d 1362, 1364–66 (8th Cir. 1990). Others assert, with little or no analysis, that the application of law to fact is reviewed *de novo*. *See*, *e.g., Henry v. Champlain Enters., Inc.*, 445 F.3d 610, 617–18 (2d Cir. 2006); *Foley v. Int'l Bhd. of Elec. Workers Local Union 98 Pension Fund*, 271 F.3d 551, 555 (3d Cir. 2001); *Rawl v. United States*, 778 F.2d 1009, 1014 & n.9 (4th Cir. 1985). A few appellate opinions conversely declare that applications of law to fact should, as a rule, be reviewed for clear error. *See, e.g., Pinkston v. Madry*, 440 F.3d 879, 888 (7th Cir. 2006); *Verhoeven v. Brunswick Sch. Comm.*, 207 F.3d 1, 5 (1st Cir. 1999); *G.J. Leasing Co. v. Union Elec. Co.*, 54 F.3d 379, 382 (7th Cir. 1995). And, occasionally, a court simply avoids judgment on the issue. *See, e.g., Primeaux v. United States*, 181 F.3d 876, 881 (8th Cir. 1999) (en banc) ("[W]e note some uncertainty whether we should review this question under the clearly erroneous or the *de novo* standard of review. We put this question aside, however, because the district court's judgment must be affirmed under either standard.").

The Supreme Court has definitively characterized as law or as fact certain mixed findings supporting Rule 52 judgments. *See, e.g., Gingles*, 478 U.S. at 77–79 (vote dilution under § 2 of the Voting Rights Act is a question of fact); *Bose*, 466 U.S. at 511 (actual malice in defamation case is a question of law); *United States v. Gen. Motors Corp.*, 384 U.S. 127, 141 n.16 (1966) ("[T]he ultimate conclusion by the trial judge, that the defendants' conduct did not constitute a combination or conspiracy in violation of the Sherman Act, is not to be shielded by the 'clearly erroneous' test. . . ."); *Duberstein*, 363 U.S. at 286–89 (meaning of "gift" in the income tax code is a question of fact). But absent such a decision, the standard of review applicable to a particular mixed question can only be reliably determined through issue-specific research in the circuit in which the appeal is being heard.

Chapter V

DECISIONS COMMITTED TO A DISTRICT JUDGE'S DISCRETION: GIVING MEANING TO THE VARIABLE ABUSE OF DISCRETION STANDARD

"[E]xpress language in statutes and rules, . . . judicial interpretation of rules that are silent on the matter, and . . . decisions in common law areas that are not subject to formal rules" may indicate that a particular question admits of more than one legally correct answer and is, therefore, committed to the discretion of the district judge. Rosenberg, *Appellate Review of Trial Court Discretion*, 79 F.R.D. 173, 175 (1978); *see also Wheat v. United States*, 486 U.S. 153, 164 (1988) (just because "[o]ther district courts might have reached differing or opposite conclusions with equal justification, . . . does not mean that one conclusion was 'right' and the other 'wrong' "). In the federal system, many decisions pertaining to a range of issues are discretionary. *See* Rosenberg, *Appellate Review of Trial Court Discretion*, 79 F.R.D. at 173; *see also Toussaint v. McCarthy*, 801 F.2d 1080, 1087–88 (9th Cir. 1986). "It is especially common for issues involving what can broadly be labeled 'supervision of litigation' . . . to be given abuse-of-discretion review." *Pierce v. Underwood*, 487 U.S. 552, 558 n.1 (1988). In addition, it is generally true "that abuse of discretion is the proper standard of review of a district court's evidentiary rulings." *Gen. Elec. Co. v. Joiner*, 522 U.S. 136, 141 (1997). But there are also matters of a more substantive nature which are reviewed under an abuse of discretion standard. *See, e.g., Cooper Indus., Inc. v. Leatherman Tool Group, Inc.*, 532 U.S. 424, 433 (2001) (noting that if no constitutional issue is raised, federal district court determination that state jury award is within the confines of a state punitive damages statute is reviewed for abuse of discretion only).

Although "deference" is the "hallmark of abuse-of-discretion review," *Gen. Elec. Co.*, 522 U.S. at 143, the variety of matters committed to the discretion of district judges means that the standard is necessarily variable. It implies no single level of scrutiny by the appellate courts. *See* Friendly, *Indiscretion About Discretion*, 31 EMORY L.J. 747, 762–64 (1982); Rosenberg, *Judicial Discretion of the Trial Court, Viewed from Above*, 22 SYRACUSE L. REV. 635, 650–53 (1971). Rather, the abuse of discretion standard "is a legal term of art[,] . . . not a wooden term but one of flexibility, dependent on the type of case in which it is to be applied and the posture of the case when it arises." *Direx Israel, Ltd. v. Breakthrough Med. Corp.*, 952 F.2d 802, 814 (4th Cir. 1991).

Abuse of discretion can thus be fairly characterized as "cover[ing] a family of review standards ... whose members differ greatly in the actual stringency of review." *Am. Hosp. Supply Corp. v. Hosp. Prods. Ltd.*, 780 F.2d 589, 594 (7th Cir. 1986). This does not mean, however, that discretionary decisions are "unfettered by meaningful standards or shielded from thorough appellate" scrutiny. *Albemarle Paper Co. v. Moody*, 422 U.S. 405, 416 (1975). "[D]iscretionary choices are not left to ... inclination, but to ... judgment; and ... judgment is to be guided by sound legal principles." *Id.*

The most basic of the legal principles guiding review of discretionary decisions pertain to the trial judge's identification and application of the controlling law and the accuracy of his or her assessment of the evidence. "A district court would necessarily abuse its discretion if it based its ruling on an erroneous view of the law or on a clearly erroneous assessment of the evidence." *Cooter & Gell v. Hartmarx Corp.*, 496 U.S. 384, 405 (1990). Moreover, decisions based on outright caprice are not tolerated in our legal system: a patently arbitrary application of the controlling law to the relevant facts thus amounts to an abuse of discretion. Otherwise, "[w]hether discretion has been abused depends ... on the bounds of that discretion and the principles that guide its exercise." *United States v. Taylor*, 487 U.S. 326, 336 (1988).

It is commonly said that discretionary decisions will not be disturbed so long as they remain within the range of choices permitted to the district court. *See, e.g., United States v. Frazier*, 387 F.3d 1244, 1259 (11th Cir. 2004) (en banc); *Verizon Commc'ns, Inc. v. Inverizon Int'l, Inc.*, 295 F.3d 870, 872–73 (8th Cir. 2002); *Zervos v. Verizon N.Y., Inc.*, 252 F.3d 163, 168–69 (2d Cir. 2001); *United States v. Dockery*, 955 F.2d 50, 54 (D.C. Cir. 1992). Although useful, this definition only goes so far. Abuse is also determined by the manner in which discretion is exercised. As the Eighth Circuit cogently explains, an abusive exercise of discretion occurs "[1] when a relevant factor that should have been given significant weight is not considered; [2] when an irrelevant or improper factor is considered and given significant weight; and [3] when all proper factors, and no improper ones, are considered, but the court, in weighing those factors, commits a clear error of judgment." *Verizon Commc'ns*, 295 F.3d at 873; *see also Sheppard v. River Valley Fitness One, L.P.*, 428 F.3d 1, 6 (1st Cir. 2005) (same); *Nat'l Wildlife Fed'n v. Nat'l Marine Fisheries Serv.*, 422 F.3d 782, 798 (9th Cir. 2005) (per curiam) (An abuse of discretion is "discretion exercised to an end not justified by the evidence, a judgment that is clearly against the logic and effect of the facts as are found."). In other words, when reviewing for abuse of discretion, a court of appeals must not only determine whether the trial court's decision was outside the choices permitted to it, but also whether, in light of the particular factual circumstances, the trial court erred in the weighing process by which it exercised its discretion.

A. ASSESSING THE EXERCISE OF CLOSELY CONFINED DISCRETION

How are the bounds of discretion determined? In *Albemarle Paper Co. v. Moody*, the Supreme Court explained that the starting point with respect to discretion delegated by Congress is congressional purpose. 422 U.S. at 417, 421–22. In that case, the Court granted *certiorari* to resolve, among other things, the standard governing back pay awards under Title VII. *Id.* at 413. The district judge found that the defendants had discriminated against the plaintiffs and consequently granted injunctive relief. *Id.* at 409. However, he refused the plaintiffs' request for back pay. *Id.* at 410. In denying back pay, the trial judge relied on two factors: (1) the absence of any evidence of bad faith on the part of the defendants and (2) his conclusion that an award of back pay would substantially prejudice the defendants in light of the plaintiffs' failure to file their back pay claim until nearly five years after the lawsuit was instituted. *Id.* at 413. According to the district court, "[t]he defendants might have chosen to exercise unusual zeal in having this court determine their rights at an earlier date had they known that back pay would be at issue." *Id.* at 410. The court of appeals reversed the district court's exercise of discretion, holding that "a plaintiff ... who is successful in obtaining an injunction under Title VII ... should ordinarily be awarded back pay unless special circumstances would render such an award unjust." *Id.* at 412.

Before the Supreme Court, the petitioning defendants argued that the district court's back pay decision should not have been overturned, since "the statutory scheme provides no guidance, beyond indicating that backpay awards are within the District Court's discretion." *Id.* at 415. The relevant remedial provision, in fact, did not set out factors for the district court to consider in awarding back pay. It stated only that a "court may ... order such affirmative action as may be appropriate, which may include, but is not limited to, reinstatement or hiring of employees, with or without back pay ... or any other equitable relief as the court deems appropriate." *Id.* at 415 n.9.

Looking to the overall scheme of Title VII, its legislative history, and analogous statutes, the Supreme Court rejected the defendants' argument. It concluded that "[t]he power to award backpay was bestowed by Congress, as part of a complex legislative design directed at a historic evil of national proportions." *Id.* at 416; *see also id.* at 417–21. The equitable nature of the remedial power granted did not, the Court found, excuse the district courts from exercising that "power in light of the large objectives of the Act." *Id.* at 416. "Congress' purpose in vesting a variety of [remedial] discretionary powers in the courts was not to limit appellate review of trial courts, or to invite inconsistency and caprice, but rather to make possible the fashioning of the most complete relief possible." *Id.* at 421. "It follows," the Court reasoned "that, given a finding of unlawful discrimination, backpay should be denied only for reasons which, if applied generally, would not frustrate the central statutory purposes of eradicating discrimination throughout the economy and making persons whole for injuries suffered through past discrimination." *Id.* The Court also admonished that "courts of appeals must maintain a consistent and principled application of the backpay provision, consonant with the twin statutory objectives, while at the same time recognizing that the trial court will often have the keener appreciation of those facts and circumstances peculiar to particular cases." *Id.* at 421–22. In order to facilitate this review, the Court declared that district courts declining back pay awards must "carefully articulate [their] reasons." *Id.* at 421 n.14. It placed no such burden on district courts awarding back pay.

Measuring the district court's decision against the purposes underlying Title VII, the Court held that the mere absence of bad faith on the part of an employer cannot justify the denial of back pay. *Id.* at 422–23. "If backpay were awardable only upon a showing of bad faith, the remedy would become a punishment for moral turpitude, rather than a compensation for workers' injuries. This would read the 'make whole' purpose right out of Title VII...." *Id.* at 422. With respect to the plaintiffs' late filing, the Court held that "[o]n these issues of procedural regularity and prejudice, the broad aims of Title VII provide no ready solution." *Id.* at 425. "Whether the [defendants] were in fact prejudiced, and whether the [plaintiffs'] trial conduct was excusable, are questions that will be open to review by the Court of Appeals, if the District Court, on remand, decides again to decline to make any award of backpay." *Id.* at 424. In such a case, the Court concluded, the court of appeals should review the district court's factual findings for clear error and its exercise of discretion for abuse in light of the circumstances peculiar to the case. *Id.* at 424–25.

The *Albemarle* opinion makes clear that the bounds of discretion are determined, in significant part, by the reasons why discretion is delegated to district courts in the first place. It also exemplifies how appellate courts, through their law-declaring powers, define the bounds of discretion. When, looking to the purposes and history of Title VII, the *Albemarle* Court held that the mere absence of bad faith on the part of an employer is never sufficient to deny back pay, it established as a matter of law that a decision based on nothing more than the absence of bad faith is outside the bounds of permissible choice. It thus placed a clear perimeter around what, under the language of the remedial provision, had appeared to be unbounded discretion.

In addition, the *Albemarle* opinion demonstrates how an appellate court, through the use of presumptions, can affect the weighing process at the heart of discretionary decisionmaking. In finding that the purposes of Title VII justified a strong presumption in favor of back pay whenever unlawful discrimination was found, the Supreme Court weighted the scales, making it clear that a decision to deny back pay in the face of a finding of unlawful discrimination would require special justification. *See City of L.A. Dep't of Water & Power v. Manhart*, 435 U.S. 702, 719 (1978). While not characterizing as impermissible every denial of back pay, the Court made clear that decisions denying such claims would be subject to closer scrutiny than those granting them, and consequently required a district court denying an award to "carefully articulate its reasons." *Albemarle*, 422 U.S. at 421 & n.14.

In *United States v. Taylor*, the Supreme Court again emphasized the central role that congressional purpose plays in abuse of discretion review. 487 U.S. at 336–37. The question in *Taylor* was whether a district court abused its discretion when it dismissed an indictment with prejudice under the Speedy Trial Act. *See id.* at 332. In ascertaining the bounds of the discretion afforded trial judges by the Act, the Supreme Court looked first to the statutory language, which stated:

> In determining whether to dismiss the case with or without prejudice, the court shall consider, among others, each of the following factors: [1] the seriousness of the offense; [2] the facts and circumstances of the case which led to the dismissal; and [3] the impact of a reprosecution on the administration of [the Speedy Trial Act] and on the administration of justice.

Id. at 332–33. Congressional delineation of these factors, the Court found, made "plain" that "[district] courts are not free simply to exercise their equitable powers in fashioning an appropriate remedy." *Id.* at 333. However, because the factors described were "somewhat broad and open-ended," the Court turned to the legislative history of the Act "for some additional indication of how the contemplated choice of remedy should be made." *Id.* Based on that history, the Court concluded that prejudice to the defendant also was to be weighed in determining whether to bar reprosecution and that neither a "with" nor a "without prejudice" dismissal was to serve as the presumptive remedy for violations of the Act. *See id.* at 333–35.

Although acknowledging that "the role of an appellate court is not to substitute its judgment for that of the trial court," the Court stated that abuse of discretion review must "ensure that the purposes of the Act and the legislative compromise it reflects are given effect." *Id.* at 336. When a discretionary decision is governed by legislatively defined factors, a trial court "must carefully consider those factors as applied to the particular case and, whatever its decision, clearly articulate their effect in order to permit meaningful appellate review." *Id.* at 336–37. "Only then," the Court concluded, "can an appellate court ascertain whether a district court has ignored or slighted a factor that Congress has deemed pertinent to the choice of remedy, thereby failing to act within the limits prescribed by Congress." *Id.* at 337.

B. ASSESSING THE EXERCISE OF BROAD OR UNDEFINED DISCRETION

Many discretionary decisions are not as narrowly confined as those at issue in *Albemarle* and *Taylor*. When it comes to questions of trial process, Congress rarely articulates legislative goals or decisional criteria that define a clear boundary between permissible and impermissible choices or mandate generally applicable presumptions in the weighing of relevant factors. Many of these questions, as well as a number governed by common-law doctrine, are said to be committed to the "sound discretion" of the trial judge. *See, e.g., Piper Aircraft Co. v. Reyno*, 454 U.S. 235, 257 (1981) (determining *forum non conveniens*); *Cornwell v. Electra Cent. Credit Union*, 439 F.3d 1018, 1026–27 (9th Cir. 2006) (management of discovery).

When the bounds of discretion are broad, appellate scrutiny is "necessarily ... limited," *Taylor*, 487 U.S. at 336, and reversal generally requires a "clear abuse of discretion," a "definite and firm conviction" that the court below committed a "clear error of judgment," or some similar finding evidencing substantial appellate deference. *See, e.g., Am. Dredging Co. v. Miller*, 510 U.S. 443, 455 (1994) (*forum non conveniens* finding); *Nystrom v. TREX Co.*, 424 F.3d 1136, 1150 (Fed. Cir. 2005) (imposition on counsel of 28 U.S.C. § 1927 liability for excessive costs); *Taucher v. Brown–Hruska*, 396 F.3d 1168, 1172–73 (D.C. Cir. 2005) ("substantial justification" finding in Equal Access to Justice Act context); *Frazier*, 387 F.3d at 1259 (exclusion of expert testimony); *FDIC v. Rocket Oil Co.*, 865 F.2d 1158, 1160 n.1 (10th Cir. 1989) (per curiam) (prejudgment interest determination). Reasonableness and relevance, two fluid concepts that gain meaning from the factual context in which they are examined, become the touchstones of review. "[S]ubstantial deference" will be accorded a district judge's decision if she has "considered all relevant public and private interest factors" and the "balancing of [those] factors is reasonable." *Piper Aircraft*, 454 U.S. at 257; *see Taylor*, 487 U.S. at 336.

Although highly deferential, this standard does not preclude reversal. The Supreme Court's opinion in *Clinton v. Jones*, 520 U.S. 681 (1997), illustrates the point. The question there was whether the district court had abused the "broad discretion" accorded it to stay trial proceedings. *Id.* at 706. The plaintiff had sued the President while he was in office for actions allegedly taken before his term began. *Id.* at 684. Although the district court denied a motion to dismiss on immunity grounds, it nevertheless stayed the trial proceedings ruling that "the public interest in avoiding litigation that might hamper the President in conducting the duties of his office outweighed any demonstrated need for an immediate trial." *Id.* at 687. The district judge also relied, in part, on the fact that the plaintiff "had failed to bring her complaint until" two days before the statute of limitations ran. *Id.* On appeal, the appellate court described the discretionary stay as the functional equivalent of a temporary grant of immunity. *Id.* at 706. Because it found that the President was not entitled to such immunity, it reversed. *Id.*

Rejecting the court of appeals' characterization of the stay, the Supreme Court reviewed the district court's decision for abuse of discretion. Preliminarily, the Court explained that district courts, "as an incident to [their] power to control [their] own docket[s]," are accorded "broad discretion" in deciding motions to stay. *Id.* at 706–07. It cited an earlier opinion in which it had described a trial court's discretion to grant or deny a stay as "incidental to the power inherent in every court to control the disposition of the causes on its docket with economy of time and effort for itself, for counsel, and for litigants. How this can best be done calls for the exercise of judgment, which must weigh competing interests and maintain an even balance." *Landis v. N. Am. Co.*, 299 U.S. 248, 254–55 (1936). The Court then noted that, "especially in cases of extraordinary public moment, a plaintiff may be required to submit to delay not immoderate in extent and not oppressive in its consequences if the public welfare or convenience will thereby be promoted." *Clinton*, 520 U.S. at 707.

Turning to the public and private interest factors cited by the district court, the Supreme Court determined that the district judge "may have given undue weight to the concern that a trial might generate unrelated civil actions that could conceivably hamper the President in conducting the duties of his office." *Id.* at 708. This conclusion, the Court found, was premature. *Id.* At the time the stay was granted, there was "nothing in the record," "[o]ther than the fact that a trial may consume some of the President's time and attention," "to enable a judge to assess the potential harm that may [have] ensue[d] from scheduling the trial promptly after discovery [was] concluded." *Id.* The Court also noted that the lengthy stay took "no account whatever of the [plaintiff's] interest in bringing the case to trial." *Id.* at 707. Although noting that the suit was filed just short of the running of the statute of limitations, the Court nevertheless concluded that "delaying trial would increase the danger of prejudice resulting from the loss of evidence." *Id.* at 707–08.

Of course, in the process of reviewing a particular exercise of discretion, appellate courts often identify factors relevant to that decision. However, unless such factors are held to be exclusive or mandatory, they generally do not bind the lower courts. Rather, they merely provide "useful guidance." *See, e.g., Wilton v. Seven Falls Co.*, 515 U.S. 277, 282–83, 288–90 (1995) (describing nonexclusive factors guiding district court dismissals of federal declaratory injunction actions in favor of parallel state litigation).

Moreover, because trial courts often are granted broad discretion so that they can address "fact-intensive, close calls" that "utterly resist generalization," *Cooter & Gell*, 496 U.S. at 404, presumptions regarding the weight to be given one factor or set of factors over others are generally disfavored. Thus, for example, the Supreme Court in *Piper Aircraft* rejected the use of a rule of presumption, noting that "[i]f central emphasis were placed on any one factor, the *forum non conveniens* doctrine would lose much of the very flexibility that makes it so valuable." 454 U.S. at 249–50. This is not to say that courts of appeals are prohibited from articulating controlling presumptions based on the consistent practice of lower courts under their supervision, *see, e.g., Noonan v. Cunard S.S. Co.*, 375 F.2d 69, 70 (2d Cir. 1967), the perceived importance of the right at issue, *see, e.g., Daniel Int'l Corp. v. Fischbach*

& Moore, Inc., 916 F.2d 1061, 1064 (5th Cir. 1990), or some other principle of reason. However, such presumptions may well lead to the narrowing of discretion in opposite directions in different circuits. *See, e.g., Rowlett v. Anheuser–Busch, Inc.*, 832 F.2d 194, 199–200 (1st Cir. 1987), *overruled on other grounds by Iacobucci v. Boulter*, 193 F.3d 14 (1st Cir. 1999) (comparing the ways in which discretion to grant late requests for jury trials pursuant to Federal Rule of Civil Procedure 39(b) has been narrowed in opposite directions in different circuits).

In addition, discretionary issues that are unconfined by congressional intent or legislatively defined criteria, may nevertheless be subject to more or less appellate scrutiny as a result of constitutional considerations implicit in the posture of the case on appeal. Review of rulings on motions for new trials in civil jury cases provide one example. Although it is generally understood that "motions for a new trial are committed to the discretion of the district court," *McDonough Power Equip., Inc. v. Greenwood*, 464 U.S. 548, 556 (1984), the actual degree of scrutiny exercised by some appellate courts varies significantly with whether the rulings are in keeping with or contrary to the jury's verdict. Thus, when a district court denies a motion for a new trial, appellate review may be "especially deferential because in that instance deference to the district court operates in harmony with deference to the jury's determination of the weight of the evidence and the constitutional allocation to the jury of questions of fact." *Diaz v. Methodist Hosp.*, 46 F.3d 492, 495 (5th Cir. 1995); *see also Baker v. Dorfman*, 239 F.3d 415, 422 (2d Cir. 2000). In contrast, when a district court judge, contrary to the finding of the jury, grants a motion for a new trial, appellate review often will be calibrated to ensure that "a judge's nullification of the jury's verdict" did not "encroach on the jury's important fact-finding function." *Vander Zee v. Karabatsos*, 589 F.2d 723, 729 (D.C. Cir. 1978). "Such ... close scrutiny is required in order to protect the litigants' right to jury trial." *Lind v. Schenley Indus. Inc.*, 278 F.2d 79, 90 (3d Cir. 1960) (en banc); *see also McNeal v. Hi–Lo Powered Scaffolding, Inc.*, 836 F.2d 637, 646–47 (D.C. Cir. 1988).

Chapter VI

PRESERVING, FORFEITING, AND WAIVING ERROR: HOW A PARTY'S ACTIONS BEFORE THE TRIAL COURT CAN AFFECT OR PRECLUDE APPELLATE REVIEW

The vast majority of errors committed by trial judges do not warrant automatic reversal. Rather, as a rule, appellate courts must disregard errors that "do not affect the substantial rights" of a complaining party. 28 U.S.C. § 2111; *see also* FED. R. CRIM. P. 52(a), (b); FED. R CRIM. P. 30(d); FED. R. CIV. P. 61; FED. R. CIV. P. 51(d); FED. R. EVID. 103(a), (d); *Kotteakos v. United States*, 328 U.S. 750 (1946); *Chapman v. California*, 386 U.S. 18 (1967); *United States v. Olano*, 507 U.S. 725 (1993). The exceptions to this practice are limited, consisting principally of jurisdictional errors, which can never be harmless, *see, e.g., Torres v. Oakland Scavenger Co.*, 487 U.S. 312, 317 n.3 (1988); a few nonconstitutional errors with respect to which Congress has explicitly or implicitly repealed the "affects substantial rights" prerequisite, *see, e.g., Zedner v. United States*, ___ U.S. ___, ___, 126 S. Ct. 1976, 1989–90 (2006) (finding in the Speedy Trial Act an implied repeal of the harmless error rule with respect to procedural errors committed in the application of the Act); and, assuming they are preserved, a handful of constitutional errors that "defy analysis by harmless-error standards because they affect the framework within which [a criminal] trial proceeds," *see United States v. Gonzalez–Lopez*, ___ U.S. ___, ___, 126 S. Ct. 2557, 2564 (2006).

An appellate court's approach to assessing whether a particular error affected substantial rights is initially determined by whether the error was "preserved" or "forfeited." If an alleged error is preserved, an appellate court that concludes pursuant to clearly erroneous, *de novo*, or abuse of discretion review that the trial court erred, applies the harmless error doctrine to determine whether the error should be remedied or disregarded. *See* Part One, Chapter VII, *infra*. In contrast, if a party forfeits an alleged error by failing to preserve it, the clearly erroneous, *de novo*, and abuse of discretion standards, as well as the harmless error doctrine, are replaced by or, perhaps more accurately, subsumed within the plain error standard of review. Pursuant to plain error review, an appellant must demonstrate (1) that there was an error, (2) that the error was clear or obvious, (3) that it affected the appellant's substantial rights, and (4) that it seriously affected the fairness, integrity, or public

75

reputation of the judicial proceedings. *See Olano*, 507 U.S. at 732–37. Because the plain error standard affords significant deference to a trial judge's decisions and, pursuant to the fourth prong, vests appellate courts with the discretion to disregard even harmful errors, it generally proves a difficult hurdle for appealing parties. *See* Part One, Chapter VIII, *infra*.

To preserve a claim of error, a party typically must raise the issue before the trial court. *See, e.g.*, FED. R. CRIM. P. 51(b) ("A party may preserve a claim of error by informing the court – when the court ruling or order is made or sought – of the action the party wishes the court to take, or the party's objection to the court's action and the grounds for that objection."); FED. R. CIV. P. 46 (virtually the same); FED R. CRIM. P. 30(d) (describing the requirements for preserving alleged error in criminal jury instructions); FED. R. CIV. P. 51(c), (d) (describing the requirements for preserving alleged error in civil jury instructions); FED. R. EVID. 103(a) (describing the requirements for preserving alleged error in evidentiary rulings). "No procedural principle is more familiar . . . than that a . . . right may be forfeited in criminal as well as civil cases by the failure to make timely assertion of the right before a tribunal having jurisdiction to determine it." *See Yakus v. United States*, 321 U.S. 414, 444 (1944). Notably, however, Federal Rule of Civil Procedure 52 excepts from this requirement challenges to the sufficiency of the evidence supporting findings of fact underlying judgments in civil bench trials. FED. R. CIV. P. 52(a)(5); *see also* 9A WRIGHT & MILLER, FEDERAL PRACTICE & PROCEDURE § 2581 (1995 & Supp. 2006).

Errors also may be waived. As defined by the Supreme Court in *Olano*, a waiver involves the "intentional relinquishment or abandonment of a known right." 507 U.S. at 733. With the exception of matters affecting the court's jurisdiction, which can never be waived, *see Torres*, 487 U.S. at 317 n.3, waived errors are "extinguish[ed]" and generally may not be argued on appeal even under the plain error standard, *Olano*, 507 U.S. at 733–34. Of course, "[w]hether a particular right is waivable; whether the defendant must participate personally in the waiver; whether certain procedures are required for waiver; and whether the defendant's choice must be particularly informed or voluntary, all depend on the right at stake." *Id.* at 733. And any of these matters may be the subject of appellate litigation. *See, e.g.*, *Zedner*, ___ U.S. ___, 126 S. Ct. 1976 (resolving intercircuit conflict regarding waiver under the Speedy Trial Act). Moreover, in some situations, the mere failure to object to an alleged error amounts to a waiver that forecloses appellate review. *See, e.g.*, *Unitherm Food Sys., Inc. v. Swift–Eckrich, Inc.*, 546 U.S. 394, 404 (2006) (sufficiency challenges to civil verdicts foreclosed if party fails to object as prescribed by Federal Rule of Civil Procedure 50); FED. R. CRIM. P. 12(e) (interpreted in most circuits to foreclose appellate challenges based on certain Rule 12(b)(3) defenses, objections, and requests if not raised within the prescribed deadlines, unless relief from waiver is granted for good cause); FED. R. CIV. P. 12(h)(1) (foreclosing appellate challenges based on certain Rule 12(b) defenses if prescribed procedures are not followed). Care must be taken, however, not to confuse these relatively few situations with the not infrequent judicial misuse of the term "waiver" to describe what are, in fact, forfeitures. *See Brickwood Contractors, Inc. v. Datanet Eng'g, Inc.*, 369 F.3d 385, 395 n.7 (4th Cir. 2004) (en banc); *Chestnut v. City of Lowell*, 305 F.3d 18, 20 (1st Cir. 2002) (en banc) (per curiam).

In reality, most claims brought before appellate courts are reviewed pursuant to the clearly erroneous, *de novo*, or abuse of discretion standards and, if error is found, are subject to the harmless error doctrine. Good advocates rarely make the mistake of raising waived claims of error, and those with a choice avoid the heavy burden (and likely loss) involved in arguing plain error. Although plain error review is available to civil litigants, individuals convicted of crimes are more likely to pursue unpreserved claims of error since the stakes (conviction and incarceration) are always high and important constitutional questions are often at issue.

Chapter VII

THE HARMLESS ERROR DOCTRINE: LIMITING THE REMEDIAL RESPONSE TO PRESERVED FACTUAL, LEGAL, AND DISCRETIONARY ERROR

A. AN OVERVIEW

Pursuant to the harmless error doctrine, appellate courts must disregard preserved trial errors that do not affect the substantial rights of a complaining party. The doctrine is straightforwardly articulated in 28 U.S.C. § 2111:

> On the hearing of any appeal or writ of certiorari in any case, the court shall give judgment after an examination of the record without regard to errors or defects which do not affect the substantial rights of the parties.

This principle is also described in the criminal and civil rules of procedure. Federal Rule of Criminal Procedure 52(a), which applies to both district courts and courts of appeals, FED. R. CRIM. P. 1, pointedly states:

> Any error, defect, irregularity, or variance that does not affect substantial rights must be disregarded.

Federal Rule of Civil Procedure 61, governing new trial motions, similarly provides:

> Unless justice requires otherwise, no error in admitting or excluding evidence – or any other error by the court or a party – is ground for granting a new trial, for setting aside a verdict, or for vacating, modifying, or otherwise disturbing a judgment or order. At every stage of the proceeding, the court must disregard all errors and defects that do not affect any party's substantial rights.

See McDonough Power Equip., Inc. v. Greenwood, 464 U.S. 548, 554 (1984) (although Rule 61 literally applies only to district courts, FED. R. CIV. P. 1, "appellate courts should act in accordance with the salutary policy embodied in" it). Federal Rule of Evidence 103(a), applicable to both trial and appellate courts, FED. R. EVID. 1101(a), likewise provides that "[e]rror may not be predicated upon a ruling which admits or excludes evidence unless a substantial right of the party is affected."

It is important to remember that the harmless error doctrine comes into play at the appellate level only when a party has properly preserved an issue before the trial court and raised it on appeal. *See* Part One, Chapter VI, *supra*. It is also worth noting that while the doctrine is generally applied only after error is found pursuant to the governing standard of review, courts of appeals sometimes employ a harmlessness analysis to avoid resolving difficult or close questions of error. *See, e.g., United States v. Ortiz*, 474 F.3d 976, 981–82 (7th Cir. 2007) (declining to decide a "close question" of whether admission of certain evidence was error because it was, in any event, harmless); *Betterbox Commc'ns Ltd. v. BB Techs., Inc.*, 300 F.3d 325, 329 (3d Cir. 2002) (finding it unnecessary to decide whether trial court abused its discretion in admitting expert testimony since the error, if there was one, was harmless).

Although the various harmless error rules are clear in directing appellate courts to disregard trial court mistakes that do not "affect" "substantial rights," none defines what these words mean. How does an appellate court determine whether a preserved error affected a party's substantial rights?

In the context of direct review of criminal convictions, Supreme Court precedent giving meaning to the phrase is abundant and the proper test for determining whether a particular preserved error is harmless generally is easily identified. With respect to the vast majority of such errors, harmlessness is assessed pursuant to either *Kotteakos v. United States*, 328 U.S. 750 (1946), or *Chapman v. California*, 386 U.S. 18 (1967). If an error does not implicate a defendant's constitutional rights, *Kotteakos* almost always controls. If the error is constitutional in dimension, *Chapman*'s "harmless beyond a reasonable doubt" standard usually applies.

There are, however, two notable exceptions to application of the *Chapman* standard. The first involves a handful of "structural defects" resulting from constitutional violations that are so intrinsically harmful as to require automatic reversal. *See United States v. Gonzalez–Lopez*, ___ U.S. ___, ___, 126 S. Ct. 2557, 2563–65 (2006) (describing the various criteria pursuant to which constitutional errors meriting automatic reversal are identified). The second pertains to a limited number of constitutional rights which, because proof of their violation requires a defendant to demonstrate harm, are, in essence, exempt from the usual two-part, "error/affects substantial rights" review framework. *See, e.g., id.* at 2563 (recognizing that under *Strickland v. Washington*, 466 U.S. 668 (1984), violation of the Sixth Amendment right to effective representation cannot be found unless a defendant demonstrates prejudice); *Kyles v. Whitley*, 514 U.S. 419, 433–34 (1995) ("[F]avorable evidence is material, and constitutional error results from its suppression by the government, if there is a reasonable probability that, had the evidence been disclosed to the defense, the result of the proceeding would have been different.").

In the context of civil litigation, there is only sparse Supreme Court precedent defining how the "affects substantial rights" prerequisite should be assessed. Consequently, generalizations are difficult to draw, and circuit-specific research regarding the precise error at issue is critical.

That having been said, with respect to nonconstitutional error, *Kotteakos* contains useful guidance regarding the proper application of 28 U.S.C. § 2111 and Federal Rule of Civil Procedure 61. *See Kotteakos*, 328 U.S. at 754–63; *see also O'Neal v. McAninch*, 513 U.S. 432, 436–38, 441–42 (1995) (looking to *Kotteakos*'s discussion of 28 U.S.C. § 2111 to support the conclusion that the risk of a reviewing court's grave doubt as to the harmlessness of an error – sometimes referred to as the burden of persuasion – should be on the party that benefitted from the error); *Tipton v. Socony Mobil Oil Co.*, 375 U.S. 34, 37 (1963) (per curiam) (referencing *Kotteakos* as a *cf.* cite when applying the harmless error standard of 28 U.S.C. § 2111 and Rule 61). Nevertheless, the Supreme Court has never held that *Kotteakos* prescribes the standard for harmless error review in civil cases. And while *Kotteakos* is not infrequently cited by appellate courts assessing the harmlessness of nonconstitutional error in civil cases, the standards actually applied frequently deviate from and sometimes wholly ignore the guidelines articulated in *Kotteakos*. *See, e.g., Beck v. Haik*, 377 F.3d 624, 634–36 (6th Cir. 2004).

Outside of the habeas context, trial court errors of a constitutional magnitude rarely seem to arise in Supreme Court review of civil proceedings. The "harmless beyond a reasonable doubt standard" is occasionally cited by circuit courts assessing the effect of constitutional error on a civil litigant's rights. *See, e.g., Hameed v. Mann*, 57 F.3d 217, 220–24 (2d Cir. 1995) (any due process error committed by the district court in determining that the plaintiff, a prison inmate, should remain shackled during his civil trial was harmless beyond a reasonable doubt). However, there appear to be no cases in which the Supreme Court has applied the *Chapman* standard to a claim of error in civil litigation.

There are also few, if any, Supreme Court opinions supporting automatic reversal in the case of constitutional error in civil matters. Thus, for example, although "[m]aintenance of the jury as a fact-finding body is of such importance and occupies so firm a place in our history and jurisprudence that any seeming curtailment of the right to a jury trial should be scrutinized with the utmost care," *Beacon Theatres, Inc. v. Westover*, 359 U.S. 500, 501 (1959), the improper denial of this Seventh Amendment right generally is subject to harmless error analysis. *See, e.g., Kulas v. Flores*, 255 F.3d 780, 784 (9th Cir. 2001) (denial is harmless if no reasonable jury could have found for the losing party); *Segrets, Inc. v. Gillman Knitwear Co.*, 207 F.3d 56, 64 (1st Cir. 2000) (denial is harmless if evidence meets the standard for a directed verdict). Some circuits do hold that certain statutory errors in civil cases are per se reversible. *See, e.g., Barnett v. Gen. Elec. Capital Corp.*, 147 F.3d 1321, 1323–24 (11th Cir. 1998) (referral of civil proceedings to magistrate judge in the absence of party consent required under 28 U.S.C. § 636(c)(1) can never be harmless); *Stockler v. Garratt*, 974 F.2d 730,

732–33 (6th Cir. 1992) (same). But the structural error doctrine governing review of certain constitutional defects in criminal verdicts has not been extended to civil cases.

Federal habeas corpus proceedings, of course, involve review of criminal convictions within the framework of civil litigation. In these proceedings, as in federal appellate practice generally, most constitutional deprivations are subject to harmless error analysis. However, in this context, the Supreme Court holds that *Kotteakos*, not *Chapman*, provides the standard for harmlessness review of nonstructural constitutional error. *Brecht v. Abrahamson*, 507 U.S. 619, 636–37 (1993); *O'Neal*, 513 U.S. at 438–39, 445. Harmlessness review in the habeas context involves a variety of unique considerations, which are beyond the scope of this book. An excellent discussion of the relevant issues, including the evolving body of precedent regarding the effect on harmless error review of the Antiterrorism and Effective Death Penalty Act, can be found in HERTZ & LIEBMAN, FEDERAL HABEAS CORPUS PRACTICE & PROCEDURE §§ 31.1–.5 (2005).

B. THE *KOTTEAKOS* DECISION: HARMLESSNESS REVIEW OF NONCONSTITUTIONAL ERROR

The principal decision describing what it means to "affect" "substantial rights" with respect to preserved claims of nonconstitutional error is *Kotteakos v. United States*, 328 U.S. 750. On the facts presented, it was uncontested that the trial court had erred in instructing the jury on and allowing the defendants to be "convicted of a single general conspiracy by evidence which the Government admit[ted] proved not one conspiracy but some eight or more different [smaller] ones of the same sort." *Id.* at 752; *see also id.* at 771. The only question before the Supreme Court was whether that error affected the defendants' substantial rights under the harmless error rule of 28 U.S.C. § 391, the precursor to 28 U.S.C. § 2111. *Id.* at 752, 755–58; *see also O'Neal*, 513 U.S. at 441 (*Kotteakos* "interpreted the then-existing harmless-error statute, 28 U.S.C. § 391, now codified with minor change at 28 U.S.C. § 2111.").

Although the error at issue pertained to a criminal verdict, Justice Rutledge began the Court's analysis with a description of the function of the harmless error statute in both criminal and civil cases. *Kotteakos*, 328 U.S. at 758–63. "The general object was simple: To substitute judgment for automatic application of rules," *id.* at 759–60, in particular, technical rules that had resulted in regular reversals of trial court verdicts, *id.* at 759. But "[t]he task was too big, too various in detail, for particularized treatment." *Id.* at 760. Consequently, as the Court explained, Congress chose to accomplish its goal through the simple command that reviewing courts ignore "errors, defects, or exceptions which do not affect the substantial rights of the parties." *Id.* at 757, 760.

This broad standard, the Court emphasized, necessarily leaves much to the judgment of appellate jurists. *Id.* at 761. The "discrimination" required by harmless error review "is one of judgment transcending confinement by formula or precise rule." *Id.* Thus, the Court underscored the primary importance of examining an error in the context of the whole record. *Id.* at 762. "In the final analysis," an appellate court's assessment of the effect of an error on a party's substantial rights "must be influenced by conviction resulting from examination of the proceedings in their entirety, tempered but not governed in any rigid sense of *stare decisis* by what has been done in similar situations." *Id.*; *see also id.* at 761 (an error that might be "minor and unimportant in one setting," may be "crucial in another"). As the Court summarized:

> Necessarily [1] the character of the proceeding, [2] what is at stake upon its outcome, and [3] *the relation of the error asserted to casting the balance for decision on the case as a whole*, are material factors in judgment.

Id. at 762 (emphasis added). Notably, the third factor instructs reviewing courts to consider the effect of an error on the decisionmaking process.

The opinion clarifies that Congress, in enacting the harmless error statute, placed the risk of appellate uncertainty as to the harmlessness of all but "technical" errors on the beneficiary of the trial court's mistake. *See id.* at 760–61; *see also Chapman*, 386 U.S. at 24 (noting that the common law similarly placed the risk of appellate uncertainty on the beneficiary of an error). As the Court both earlier and later explained, "technical errors" are errors "concerned with the 'mere etiquette of trials and with the formalities and minutiae of procedure.' " *O'Neal*, 513 U.S. at 440 (quoting *Bruno v. United States*, 308 U.S. 287, 294 (1939)). Thus, when a party successfully demonstrates the existence of preserved, nontechnical error, the opposing party bears the burden of persuading the appellate court that the error was harmless. *See United States v. Olano*, 507 U.S. 725, 734 (1993).

1. HARMLESSNESS REVIEW OF NONCONSTITUTIONAL ERROR IN CRIMINAL CASES

Having described generally how the harmless error statute should be applied in both criminal and civil cases, the *Kotteakos* Court turned to the specifics of the statute's application to error infecting criminal verdicts:

> [I]t is not the appellate court's function to determine guilt or innocence. Nor is it to speculate upon probable reconviction and decide according to how the speculation comes out. Appellate judges cannot escape such impressions. But they may not make them sole criteria for reversal or affirmance. Those judgments are exclusively for the jury, given always the necessary minimum evidence legally sufficient to sustain the conviction unaffected by the error.
>
> But this does not mean that the appellate court can escape altogether taking account of the outcome. To weigh the error's

effect against the entire setting of the record without relation to the verdict or judgment would be almost to work in a vacuum. In criminal causes that outcome is conviction. This is different, or may be, from guilt in fact. It is guilt in law, established by the judgment of laymen. And the question is, not were they right in their judgment, regardless of the error or its effect upon the verdict. *It is rather what effect the error had or reasonably may be taken to have had upon the jury's decision.* The crucial thing is the impact of the thing done wrong on the minds of other men, not on one's own, in the total setting.

This must take account of what the error meant to them, not singled out and standing alone, but in relation to all else that happened. And one must judge others' reactions not by his own, but with allowance for how others might react and not be regarded generally as acting without reason. This is the important difference, but one easy to ignore when the sense of guilt comes strongly from the record.

If, when all is said and done, the [reviewing court's] conviction is sure that the error did not influence the jury, or had but very slight effect, the verdict and the judgment should stand, except perhaps where the departure is from a constitutional norm or a specific command of Congress. But if one cannot say, with fair assurance, after pondering all that happened without stripping the erroneous action from the whole, that the judgment was not substantially swayed by the error, it is impossible to conclude that substantial rights were not affected.

328 U.S. at 763–65 (emphasis added).

This formulation gives unequivocal expression to the intent of Congress that the burden of demonstrating harmlessness rest on the party that benefitted from the trial court's mistake. The opinion pointedly states that if an appellate court concludes that an "error itself had substantial influence ... *or if [the court] is left in grave doubt*, the conviction cannot stand." *Id.* at 765 (emphasis added); *see also O'Neal*, 513 U.S. at 438–39 (describing *Kotteakos* as "placing the risk of doubt" on the government); *Olano*, 507 U.S. at 741 (under harmless error analysis, the government bears the "burden of showing the absence of prejudice").

The test described also reiterates the Court's general observation that the judgment required by the harmless error statute depends upon "examination of the proceedings in their entirety." *Kotteakos*, 328 U.S. at 762. Stating that "it is not the appellate court's function to determine guilt or innocence," *id.* at 763, the Court makes specific to the criminal context its earlier admonition that harmlessness review focus on the effect of an error on the decisionmaking process, *see id.* at 760–62. It explicitly instructs: "The inquiry cannot be merely whether there was enough to support the result, apart from the phase affected by the error." *Id.* at 765. Rather, it must be "whether the error *itself* had substantial influence." *Id.* (emphasis added).

Finally, this definition establishes the certainty of harmlessness necessary to sustain a verdict. Pursuant to the *Kotteakos* standard, a reviewing court must find that a defendant's substantial rights have been affected (and thus reverse) *unless* it can conclude, "with fair assurance," that the error at issue did not "substantially" influence the judgment of the decisionmaker below. *Id.* Put another way, *Kotteakos* requires reversal if the error found "may have had 'substantial influence' on the outcome of the proceeding." *Bank of Nova Scotia v. United States*, 487 U.S. 250, 256 (1988) (quoting and describing the Court's holding in *Kotteakos*).

The *Kotteakos* Court's application of these decisional principles to the facts presented aptly illustrates how the harmless error test works in practice. As noted, the government conceded that the trial court erred in instructing the jury on and allowing the defendants to be convicted of a single conspiracy when the evidence proved eight or more smaller conspiracies. *Kotteakos*, 328 U.S. at 752, 771. And, significantly, the defendants did not challenge the sufficiency of the evidence to sustain their convictions "considered apart from the alleged errors relating to the proof and the instructions." *Id.* at 753. Relying on the rationale supporting the appellate court's decision to sustain the convictions, the government argued that while "the trial judge was plainly wrong in supposing that upon the evidence there could be a single conspiracy," the error was not prejudicial because "guilt was so manifest." *Id.* at 755–56, 767. The Supreme Court firmly rejected this argument:

> It may be, as the Court of Appeals found, that the evidence concerning each petitioner was so clear that conviction would have been dictated and reversal forbidden, if it had been presented in separate trials for each offense. . . . But whether so or not is neither our problem nor that of the Court of Appeals for this case. That conviction would, or might probably, have resulted in a properly conducted trial is not the criterion of [the harmless error statute].

Id. at 776.

The government also argued that "there was no prejudice . . . because the results show[ed] that the jury exercised discrimination as among the defendants whose cases were submitted to it." *Id.* at 767. The government reasoned that because "the jury acquitted some, disagreed as to others, and found still others guilty," the Court could "conclude[] that the jury was not confused and, apparently, reached the same result as [it] would have . . . if the convicted defendants had been . . . tried separately." *Id.* In other words, the government contended that the error did not substantially affect the jury's verdict.

Based on the facts of the trial and, in particular, on an instruction delivered by the trial judge, the Supreme Court also rejected this analysis. *Id.* at 769, 776. The trial court had instructed the jurors that the indictment charged one conspiracy and had admonished them not to divide the described conspiracy, but rather to determine "whether or not each of the defendants, or which of the defendants, are members of that conspiracy." *Id.* at 767. Conceding that the government's position was not wholly illogical, the Supreme Court acknowledged that, notwithstanding the instructional error, "[i]t may be that ... the jury actually understood correctly the purport of the evidence, as the Government now concedes it to have been ... and [consequently] came to the conclusion that the [defendants] were guilty only of the separate conspiracies in which the proof shows they respectively participated." *Id.* at 769. Nevertheless, the Court held that "in the face of [the erroneous instruction] and in the circumstances of this case, we cannot assume that the lay triers of fact were so well informed upon the law or that they disregarded the permission expressly given [in the instruction] to ignore that vital difference" between the crime charged and the evidence submitted. *Id.* Thus, the Court concluded, "We think it highly probable that the error had substantial and injurious effect or influence in determining the jury's verdict." *Id.* at 776.

2. HARMLESSNESS REVIEW OF NONCONSTITUTIONAL ERROR IN CIVIL CASES

The courts of appeals do not uniformly apply *Kotteakos* in assessing the effect of nonconstitutional error on a civil litigant's substantial rights. This is not particularly surprising given the *Kotteakos* Court's acknowledgment that the absence of a distinction in the harmless error statute between civil and criminal cases "does not mean that the same criteria shall always be applied regardless of [the] difference." *Id.* at 762. As the Court explained:

> [The harmless error statute] did not make irrelevant the fact that a person is on trial for his life or his liberty. It did not require the same judgment in such a case as in one involving only some question of civil liability. There is no purpose, for instance, to abolish the historic difference between civil and criminal causes relating to the burden of proof placed in the one upon the plaintiff and in the other on the prosecution.

Id. at 763.

What is surprising, however, is the number of circuits that ignore the *Kotteakos* Court's conclusion that Congress intended, in both criminal *and* civil cases, to place the risk of appellate uncertainty regarding the harmlessness of an error on the beneficiary of that error. Although dicta, Justice Rutledge's analysis of congressional intent is telling, particularly in light of the Court's later reliance on it in *O'Neal*. In the latter case, the Supreme Court again concluded, albeit in dicta, that the "civil and criminal harmless-error standards do not differ in their treatment of grave doubt as to the harmlessness of errors." *O'Neal*, 513 U.S. at 441 (citing and discussing *Kotteakos*). Nevertheless, many circuits regularly put the risk of appellate uncertainty in civil cases on the party who properly objected before the trial court. *See, e.g., Naeem v. McKesson Drug Co.*, 444 F.3d 593, 608–09 (7th Cir. 2006); *Beck v. Haik*, 377 F.3d at 635; *Tesser v. Bd. of Educ.*, 370 F.3d 314, 319–20 (2d Cir. 2004); *Dresser-Rand Co. v. Virtual Automation Inc.*, 361 F.3d 831, 842 (5th Cir. 2004); *In re Watts*, 354 F.3d 1362, 1369 (Fed. Cir. 2004); *Bacou Dalloz USA, Inc. v. Cont'l Polymers, Inc.*, 344 F.3d 22, 29 (1st Cir. 2003); *S. Pine Helicopters, Inc. v. Phoenix Aviation Managers, Inc.*, 320 F.3d 838, 843 (8th Cir. 2003); *Frederick v. Kirby Tankships, Inc.*, 205 F.3d 1277, 1285 (11th Cir. 2000); *Coletti v. Cudd Pressure Control*, 165 F.3d 767, 773 (10th Cir. 1999).

Interestingly, the few circuits that follow *Kotteakos* in placing the risk of appellate uncertainty on the beneficiary of an error, each rely upon distinct articulations of the certainty of harmlessness required to sustain a district court outcome. Thus, the Fourth Circuit, quoting the *Kotteakos* formulation, reverses unless provided with "fair assurance" that the verdict was "not substantially swayed" by the error. *See Taylor v. Va. Union Univ.*, 193 F.3d 219, 235 (4th Cir. 1999) (en banc), *abrogated on other grounds by Desert Palace, Inc. v. Costa*, 539 U.S. 90 (2003). The Third Circuit, using different phrasing to describe what may well be a similar level of certainty, reverses unless "it is highly probable that the error[] did not affect the outcome of the case." *McQueeney v. Wilmington Trust Co.*, 779 F.2d 916, 917, 927 & n.19 (3d Cir. 1985) (holding that the same standard applies in civil and criminal cases). In contrast, the Ninth Circuit will reverse unless "it is more probable than not that the error did not materially affect the verdict." *Obrey v. Johnson*, 400 F.3d 691, 700 (9th Cir. 2005).

Somewhat oddly, the *Kotteakos* standard of certainty is often appropriated by several of the circuits that regularly place the risk of appellate uncertainty on the party who properly objected before the trial court. Needless to say, the requirement that a court have a "fair assurance" that the judgment was "not substantially swayed" is significantly different when the risk of uncertainty is on the party claiming error rather than on the party that benefitted from the error. Thus, for example, the Sixth Circuit, citing *Kotteakos*, requires that a party claiming error "deprive the appellate court of a fair assurance that the error was *not* outcome-determinative" in order to obtain a reversal. *Beck v. Haik*, 377 F.3d at 635. Pursuant to this standard, the party claiming error must show by something less than a preponderance of the evidence that the error was outcome-determinative. The Second Circuit similarly requires that a verdict be sustained unless the party claiming error can provide the court with "fair assurance" that the judgment was "substantially swayed," or, in other words, "demonstrates that it is likely that in some material respect that factfinder's judgment was swayed by the error." *Tesser*, 370 F.3d at 319–20; *see also Bacou*, 344 F.3d at 29–30 (placing on the party claiming error the risk of the appellate court's uncertainty as to whether it "can say with fair assurance ... that the judgment was not substantially swayed by the error").

C. ASSESSING THE EFFECT OF CONSTITUTIONAL ERROR IN CRIMINAL CASES

1. THE HARMLESS BEYOND A REASONABLE DOUBT TEST OF *CHAPMAN*

It is well established that most federal constitutional errors can be harmless. *Arizona v. Fulminante*, 499 U.S. 279, 306 (1991). However, pursuant to *Chapman*, a reviewing court may disregard a constitutional error only if it is "able to declare a belief that [the error] was harmless beyond a reasonable doubt." 386 U.S. at 24.

In establishing the harmless beyond a reasonable doubt standard, the *Chapman* Court rejected the argument that all constitutional errors merit automatic reversal. The Court explained that the harmless error rules, including 28 U.S.C. § 2111, "serve a very useful purpose insofar as they block setting aside convictions for small errors or defects that have little, if any, likelihood of having changed the result of [a] trial." *Id.* at 22. Pointing to the fact that neither 28 U.S.C. § 2111 nor the other harmless error rules "distinguish[] between federal constitutional errors and errors of . . . federal statutes and rules," the Supreme Court concluded that there are "constitutional errors which *in the setting of a particular case* are so unimportant and insignificant that they may, consistent with the Federal Constitution, be deemed harmless." *Id.* (emphasis added). However, pointing to the fact that the rules emphasize "an intention not to treat as harmless those constitutional errors that affect substantial rights," *id.* at 23, the Court found it inappropriate to allow a reviewing court to disregard constitutional error unless it is satisfied "beyond a reasonable doubt that the error complained of did not contribute to the verdict obtained," *id.* at 24. Following the common-law rule, *Chapman* also put "the burden on the beneficiary of the [constitutional] error either to prove that there was no injury or to suffer a reversal of his erroneously obtained judgment." *Id.*; *see also Fulminante*, 499 U.S. at 295–96 (confirming that the burden of proving harmlessness is on the government).

Significantly, the *Chapman* test, like the *Kotteakos* test, looks to the effect of an error on the decisionmaking process. "Consistent with the jury-trial guarantee, the question [the *Chapman* decision] instructs the reviewing court to consider is not what effect the constitutional error might generally be expected to have upon a reasonable jury, but rather what effect it had upon the guilty verdict in the case at hand." *Sullivan v. Louisiana*, 508 U.S. 275, 279 (1993). The government is required "to prove beyond a reasonable doubt that the error complained of *did not contribute to the verdict obtained*." *Chapman*, 386 U.S. at 24 (emphasis added). Thus, "[h]armless-error review looks . . . to the basis on which the jury *actually rested* its verdict. The inquiry, in other words, is not whether, in a trial that occurred without the error, a guilty verdict would surely have been rendered, but whether the guilty verdict actually rendered in *this* trial was surely unattributable to the error." *Sullivan*, 508 U.S. at 279.

The Court's decision in *Fulminante* exemplifies this approach to harmlessness review. The question in *Fulminante* was whether the erroneous admission of a coerced confession was harmless in light of the fact that the government had admitted into evidence a second, uncoerced confession. 499 U.S. at 283–85. Based on "the overwhelming evidence adduced from the second confession," the Arizona Supreme Court held the error harmless, finding that "if there had not been a first confession, the jury would still have had the same basic evidence to convict." *Id.* at 296–97.

In rejecting this conclusion, the *Fulminante* opinion initially emphasized that "the risk that [a coerced] confession is unreliable, coupled with the profound impact that [such a] confession has upon [a] jury, requires a reviewing court to exercise extreme caution before determining that the admission of the confession at trial was harmless." *Id.* at 296. Turning then to a detailed review of the record, including how the confession affected the development of the state's case, *id.* at 297–98, the state's jury arguments regarding the confession, *id.*, the likely effect of the first confession on the jury's assessment of the second confession, *id.* at 298–300, and the fact that the confession laid the foundation for the admission of additional prejudicial evidence, *id.* at 300, the Supreme Court held that the state "ha[d] not carried its burden" to demonstrate that the error was harmless beyond a reasonable doubt, *id.* at 296.

2. DETERMINING WHETHER CONSTITUTIONAL ERROR MERITS AUTOMATIC REVERSAL: STRUCTURAL DEFECTS

Although "most constitutional errors can be harmless," *Fulminante*, 499 U.S. at 306, the Supreme Court recognizes "a limited class of fundamental constitutional errors that defy analysis by harmless error standards." *Neder v. United States*, 527 U.S. 1, 7 (1999); *see also Sullivan*, 508 U.S. at 278–79; *Fulminante*, 499 U.S. at 309–10. "Errors of this type are so intrinsically harmful as to require automatic reversal . . . without regard to their effect on the outcome." *Neder*, 527 U.S. at 7. Commonly referred to as "structural defects," these constitutional deprivations "defy" harmless error analysis, "because they affect the framework within which the trial proceeds, and are not simply an error in the trial process itself." *Gonzalez-Lopez*, ___ U.S. at ___, 126 S. Ct. at 2564; *see also Sullivan*, 508 U.S. at 281; *Fulminante*, 499 U.S. at 309–10.

The Supreme Court applies several different criteria in determining whether a preserved constitutional error is structural. *See Gonzalez-Lopez*, ___ U.S. at ___, 126 S. Ct. at 2564 n.4. The "fundamental unfairness" of an error is one such criterion. *Id.* (citing *Neder*, 527 U.S. at 9). Alternatively, the Court will consider "the difficulty of assessing the effect of the error" on the trial proceedings. *Id.* Thus, it has held that "violation of the public-trial guarantee is not subject to harmlessness review because the benefits of a public trial are frequently intangible, difficult to prove, or a matter of chance." *Id.* (citing *Waller v. Georgia*, 467 U.S. 39, 49 n.9 (1984)). Similarly, when a petit jury is selected according to certain improper criteria or "has been exposed to prejudicial publicity," automatic reversal is required "because the effect of the violation cannot be ascertained." *Id.* (quoting *Vasquez v. Hillery*, 474 U.S. 254, 263 (1986) (plurality opinion)). The "erroneous deprivation of the right to [retained] counsel of choice, with consequences that are necessarily unquantifiable and indeterminate," also "unquestionably qualifies as structural error." *Id.* at 2564. So, too, is the deprivation of the right to trial by jury as a result of a constitutionally deficient reasonable doubt instruction considered structural given the "necessarily unquantifiable and indeterminate" consequences of such an error. *Sullivan*, 508 U.S. at 281–82.

In addition, the Court has relied "on the irrelevance of harmlessness" in concluding that an error is structural. *Gonzalez-Lopez*, ___ U.S. at ___, 126 S. Ct. at 2564 n.4. On the basis of this criteria, it has found that "[s]ince the right [of] self-representation is a right that when exercised usually increases the likelihood of a trial outcome unfavorable to the defendant, its denial is not amenable to harmless error analysis." *Id.* (quoting *McKaskle v. Wiggins*, 465 U.S. 168, 177 n.8 (1984)).

To be sure, the category of preserved errors qualifying for automatic reversal is small. The Supreme Court has several times underscored this fact, stating: " 'If the defendant had counsel and was tried by an impartial adjudicator, there is a strong presumption that any other constitutional errors that may have occurred are subject to harmless-error analysis.' " *Neder*, 527 U.S. at 8 (quoting *Rose v. Clark*, 478 U.S. 570, 579 (1986)); *see also Washington v. Recuenco*, ___ U.S. ___, ___, 126 S. Ct. 2546, 2551 (2006). Nevertheless, applying the above described criteria, the Court has characterized a variety of errors as structural, including the denial of the right of self-representation, *see McKaskle*, 465 U.S. at 177 n.8; the denial of the right to public trial, *see Waller*, 467 U.S. at 49 n.9; the denial of the right to trial by jury resulting from a defective reasonable doubt instruction, *see Sullivan*, 508 U.S. at 281–82; the denial of due process resulting from trial by a biased judge, *see Neder*, 527 U.S. at 8 (citing *Tumey v. Ohio*, 273 U.S. 510 (1927)); the denial of equal protection resulting from racial discrimination in the selection of a grand jury, *see Vasquez*, 474 U.S. at 262–63 (majority opinion); the complete denial of counsel, *see Neder*, 527 U.S. at 8 (citing *Gideon v. Wainwright*, 372 U.S. 335 (1963)); and the denial of the right to retained counsel of choice, *see Gonzalez–Lopez*, ___ U.S. at ___, 126 S. Ct. at 2564.

Chapter VIII

PLAIN ERROR REVIEW: ASSESSING AND REMEDYING UNPRESERVED ERROR

The plain error standard of review controls when a party seeks an appellate remedy for error that was not properly preserved in the trial court. As with harmless error analysis, when conducting plain error review, a court must look to whether a demonstrated error affected the substantial rights of the individual claiming it. Federal Rule of Criminal Procedure 52(b) broadly provides:

> A plain error that affects substantial rights may be considered even though it was not brought to the court's attention.

See also FED. R. CRIM. P. 30(d) (making the "affects substantial rights" standard of Rule 52(b) applicable to unpreserved claims of instructional error in criminal jury trials). Federal Rule of Evidence 103(d), applicable to both criminal and civil cases, similarly states:

> Nothing in this rule precludes taking notice of plain errors affecting substantial rights although they were not brought to the attention of the court.

Moreover, while there is no broadly applicable rule of civil procedure comparable to Criminal Rule 52(b), it is well accepted that plain error review is generally available for unpreserved claims of error affecting substantial rights in civil cases. *See United States v. Olano*, 507 U.S. 725, 736 (1993) (citing *Connor v. Finch*, 431 U.S. 407, 421 n.19 (1977)); *see also, e.g., Brickwood Contractors, Inc. v. Datanet Eng'g, Inc.*, 369 F.3d 385, 396–97 (4th Cir. 2004) (en banc); *Douglass v. United Servs. Auto. Ass'n*, 79 F.3d 1415, 1424 (5th Cir. 1996) (en banc). *See also* FED. R. CIV. P. 51(d)(2) (applying the "affects substantial rights" standard to unpreserved claims of instructional error in civil jury trials).

In *United States v. Olano*, 507 U.S. 725, the principal opinion describing plain error review, the Supreme Court held that pursuant to Federal Rule of Criminal Procedure 52(b), appellate courts may correct unpreserved error only when (1) there is an "error," (2) that is "plain," (3) that affects the complaining party's "substantial rights," and (4) that "seriously affects the fairness, integrity or public reputation of judicial proceedings." 507 U.S. at 732. The Court made clear that the burden of demonstrating the appropriateness of an appellate remedy rests with the party who forfeited an alleged error by failing to raise it below. *Id.* at 734; *see also United States v. Vonn*, 535 U.S. 55, 62–63 (2002) ("When an appellate court considers error that qualifies as plain," the complaining party "who sat silent at trial has the burden to show that his substantial rights were affected [and] ... that the error 'seriously affected the fairness, integrity or public reputation of judicial proceedings.' "). In articulating this four-part test, the Court also noted that the plain error standard embodied in Rule 52(b), "was intended as a restatement of existing law." *Olano*, 507 U.S. at 731; *see also id.* at 735–36. It is perhaps not surprising, then, that circuit courts addressing unpreserved claims of error (especially in civil cases) not infrequently continue to rely on the pre-*Olano* interest of justice, miscarriage of justice, and manifest injustice formulations of the test for determining when unpreserved error merits appellate remedy. *See, e.g., Morales-Fernandez v. INS*, 418 F.3d 1116, 1120 (10th Cir. 2005); *Brickwood Contractors*, 369 F.3d at 397 n.8.

Turning to what it means for an error to be "plain," the *Olano* Court stated that " '[p]lain' is synonymous with 'clear' or, equivalently, 'obvious.' " 507 U.S. at 734. However, it "refrained from deciding *when* an error must be plain to be reviewable," *Johnson v. United States*, 520 U.S. 461, 467 (1997), saying only that, "[a]t a minimum, a court of appeals cannot correct an error pursuant to [plain error review] unless the error is clear under current law," *Olano*, 507 U.S. at 734. In *Johnson v. United States*, the Court refined this formulation, holding that when "the law at the time of trial was settled and clearly contrary to the law at the time of appeal ... it is enough that an error be 'plain' at the time of appellate consideration." 520 U.S. at 468.

What the Supreme Court has yet to decide is whether an error will be considered plain when it is clear under the law at the time of appeal, but the law at the time of trial was unsettled. *See Olano*, 507 U.S. at 734. Only the Ninth and Eleventh Circuits appear to have definitively resolved this question, though in opposite directions. The Ninth Circuit holds that "[w]hen the state of the law is unclear at trial and only becomes clear as a result of later authority, the district court's error is perforce not plain." *United States v. Turman*, 122 F.3d 1167, 1170 (9th Cir. 1997). In contrast, the Eleventh Circuit holds that a defendant does not have to establish that the error alleged was plain at the time of trial. The error need only "be plain at the time of appellate consideration." *United States v. Smith*, 459 F.3d 1276, 1283 (11th Cir. 2006). In the post-*Johnson* era, dicta in cases from a number of circuits suggest that they, like the Eleventh Circuit, are likely to hold that plainness is measured at the time of appeal, even when the law was unsettled at the time of trial. *See, e.g., United States v. Maxwell*, 285 F.3d 336, 342 (4th Cir. 2002); *United States v. Weintraub*, 273 F.3d 139, 152 (2d Cir. 2001); *Crawford v. Falcon Drilling Co.*, 131 F.3d 1120, 1125 & n.6 (5th Cir. 1997); *United States v. Barone*, 114 F.3d 1284, 1293–94 (1st Cir. 1997). *But see United States v. Rivera–Rosario*, 300 F.3d 1, 18 n.20 (1st Cir. 2002). *See also United States v. Baugham*, 449 F.3d 167, 183 (D.C. Cir. 2006) (recognizing that the question is open); *United States v. Blazek*, 431 F.3d 1104, 1107–08 (8th Cir. 2005) (same).

With respect to the phrase "affects substantial rights," the *Olano* opinion established that the inquiry required is – "with one important difference" – normally the same as that pursuant to which the harmlessness of a preserved error is determined under Federal Rule of Criminal Procedure 52(a). 507 U.S. at 734. The difference pertains to "who bears the burden of persuasion with respect to prejudice." *Id.* Under plain error review, the defendant, rather than the government, bears the burden. "This burden shifting," the Court explained, "is dictated by a subtle but important difference in language between the two parts of Rule 52: While Rule 52(a) precludes error correction only if the error 'does *not* affect substantial rights,' Rule 52(b) authorizes no remedy unless the error *does* 'affect substantial rights.' " *Id.* at 734–35.

Regarding the nature of the burden borne by the appealing party, the Court, citing three harmless error cases, explained that "[i]n most cases [the phrase 'affects substantial rights'] means that the error must have been prejudicial: It must have affected the outcome of the district court proceedings." *Id.* at 734. Additional definition of what it means to "affect[] the outcome of district court proceedings" is found in the cited harmless error cases: *Bank of Nova Scotia v. United States*, 487 U.S. 250 (1988); *United States v. Lane*, 474 U.S. 438 (1986); and *Kotteakos v. United States*, 328 U.S. 750 (1946). In each, the Court concluded that substantial rights are affected if an appellate court finds that an "error *may* have had a substantial influence on the outcome of the proceedings." *Bank of Nova Scotia*, 487 U.S. at 256 (emphasis added); *see also Lane*, 474 U.S. at 458–61 (Brennan, J., concurring in part and dissenting in part) (quoting *Kotteakos* at length and characterizing it as holding that "error is harmless unless it had 'substantial influence' on the outcome *or leaves one in 'grave doubt' as to whether it had such effect*" (emphasis added)).

In *United States v. Dominguez Benitez*, 542 U.S. 74 (2004), the Supreme Court gave further meaning to the "affects substantial rights" requirement of plain error review. The issue raised involved the trial court's consideration of a plea agreement under Rule 11 of the Federal Rules of Criminal Procedure. Citing Rule 52, the Court first stated that in the plain error context a moving party must show "error that affects substantial rights." *Id.* at 81. The Court then said: "In cases where the burden of demonstrating prejudice (or materiality) is on the defendant seeking relief, we have invoked a standard with similarities to the *Kotteakos* formulation in requiring the showing of 'a reasonable probability that, but for the error claimed, the result of the proceeding would have been different.' " *Id.* at 81–82 (quoting *United States v. Bagley*, 473 U.S. 667, 682 (1985) (opinion of Blackmun, J.)). "A defendant must thus satisfy the judgment of the reviewing court, informed by the entire record, that the probability of a different result is sufficient to undermine confidence in the outcome of the proceeding." *Id.* at 83. Most significantly, however, the Court made clear that this "reasonable-probability standard is not the same as, and should not be confused with, a requirement that a defendant prove by a preponderance of the evidence that but for error things would have been different." *Id.* at 83 n.9. In other words, the Court clarified – over objection in Justice Scalia's concurrence, *id.* at 87 (Scalia, J., concurring in the judgment) – that, at least in the Rule 11 context, plain error analysis does *not* require the defendant to show that there is a greater than 50 percent possibility that the outcome would have been different absent the error.

Pursuant to the fourth prerequisite to appellate remedy under the plain error standard, the *Olano* opinion made clear that correction of unpreserved errors "is permissive, not mandatory." 507 U.S. at 735. As the Court explained in *Johnson*:

> [E]ven assuming that [an error] "affected substantial rights," it [still may] not meet the final requirement of *Olano*. When the first three parts of *Olano* are satisfied, an appellate court must then determine whether the forfeited error "seriously affects the fairness, integrity or public reputation of judicial proceedings" before it may exercise its discretion to correct the error.

520 U.S. at 469–70 (quoting *Olano*, 507 U.S. at 736). Thus, an appellate court may not remedy a plain error – even one with respect to which there is a reasonable probability that it affected the complaining party's substantial rights – if the court determines that the error did not "seriously affect[] the fairness, integrity, or public reputation of the judicial proceedings." This is not to say, however, that in criminal cases plain error reversal is available only upon a showing of actual innocence. The *Olano* Court explicitly rejected this possibility, stating:

> We previously have explained that the discretion conferred by Rule 52(b) should be employed in those circumstances in which a miscarriage of justice would otherwise result. In our collateral-review jurisprudence, the term "miscarriage of justice" means that the defendant is actually innocent. The court of appeals should no doubt correct a plain forfeited error that causes the conviction or sentencing of an actually innocent defendant, but we have never held that a Rule 52(b) remedy is *only* warranted in cases of actual innocence.
>
> Rather, the standard that should guide the exercise of remedial discretion under Rule 52(b) was articulated in *United States v. Atkinson*, 297 U.S. 157 (1936). The court of appeals should correct a plain forfeited error affecting substantial rights if the error "seriously affects the fairness, integrity or public reputation of judicial proceedings."

507 U.S. at 736.

Part Two

REVIEW OF AGENCY ACTIONS

---

*

Chapter IX

WHAT ARE ADMINISTRATIVE AGENCIES?

Federal administrative agencies exercise significant power in contemporary American life. Pursuant to congressionally delegated authority, they administer numerous federal statutes, undertaking myriad actions addressing health, welfare, safety, security, economic, and environmental issues. Some agency actions take the form of legislative rulemakings that produce forward-looking regulations of general applicability having the force of law. Others are achieved through case-by-case adjudications resulting in trial-like records that provide the factual bases for judgments that also have the force of law. Still others involve the investigation and prosecution of entities or individuals alleged to have violated the statutes and regulations an agency is authorized to enforce. Agencies are also authorized to use a variety of informal measures – such as policy statements, advisory letters, reports, warning notices, information sheets, web sites, hearings, and surveys – to advance their missions without making law.

Administrative agencies generally are understood to include "each authority of the Government of the United States," 5 U.S.C. § 701(b)(1), excluding the President, Congress, and the courts. *See Franklin v. Massachusetts*, 505 U.S. 788, 800–01 (1992). Unlike the three constitutionally designated branches of the federal government, these authorities, which are variously referred to as agencies, commissions, boards, or departments, have no existence absent statutory authorization by Congress. Agencies normally are established by "organic" statutes in which Congress sets forth the basic mission of an agency, its principal responsibilities, and its authority to act. An agency's policymaking, adjudicatory, enforcement, or administrative responsibilities also may be amplified in "authorizing" or "enabling" statutes enacted by Congress. References to authorizing and enabling statutes sometimes denote organic statutes.

"Some agencies are regulatory commissions, headed by multi-member bodies; these are usually free-standing bodies whose members can be removed from office by the President only for 'cause,' and accordingly are sometimes called 'independent' agencies." STRAUSS, RAKOFF & FARINA, GELLHORN & BYSE'S ADMINISTRATIVE LAW CASES & COMMENTS 10 (2003). Prominent independent agencies include the Civil Aeronautics Board, Federal Communications Commission, National Labor Relations Board, Nuclear Regulatory Commission, Federal Energy Regulatory Commission, Federal Trade Commission, and Securities and Exchange

Commission. Other agencies, sometimes denominated "executive," operate under the leadership of "a single administrator who serves at the President's pleasure, and these are often nestled within larger entities headed by members of the President's Cabinet, whom the President can also discharge." *Id.* For example, the National Highway Traffic Safety Administration operates within the Department of Transportation – both are administrative agencies.

It has been suggested that the President, by virtue of his control of agency leadership, has greater influence over the work of executive agencies than over independent agencies. It is unclear whether this is an accurate assessment of the President's power. *See* Symposium, *The Independence of Independent Agencies*, 1988 DUKE L.J. 215 (1988). What is beyond question, however, is that administrative agencies are powerless to act absent congressionally delegated authority.

Although agencies may not act absent congressionally delegated authority, Congress may not, in the process of authorizing agency action, "interfere with the President's exercise of the 'executive power' and his constitutionally appointed duty to 'take care that the laws be faithfully executed' under Article II." *Morrison v. Olson*, 487 U.S. 654, 689–90 (1988). "[S]pecial considerations control when the Executive Branch's interests in maintaining the autonomy of its office and safeguarding the confidentiality of its communications are implicated." *Cheney v. U.S. Dist. Court for D.C.*, 542 U.S. 367, 385 (2004). Therefore, if an agency's statutorily mandated operating scheme abridges the President's Article II authority, serious separation of powers concerns arise. *See, e.g., Bowsher v. Synar*, 478 U.S. 714 (1986).

Separation of powers questions also may be implicated when Congress authorizes the adjudication of private rights by a non-Article III tribunal. *See, e.g., Commodity Futures Trading Comm'n v. Schor*, 478 U.S. 833 (1986). Moreover, significant constitutional issues may arise under the Sixth and Seventh Amendments when Congress empowers an agency to adjudicate disputes without a jury. *See, e.g., Atlas Roofing Co. v. Occupational Safety & Health Review Comm'n*, 430 U.S. 442 (1977). And the courts are occasionally required to determine whether Congress has statutorily delegated legislative power to an agency in violation of Article I, Section 1 of the Constitution. *See, e.g., Whitman v. Am. Trucking Ass'ns*, 531 U.S. 457 (2001).

Questions such as these, concerning the constitutional limits on congressional authority to confer regulatory and adjudicatory powers on administrative agencies, undoubtedly are important. These matters are beyond the scope of this book, however. Rather, the focus here is on the standards of review governing judicial challenges to agency actions that allegedly exceed a constitutionally permissible congressional delegation of authority, contravene the strictures of an agency's organic or authorizing statute, or violate the applicable provisions of the Administrative Procedure Act ("APA").

Chapter X

THE PRINCIPAL FRAMEWORK
FOR REVIEW OF AGENCY
DECISIONS

A federal agency "literally has no power to act ... unless and until Congress confers power upon it." *La. Pub. Serv. Comm'n v. FCC*, 476 U.S. 355, 374 (1986). The organic and authorizing statutes that confer authority upon an agency also may prescribe whether and how closely agency actions will be reviewed by the courts. To the degree that such statutes do not preemptively define the scope and standards of judicial review, these norms are prescribed by the Administrative Procedure Act. *See* 5 U.S.C. §§ 701–706.

There are many instances in which authorizing statutes grant the courts of appeals jurisdiction over challenges to final agency action and over agency petitions seeking judicial enforcement. In such situations, district court review of agency action is implicitly precluded. *See Thunder Basin Coal Co. v. Reich*, 510 U.S. 200 (1994). However, absent such authorization, judicial review commences in district court. *See, e.g., Troy Corp. v. Browner*, 120 F.3d 277 (D.C. Cir. 1997) (chemical companies and related associations brought action to invalidate an EPA rulemaking); *United States v. Nova Scotia Food Prods. Corp.*, 568 F.2d 240 (2d Cir. 1977) (U.S. Attorney brought action to compel processor of whitefish to comply with FDA regulations).

But the starting point of judicial review is of no moment in determining the standards governing appellate review. Appellate courts "do not defer to a district court's review of an agency [action] any more than the Supreme Court defers to a court of appeals' review of such a decision." *Novicki v. Cook*, 946 F.2d 938, 941 (D.C. Cir. 1991); *see also Holland v. Nat'l Mining Ass'n*, 309 F.3d 808, 814 (D.C. Cir. 2002). This is because, when an agency acts pursuant to congressionally delegated authority and the action has the force of law, "the agency itself is typically owed deference with respect to its fact-finding, *see NLRB v. Brown*, 380 U.S. 278, 292 (1965), its application of law to facts, *see Citizens to Pres. Overton Park, Inc. v. Volpe*, 401 U.S. 402, 416 (1971), and its interpretation of the governing statute or regulation, *see Chevron U.S.A. Inc. v. Natural Res. Def. Council, Inc.*, 467 U.S. 837, 843 (1984)." *Novicki*, 946 F.2d at 941. And if deference is owed to the agency, "it is anomalous ([and] if the agency and district court disagree analytically impossible) to defer also to another court's review of the agency's action." *Id.*; *see also Senior Res. v. Jackson*, 412 F.3d 112, 117 (D.C. Cir. 2005) (appellate court reviews *de novo* a district court's review of agency action pursuant to 5 U.S.C. § 706(2)(A)).

The standards of review prescribed by the APA and the various statutes authorizing administrative action, as well as by judicial decisions interpreting those statutes, reflect judgments about the degree to which courts should defer to agency decisionmaking. Although the standard of review varies with the type of agency action at issue, there are numerous situations in which significant deference is afforded the substantive judgments rendered by administrative agencies. Why? Because many agency actions having the force of law require expertise that the courts do not possess and involve policy choices more appropriately overseen by a politically accountable branch of the government. As the Supreme Court explained in *Chevron U.S.A. Inc. v. Natural Resources Defense Council, Inc.*:

> We have long recognized that considerable weight should be accorded to an executive department's construction of a statutory scheme it is entrusted to administer, and the principle of deference to administrative interpretations has been consistently followed by this Court whenever decision as to the meaning or reach of a statute has involved reconciling conflicting policies, and a full understanding of the force of the statutory policy in the given situation has depended upon more than ordinary knowledge respecting the matters subjected to agency regulations.
>
> . . . .
>
> Judges are not experts in [pollution-emitting devices], and are not part of either political branch of the Government. Courts must, in some cases, reconcile competing political interests, but not on the basis of the judges' personal policy preferences. In contrast, an agency to which Congress has delegated policymaking responsibilities may, within the limits of that delegation, properly rely upon the incumbent administration's views of wise policy to inform its judgments. While agencies are not directly accountable to the people, the Chief Executive is, and it is entirely appropriate for this political branch of the Government to make such policy choices – resolving the competing interests which Congress itself either inadvertently did not resolve, or intentionally left to be resolved by the agency charged with the administration of the statute in light of everyday realities.

467 U.S. at 844, 865–66.

Although a court must give appropriate deference to agency decisionmaking where it is called for, it may not uphold an agency action "on a basis containing any element of discretion ... that is not the basis the agency used." *ICC v. Bhd. of Locomotive Eng'rs*, 482 U.S. 270, 283

(1987). This "simple but fundamental rule of administrative law" was explained by the Supreme Court in *SEC v. Chenery Corp.*, 332 U.S. 194 (1947):

> [A] reviewing court, in dealing with a determination or judgment which an administrative agency alone is authorized to make, must judge the propriety of such action solely by the grounds invoked by the agency. If those grounds are inadequate or improper, the court is powerless to affirm the administrative action by substituting what it considers to be a more adequate or proper basis. To do so would propel the court into the domain which Congress has set aside exclusively for the administrative agency.

Id. at 196.

Judicial review of the procedures pursuant to which an agency acts is also circumscribed. The Supreme Court in *Vermont Yankee Nuclear Power Corp. v. Natural Resources Defense Council, Inc.*, 435 U.S. 519 (1978), held that a court may not impose procedural requirements on an agency that exceed those prescribed by the APA, the agency's authorizing statute, or any rules adopted by the agency pursuant to its enabling statute. The Court explained:

> [G]enerally speaking [the APA] established the maximum procedural requirements which Congress was willing to have the courts impose upon agencies in conducting rulemaking procedures. Agencies are free to grant additional procedural rights in the exercise of their discretion, but reviewing courts are generally not free to impose them if the agencies have not chosen to grant them. This is not to say necessarily that there are no circumstances which would ever justify a court in overturning agency action because of a failure to employ procedures beyond those required by the statute. But such circumstances, if they exist, are extremely rare.
>
> Even apart from the Administrative Procedure Act this Court has for more than four decades emphasized that the formulation of procedures was basically to be left within the discretion of the agencies to which Congress had confided the responsibility for substantive judgments.

Id. at 524.

Although the courts must give appropriate deference to certain agency judgments, this does not mean that judicial review of administrative action is meaningless. The APA, as well as many statutes authorizing agency action, imposes fairly precise limits on the discretionary authority delegated to agencies and prescribes in some detail how agency authority is to be exercised. And the APA gives the courts the power to enforce these statutory commands. *See* 5 U.S.C. §§ 701–706.

Section 706 of the APA establishes the principal framework for judicial review of administrative action, setting forth both the applicable scope of review and the controlling standards of review. It provides:

To the extent necessary to decision and when presented, the reviewing court shall decide all relevant questions of law, interpret constitutional and statutory provisions, and determine the meaning or applicability of the terms of an agency action. The reviewing court shall –

(1) compel agency action unlawfully withheld or unreasonably delayed; and

(2) hold unlawful and set aside agency action, findings, and conclusions found to be –

(A) arbitrary, capricious, an abuse of discretion, or otherwise not in accordance with law;

(B) contrary to constitutional right, power, privilege, or immunity;

(C) in excess of statutory jurisdiction, authority, or limitations, or short of statutory right;

(D) without observance of procedure required by law;

(E) unsupported by substantial evidence in a case subject to sections 556 and 557 of this title or otherwise reviewed on the record of an agency hearing provided by statute; or

(F) unwarranted by the facts to the extent that the facts are subject to trial de novo by the reviewing court.

In making the foregoing determinations, the court shall review the whole record or those parts of it cited by a party, and due account shall be taken of the rule of prejudicial error.

5 U.S.C. § 706. Some agency authorizing statutes supplement or preempt the scope and standards of review set forth in § 706. More often than not, however, § 706 sets the parameters for judicial review of agency action. And, as countless federal judicial decisions vacating and reversing agency actions demonstrate, this provision assigns the courts a significant role in reviewing administrative action.

Section 706(1) provides that a reviewing court "shall compel agency action unlawfully withheld or unreasonably delayed." 5 U.S.C. § 706(1). "[T]he only agency action that can be compelled under [§ 706(1)] is action legally *required*." *Norton v. S. Utah Wilderness Alliance*, 542 U.S. 55, 63 (2004). "Thus, a claim under § 706(1) can proceed only where a plaintiff asserts that an agency failed to take a *discrete* agency action that it is *required to take*." *Id.* at 64.

Section 706(2), in turn, enumerates six different grounds upon which a reviewing court may "hold unlawful and set aside agency action, findings, and conclusions." 5 U.S.C. § 706(2).

In all cases agency action must be set aside if the action was "arbitrary, capricious, an abuse of discretion, or otherwise not in accordance with law" or if the action failed to meet statutory, procedural, or constitutional requirements. 5 U.S.C. § 706(2)(A), (B), (C), (D). In certain narrow, specifically limited situations, the agency action is to be set aside if the action was not supported by "substantial evidence." And in other equally narrow circumstances the reviewing court is to engage in a *de novo* review of the action and set it aside if it was "unwarranted by the facts." 5 U.S.C. § 706(2)(E), (F).

Overton Park, 401 U.S. at 413–14.

The "substantial evidence" standard of paragraph (E) applies only to review of factual findings emanating from formal, on-the-record hearings, as required either by §§ 556 and 557 of the APA or pursuant to an agency's authorizing statute. 5 U.S.C. § 706(2)(E). Paragraph (F) applies in equally limited circumstances, authorizing a reviewing court to engage in *de novo* review of an agency's factual findings only when "the action is adjudicatory in nature and the agency factfinding procedures are inadequate" or "when issues that were not before the agency are raised in a proceeding to enforce nonadjudicatory agency action." *Overton Park*, 401 U.S. at 415.

The provisions of § 706(2) are cumulative. "Thus, an agency action which is supported by the required substantial evidence may in another regard be 'arbitrary, capricious, an abuse of discretion, or otherwise not in accordance with law' – for example, because it is an abrupt and unexplained departure from agency precedent." *Ass'n of Data Processing Serv. Orgs. v. Bd. of Governors of the Fed. Reserve Sys.*, 745 F.2d 677, 683 (D.C. Cir. 1984). It is also important to recognize that paragraphs (B) through (F) in § 706(2) are confined to particular types of claims, whereas paragraph (A), the arbitrary-and-capricious provision, "is a catchall, picking up administrative misconduct not covered by the other more specific paragraphs." *Id.* This means, for example, that agency action that is not "in excess of statutory authority," as required by paragraph (C), and is properly supported by "substantial evidence," as required by paragraph (E), may nevertheless be struck down as arbitrary and capricious for want of reasoned decisionmaking. Or, "in those situations where paragraph (E) has no application (informal rulemaking, for example, which is not governed by §§ 556 and 557 to which paragraph (E) refers), paragraph (A) takes up the slack, so to speak, enabling the courts to strike down, as arbitrary, agency action that is devoid of needed factual support." *Id.* The Supreme Court also has indicated that "[s]ubstantive review of an agency's interpretation of its regulations is governed only by [§ 706(2)(A)]." *Allentown Mack Sales & Serv., Inc. v. NLRB*, 522 U.S. 359, 377 (1998); *see also Thomas Jefferson Univ. v. Shalala*, 512 U.S. 504, 512 (1994).

The table below identifies some of the principal Supreme Court decisions interpreting and applying the scope and standards of review under § 706.

APA	Text	Principal Judicial Authorities
5 U.S.C § 706	To the extent necessary to decision and when presented, the reviewing court shall decide all relevant questions of law, interpret constitutional and statutory provisions, and determine the meaning or applicability of the terms of an agency action. The reviewing court shall –	
§ 706(1)	compel agency action unlawfully withheld or unreasonably delayed; and	*Norton v. S. Utah Wilderness Alliance*, 542 U.S. 55, 63-64 (2004)
§ 706(2)	hold unlawful and set aside agency action, findings, and conclusions found to be –	
§ 706(2)(A)	arbitrary, capricious, an abuse of discretion, or otherwise not in accordance with law;	*Citizens to Pres. Overton Park v. Volpe*, 401 U.S. 402, 413-14, 416 (1971); *Motor Vehicle Mfrs. Ass'n of the U.S. v. State Farm Mut. Auto. Ins. Co.*, 463 U.S. 29 (1983); *Thomas Jefferson Univ. v. Shalala*, 512 U.S. 504, 512 (1994); *Allentown Mack Sales & Serv., Inc. v. NLRB*, 522 U.S. 359, 377 (1998)
§ 706(2)(B)	contrary to constitutional right, power, privilege, or immunity;	*Webster v. Doe*, 486 U.S. 592 (1988); *FCC v. Beach Commc'ns, Inc.*, 508 U.S. 307 (1993)
§ 706(2)(C)	in excess of statutory jurisdiction, authority, or limitations, or short of statutory right;	*Chevron U.S.A. Inc. v. Natural Res. Def. Council, Inc.*, 467 U.S. 837 (1984); *United States v. Mead Corp.*, 533 U.S. 218 (2001); *Gonzales v. Oregon*, 546 U.S. 243 (2006); *Christensen v. Harris County*, 529 U.S. 576, 587 (2000); *Skidmore v. Swift & Co.*, 323 U.S. 134 (1944)
§ 706(2)(D)	without observance of procedure required by law;	*Vermont Yankee Nuclear Power Corp. v. Natural Res. Def. Council, Inc.*, 435 U.S. 519 (1978)
§ 706(2)(E)	unsupported by substantial evidence in a case subject to sections 556 and 557 of this title or otherwise reviewed on the record of an agency hearing provided by statute; or	*Universal Camera Corp. v. NLRB*, 340 U.S. 474 (1951); *Allentown Mack Sales & Serv., Inc. v. NLRB*, 522 U.S. 359 (1998)
§ 706(2)(F)	unwarranted by the facts to the extent that the facts are subject to trial de novo by the reviewing court.	*Citizens to Pres. Overton Park, Inc. v. Volpe*, 401 U.S. 402 (1971); *Camp v. Pitts*, 411 U.S. 138 (1973) (per curiam)
5 U. S. C. §706	In making the foregoing determinations, the court shall review the whole record or those parts of it cited by a party, and due account shall be taken of the rule of prejudicial error.	*National Ass'n of Home Builders v. Defenders of Wildlife*, ___ U.S. ___, 127 S.Ct. 2518 (2007)

The sections that follow first address threshold jurisdictional and prudential limitations on judicial review of agency action (including subject matter jurisdiction, standing, mootness, sovereign immunity, finality, ripeness, exhaustion, and issue waiver). These matters are given significant treatment, because, in the administrative context, jurisdictional and prudential limitations often function as something akin to first order standards of review, governing if and to what degree the judiciary will oversee administrative action. The important presumption of reviewability and its exceptions are addressed next. The discussion then turns to the standards controlling review of the bulk of judicial challenges to agency decisionmaking, including claims that an agency acted

- without congressionally delegated authority;

- contrary to a congressional directive on the precise question at issue (*Chevron* Step One);

- pursuant to a purported express delegation of authority, but in a manner manifestly contrary to its authorizing statute (*Chevron* Step Two);

- pursuant to a purported implicit delegation of authority, but in an unreasonable manner (*Chevron* Step Two);

- without the force of law (*Skidmore*);

- in an arbitrary and capricious manner;

- without substantial evidentiary support in an action subject to § 706(2)(E) or a like provision in the agency's authorizing statute; or

- in a plainly erroneous manner in interpreting its own regulations (*Auer*).

In addressing these and other claims seeking judicial review of administrative agency action, the intent here is to illuminate the scope of review while highlighting and amplifying the applicable standards of review. Most of the cases that are discussed fall within the framework of 5 U.S.C. § 706. The principal standards of review, some of which are denominated by a case name, include *de novo*, *Chevron* Step One, *Chevron* Step Two, *Skidmore* review, *Auer* review, arbitrary and capricious, and substantial evidence.

*

Chapter XI

THRESHOLD JURISDICTIONAL AND PRUDENTIAL LIMITATIONS ON JUDICIAL REVIEW

Although federal jurisdiction is not the focus of this book, it makes little sense to consider the standards controlling federal judicial review of administrative agency actions without providing at least an overview of subject matter jurisdiction, sovereign immunity, standing, mootness, finality, ripeness, exhaustion of remedies, and issue waiver – all doctrines that pose potential barriers to judicial review. These oft-recurring issues address important questions "about the appropriate role of the judiciary in the regulatory process," STRAUSS, RAKOFF & FARINA, GELLHORN & BYSE'S ADMINISTRATIVE LAW CASES & COMMENTS 1117 (2003), and thus take on something of the character of standards of review, determining if, when, and to what extent the courts will oversee the regulatory programs created and administered by the other branches of government.

Standing, in particular, is a consuming issue in the case law defining the availability of judicial review of agency action.

> Standing is the key to the courthouse door; those who possess the key, possess power. To be sure, being permitted to complain about agency behavior is a long way from having that complaint legally validated and judicially remedied. Still, from the agency's perspective, the very act of being haled into court and required to defend its action involves considerable costs. Hence, parties who are capable of imposing such costs at the *end* of the regulatory process become parties whose interests must be reckoned with *during* the regulatory process. . . .

> [A court's decision as to] who, if anyone, shall be entitled to trigger judicial scrutiny of agency conduct [has] significant implications for the Executive Branch that administers regulatory programs and for the Legislative Branch that creates them.

Id.

Although standing is significant, the other jurisdictional and prudential limitations on judicial review are no less critical to the questions of whether and to what degree the courts may become involved in the

107

oversight of administrative agencies. Indeed, the APA explicitly covers sovereign immunity, 5 U.S.C. § 702, prudential ("zone-of-interest") standing, *id.*, finality, *id.* § 704, and exhaustion, *id.* And there are countless judicial decisions that address these matters and the other jurisdictional and prudential limitations.

A. SUBJECT MATTER JURISDICTION

"[S]ubject-matter jurisdiction, because it involves a court's power to hear a case, can never be forfeited or waived." *Arbaugh v. Y & H Corp.*, 546 U.S. 500, 514 (2006). Moreover, the courts "have an independent obligation to determine whether subject-matter jurisdiction exists, even in the absence of a challenge from any party." *Id.* Absent a statutory grant of jurisdiction, a federal court has no authority to decide a claim. Thus, it is generally said that a federal court may not "assum[e] jurisdiction for the purpose of deciding the merits" of a case. *Steel Co. v. Citizens for a Better Env't*, 523 U.S. 83, 94 (1998).

Although the majority of challenges to agency action are brought under the APA, the APA itself does not grant the federal courts subject matter jurisdiction to review agency action. *See Califano v. Sanders*, 430 U.S. 99, 107 (1977). Rather, judicial challenges brought under the APA fall within the ambit of 28 U.S.C. § 1331, the general federal question statute, which vests district courts with "original jurisdiction of all civil actions arising under the Constitution, laws, or treaties of the United States." *See Chrysler Corp. v. Brown*, 441 U.S. 281, 317 n.47 (1979).

There are also many authorizing statutes that vest exclusive jurisdiction over challenges to final agency action in the appellate courts. In such instances, it is normally assumed that, "[b]y lodging review of agency action in the Court of Appeals, Congress manifested an intent that the appellate court exercise sole jurisdiction over the class of claims covered by the statutory grant of review power." *Telecomms. Research & Action Ctr. v. FCC*, 750 F.2d 70, 77 (D.C. Cir. 1984) (*TRAC*). Consequently, even when the jurisdictional provision in an enabling statute refers to "final agency action," the appellate court's "exclusive jurisdiction" extends to § 706(1) claims seeking to compel agency action unreasonably delayed – if that action, once taken, would be reviewable in the court of appeals. In other words, an "appellate court has exclusive jurisdiction to hear suits seeking relief that might affect its future statutory power of review." *Id.* at 72.

In *TRAC*, for example, the statutory commitment of review to the court of appeals of final Federal Communications Commission actions, read in conjunction with the All Writs Act, 28 U.S.C. § 1651(a), was held to afford the appellate court exclusive jurisdiction over claims seeking mandamus relief from unreasonable Commission delay. The court reasoned that "[i]t would be anomalous to hold that [the grant of exclusive jurisdiction to the court of appeals] only strips the District Court of general federal question jurisdiction under 28 U.S.C. § 1331 when the Circuit Court has present jurisdiction under a special review statute, but not when the Circuit Court has immediate jurisdiction under the All Writs Act in aid of its future statutory review power." *TRAC*, 750 F.2d at 77.

Although the APA does not grant the federal courts subject matter jurisdiction to review agency action, it does afford several causes of action to parties seeking to challenge disputed agency actions. *See Arbaugh*, 546 U.S. at 510–16 (explaining the difference between statutory provisions granting subject matter jurisdiction and statutory provisions defining the elements of a party's cause of action). The APA, by its terms,

> waives sovereign immunity in actions "seeking relief other than money damages and stating a claim that an agency or an officer or employee thereof acted or failed to act in an official capacity or under color of legal authority," 5 U.S.C. § 702,

> allows judicial review for persons "suffering legal wrong because of agency action, or adversely affected or aggrieved by agency action within the meaning of a relevant statute," *id.*,

> makes clear that "[a]gency action made reviewable by statute and final agency action for which there is no other adequate remedy in a court are subject to judicial review," *id.* § 704,

> "and applies universally 'except to the extent that – (1) statutes preclude judicial review; or (2) agency action is committed to agency discretion by law,' § 701(a)," *Bennett v. Spear*, 520 U.S. 154, 175 (1997).

Consistent with these provisions, an aggrieved party may have a cause of action under § 706(1) of the APA to compel agency action unlawfully delayed, 5 U.S.C. § 706(1), or under § 706(2) to challenge agency action on one of the six different grounds upon which a reviewing court may "hold unlawful and set aside agency action, findings, and conclusions," *id.* § 706(2).

B.   SOVEREIGN IMMUNITY

The federal government and federal administrative agencies are immune from suit absent an express waiver of sovereign immunity. *See Lane v. Pena*, 518 U.S. 187, 192 (1996). The general grant of federal question jurisdiction under 28 U.S.C. § 1331 is not consent by the government to be sued for claims arising under federal law. *See Voluntary Purchasing Groups, Inc. v. Reilly*, 889 F.2d 1380, 1385 (5th Cir. 1989). Any waiver of sovereign immunity must be expressed unequivocally in statutory text. *See United States v. Nordic Village, Inc.*, 503 U.S. 30, 33–34, 37 (1992).

In 1976, Congress amended the APA to remove sovereign immunity as a defense to judicial review of federal administrative action. *See* 5 U.S.C. § 702 note (Amendments). This waiver of sovereign immunity is not limited to causes of action arising under the APA, but rather extends to any action in which a party "seek[s] relief other than money damages and stat[es] a claim that an agency or an officer or employee thereof acted or failed to act in an official capacity or under color of legal authority." *Id.*; *see also Presbyterian Church (U.S.A.) v. United States*, 870 F.2d 518, 523–26 (9th Cir. 1989) (finding waiver of sovereign immunity pursuant to 5 U.S.C. § 702 when First and Fourth Amendment claims were asserted and alleged activity did not constitute "agency action"). Section 702 preserves "the defense of sovereign immunity only when another statute expressly or implicitly forecloses" an action against an agency or an officer or employee of the United States. *Schnapper v. Foley*, 667 F.2d 102, 108 (D.C. Cir. 1981).

C. STANDING REQUIREMENTS

1. ARTICLE III STANDING

Article III of the Constitution confines the federal courts to the adjudication of actual "cases" or "controversies." The case or controversy requirement embraces "the idea of separation of powers on which the Federal Government is founded." *Allen v. Wright*, 468 U.S. 737, 750 (1984). The various doctrines that give content to Article III, including standing, mootness, and ripeness, are "founded in concern about the proper – and properly limited – role of the courts in a democratic society." *Warth v. Seldin*, 422 U.S. 490, 498 (1975). "The Art. III doctrine that requires a litigant to have 'standing' to invoke the power of a federal court is perhaps the most important of these doctrines." *Allen v. Wright*, 468 U.S. at 750.

A party invoking federal jurisdiction bears the burden of establishing standing. In *Lujan v. Defenders of Wildlife*, 504 U.S. 555 (1992), the Court explained:

> [T]he irreducible constitutional minimum of standing contains three elements. First, the plaintiff must have suffered an injury in fact – an invasion of a legally protected interest which is (a) concrete and particularized, and (b) actual or imminent, not conjectural or hypothetical. Second, there must be a causal connection between the injury and the conduct complained of – the injury has to be fairly ... traceable to the challenged action of the defendant, and not ... the result of the independent action of some third party not before the court. Third, it must be likely, as opposed to merely speculative, that the injury will be redressed by a favorable decision.

Id. at 560–61. The Court also made it clear that the element of "particularized" injury normally requires a plaintiff to establish that the injury suffered was personal and individual. *Id.* at 560 n.1, 561–62.

In *Massachusetts v. EPA*, ___ U.S. ___, 127 S. Ct. 1438 (2007), the Supreme Court explained that the normal standing requirements for imminency and redressability need not be met when a party asserts a "procedural right" in challenging agency action or inaction. In that case, Massachusetts and other parties sought judicial review of EPA's refusal to regulate greenhouse gas emissions under the Clean Air Act. In addressing the question of standing, the Court held: "When a litigant is vested with a procedural right, that litigant has standing if there is some possibility that the requested relief will prompt the injury-causing party to reconsider the decision that allegedly harmed the litigant." *Id.* at 1453 (citing *Lujan v. Defenders of Wildlife*, 504 U.S. at 572 n.7). In finding that the requirements of Article III standing had been satisfied, the Court noted Massachusetts' "special position and interest" as "a sovereign State" and its procedural right under the statute to challenge EPA's rejection of its rulemaking petition:

> Congress has ordered EPA to protect Massachusetts (among others) by prescribing standards applicable to the "emission of any air pollutant from any class or classes of new motor vehicle engines, which in [the Administrator's] judgment cause, or contribute to, air pollution which may reasonably be anticipated to endanger public health or welfare." 42 U.S.C. § 7521(a)(1). Congress has moreover recognized a concomitant procedural right to challenge the rejection of [a party's] rulemaking petition as arbitrary and capricious. § 7607(b)(1). Given that procedural right and Massachusetts' stake in protecting its quasi-sovereign interests, the Commonwealth is entitled to special solicitude in our standing analysis.

> . . . .

> . . . [I]t is clear that petitioners' submissions as they pertain to Massachusetts have satisfied the most demanding standards of the adversarial process. EPA's steadfast refusal to regulate greenhouse gas emissions presents a risk of harm to Massachusetts that is both "actual" and "imminent." There is, moreover, a "substantial likelihood that the judicial relief requested" will prompt EPA to take steps to reduce that risk.

Id. at 1454–55.

When a challenge to standing is raised in conjunction with an appellate court's direct review of a final order from an administrative agency, as in *Massachusetts v. EPA*, there obviously is no record from a district court. And the agency record normally will not include any findings addressing standing, because Article III standing is not a prerequisite to participation in federal agency proceedings. *See Pfizer Inc. v. Shalala*, 182 F.3d 975, 980 (D.C. Cir. 1999). However, the constitutional standing requirement imposed on a petitioner seeking direct review in an appellate court "is the same . . . as it would be if such review were conducted in the first instance by the district court." *Sierra Club v. EPA*, 292 F.3d 895, 899 (D.C. Cir. 2002). Therefore, it has been held that "[t]he petitioner's burden of production in the court of appeals is . . . the same as that of a plaintiff moving for summary judgment in the district court: it must support each element of its claim to standing by affidavit or other evidence. Its burden of proof is to show a *substantial probability* that it has been injured, that the defendant caused its injury, and that the court could redress that injury." *Id.* (emphasis added). Accordingly, a court of appeals may accept, or request and receive, evidence outside of the administrative record, as necessary, to support a petitioner's entitlement to judicial review. *See Tex. Indep. Producers & Royalty Owners Ass'n v. EPA*, 410 F.3d 964, 972–73 (7th Cir. 2005) (holding that three affidavits presented with petitioner's reply brief were inadequate to establish standing, because they merely repeated the conclusory allegations in the opening brief).

Sierra Club v. EPA holds that, in cases involving petitions for review of administrative agency actions, "a petitioner whose standing is not selfevident should establish its standing by the submission of its arguments and any affidavits or other evidence appurtenant thereto at the first appropriate point in the review proceeding." 292 F.3d at 900. The court noted that in some cases petitioners will be required to respond to motions to dismiss for want of standing, and in other cases petitioners will simply cite to record evidence and append affidavits and other extra-record evidence in their opening briefs to support standing. If parties reasonably believe that their standing is self-evident, but the court disagrees, the court may instruct the parties to submit affidavits and supplemental briefs addressing standing, *see, e.g., Am. Library Ass'n v. FCC*, 401 F.3d 489, 492, 496 (D.C. Cir. 2005), or it may dismiss, *see, e.g., Int'l Bhd. of Teamsters v. Transp. Sec. Admin.*, 429 F.3d 1130, 1135–36 (D.C. Cir. 2005) (declining to accept petitioner's supplemental submissions in support of standing, because, on the evidentiary record before the court, petitioner "could not have reasonably believed its representational standing was self-evident"). And in some instances, the appellate court may consider new materials addressing standing offered with a petition for rehearing. *See, e.g., Natural Res. Def. Council v. EPA*, 464 F.3d 1, 3, 7 n.6 (D.C. Cir. 2006).

In other words, a court may do what is necessary to fulfill its responsibility to determine whether it has jurisdiction to hear a claim. In cases in which an appellate court directly reviews a final order of an administrative agency, it will review the record and the parties' submissions and then decide whether there is "a substantial probability that, if enforced, the [agency's disputed action] will immediately harm the concrete and particularized interests" of the petitioner so as to satisfy the injury, causation, and redressability requirements of Article III standing. *Am. Library Ass'n v. FCC*, 406 F.3d 689, 697 (D.C. Cir. 2005).

2. ZONE-OF-INTEREST STANDING

In addition to determining whether a petitioner has Article III standing, a court presented with a challenge to agency action must also determine "whether the interest sought to be protected by the complainant is arguably within the zone of interests to be protected or regulated by the statute or constitutional guarantee in question." *Ass'n of Data Processing Serv. Orgs. v. Camp*, 397 U.S. 150, 153 (1970); *see also Clarke v. Sec. Indus. Ass'n*, 479 U.S. 388, 394–97 (1987). The zone-of-interest inquiry, which is "basically one of interpreting congressional intent," *Clarke*, 479 U.S. at 394, is a prudential requirement of general application that applies unless expressly negated by Congress. *See Bennett v. Spear*, 520 U.S. at 163.

The zone-of-interest standing doctrine is based largely on the Supreme Court's interpretation of the Administrative Procedure Act. Under the APA, "[a]gency action made reviewable by statute and final agency action for which there is no other adequate remedy in a court are subject to judicial review." 5 U.S.C. § 704. If the relevant authorizing statute does not provide for a private right of action, a party may seek judicial review of an administrative action under § 702 of the APA, which states:

> A person suffering legal wrong because of agency action, or adversely affected or aggrieved by agency action within the meaning of a relevant statute, is entitled to judicial review thereof.

By its terms, § 702 could be construed to require a showing of a precise "legal interest" or "an explicit provision in the relevant statute permitting suit by any party adversely affected or aggrieved." *See Clarke*, 479 U.S. at 394. However, the Supreme Court has been "unwilling to take so narrow a view of the APA's generous review provisions." *Id.* at 395. Rather, the Court has emphasized that, "[w]here statutes are concerned, the trend is toward enlargement of the class of people who may protest administrative action." *Data Processing v. Camp*, 397 U.S. at 154.

> The "zone of interest" test is a guide for deciding whether, in view of Congress' evident intent to make agency action presumptively reviewable, a particular plaintiff should be heard to complain of a particular agency decision. In cases where the plaintiff is not itself the subject of the contested regulatory action, the test denies a right of review if the plaintiff's interests are so marginally related to or inconsistent with the purposes implicit in the statute that it cannot reasonably be assumed that Congress intended to permit the suit. The test is not meant to be especially demanding; in particular, there need be no indication of congressional purpose to benefit the would-be plaintiff.

Clarke, 479 U.S. at 399–400.

In adopting the zone-of-interest test, however, the Court explicitly rejected the suggestion that Congress, in enacting § 702, meant to allow a suit by any person who could satisfy the requirements of Article III standing. Recognizing "the potential for disruption inherent in allowing every party adversely affected by agency action to seek judicial review," *id.* at 397, the Court embraced a more restrained construction of aggrievement.

> [T]o be "adversely affected or aggrieved ... within the meaning" of a statute, the plaintiff must establish that the injury he complains of (*his* aggrievement, or the adverse effect *upon him*) falls within the "zone of interests" sought to be protected by the statutory provision whose violation forms the legal basis for his complaint. Thus, for example, the failure of an agency to comply with a statutory provision requiring "on the record" hearings would assuredly have an adverse effect upon the company that has the contract to record and transcribe the agency's proceedings; but since the provision was obviously enacted to protect the interests of the parties to the proceedings and not those of the reporters, that company would not be "adversely affected within the meaning" of the statute.

Lujan v. Nat'l Wildlife Fed'n, 497 U.S. 871, 883 (1990). Congress may, of course, eliminate the constraints of the zone-of-interest test by enacting a statute that allows any aggrieved person to challenge administrative action under the relevant enabling statute. *See Bennett v. Spear*, 520 U.S. at 164–66. In such a situation, standing to sue is limited only by the requirements of Article III.

D. MOOTNESS

Because the exercise of judicial power under Article III depends upon the existence of a case or controversy, a federal court may not render advisory opinions or decide questions that do not affect the rights of parties properly before it. *See North Carolina v. Rice*, 404 U.S. 244, 246 (1971) (per curiam). A court's judgment must resolve "a real and substantial controversy admitting of specific relief through a decree of a conclusive character, as distinguished from an opinion advising what the law would be upon a hypothetical state of facts." *Id.* This means that an actual controversy must exist at all stages of judicial review, not merely when the complaint is filed. *See Roe v. Wade*, 410 U.S. 113, 125 (1973). If a case is settled, a party dies, or one side abandons the litigation, the case must be dismissed as moot.

There are two exceptions to mootness. The first pertains to situations in which "the challenged action was in its duration too short to be fully litigated prior to its cessation or expiration," yet there is a "demonstrated probability that the same controversy will recur involving the same complaining party." *Murphy v. Hunt*, 455 U.S. 478, 482 (1982) (per curiam). For example, in *Roe v. Wade*, the plaintiff challenged Texas criminal abortion statutes. Although the plaintiff's pregnancy ended before the litigation was complete, the Supreme Court held that the case was not moot, because the dispute was "capable of repetition, yet evading review." *Roe*, 410 U.S. at 125.

The second exception involves a party's "voluntary cessation" of the challenged activity. As a general rule, a defendant's "voluntary cessation of allegedly illegal conduct does not deprive [a court] of power to hear and determine the case." *County of Los Angeles v. Davis*, 440 U.S. 625, 631 (1979). Voluntary cessation will only moot a case if "there is no reasonable expectation ... that the alleged violation will recur" and "interim relief or events have completely and irrevocably eradicated the effects of the alleged violation." *Id.* The defendant carries the burden of demonstrating "that there is no reasonable expectation that the wrong will be repeated," and "[t]he burden is a heavy one." *United States v. W. T. Grant Co.*, 345 U.S. 629, 633 (1953).

Although the Article III case or controversy limitation on federal judicial authority underpins both standing and mootness, *Friends of the Earth, Inc. v. Laidlaw Environmental Services (TOC), Inc.*, 528 U.S. 167 (2000), makes clear that the two doctrines differ in important respects. In *Friends of the Earth*, the plaintiffs sued under the citizen suit provisions of the Clean Water Act to enjoin the defendant's violation of the statute and to require the defendant to pay a civil penalty to the government. The district court determined that injunctive relief was inappropriate, because the defendant's violations of the statute had ceased after litigation commenced. However, the court assessed a civil penalty against the defendant to forestall future violations. The court of appeals reversed the imposition of the fine, holding that the case was moot once the defendant fully complied with the terms of the statute. It reasoned that all elements of Article III standing must exist throughout litigation and that the only remedy available after the defendant's violations had ceased – civil penalties payable to the government – did not redress any injury to the plaintiff. The Supreme Court reversed, holding that "the Court of Appeals confused mootness with standing." *Id.* at 189.

Friends of the Earth rejects the Court's prior statements that "[t]he requisite personal interest that must exist at the commencement of the litigation (standing) must continue throughout its existence (mootness)." *Id.* "[I]f mootness were simply 'standing set in a time frame,' the exception to mootness that arises when the defendant's allegedly unlawful activity is 'capable of repetition, yet evading review,' could not exist." *Id.* at 190. More significantly, the Court looked to the distinct functions of standing and mootness to explain why "there are circumstances in which the prospect that a defendant will engage in (or resume) harmful conduct may be too speculative to support standing, but not too speculative to overcome mootness." *Id.*

> Standing doctrine functions to ensure, among other things, that the scarce resources of the federal courts are devoted to those disputes in which the parties have a concrete stake. In contrast, by the time mootness is an issue, the case has been brought and litigated, often (as here) for years. To abandon the case at an advanced stage may prove more wasteful than frugal. This argument from sunk costs does not license courts to retain

jurisdiction over cases in which one or both of the parties plainly lack a continuing interest, as when the parties have settled or a plaintiff pursuing a nonsurviving claim has died. But the argument surely highlights an important difference between the two doctrines.

Id. at 191–92.

Friends of the Earth also confirms that the standard "for determining whether a case has been mooted by the defendant's voluntary conduct is stringent: A case might become moot if subsequent events made it absolutely clear that the allegedly wrongful behavior could not reasonably be expected to recur." *Id.* at 189. As the Court explained, a defendant's voluntary cessation of a challenged practice cannot, alone, deprive a federal court of its power to determine the legality of the practice. "If it did, the courts would be compelled to leave the defendant . . . free to return to his old ways." *Id.*

The *Friends of the Earth* opinion follows easily from earlier decisions holding that if a plaintiff challenges both a specific action and the policy that underlies that action, the challenge to the policy is not necessarily mooted merely because the challenge to the particular action is moot. For example, in *Super Tire Engineering Co. v. McCorkle*, 416 U.S. 115 (1974), employers sought declaratory and injunctive relief to prevent New Jersey from granting state welfare benefits to striking workers on the ground that the state's actions violated federal labor law. The Court held that because the strike that prompted the suit ended before the case was resolved, the employer's request for an injunction preventing payment of welfare benefits during the strike was moot. However, the Court also held that the employer's request for declaratory relief was not moot, because the challenged governmental action had not ceased and the employer's relationship with the union would be continually affected by the "fixed and definite" state policy of giving welfare benefits to strikers. *Id.* at 122–24.

E. THE OVERLAPPING DOCTRINES OF FINALITY, RIPENESS, EXHAUSTION OF ADMINISTRATIVE REMEDIES, AND ISSUE WAIVER

The doctrines of finality, ripeness, exhaustion of administrative remedies, and issue waiver each require a court to determine whether there has been an adequate opportunity for an agency to fully consider a matter with respect to which judicial review is sought. Given this common focus, it is sometimes difficult to discern which doctrine controls in a given case. This is particularly true with respect to finality, ripeness, and exhaustion. *See Ticor Title Ins. Co. v. FTC*, 814 F.2d 731, 732 (D.C. Cir. 1987) (opinion of Edwards, J.).

1. THE FINALITY DOCTRINE

There is a "strong presumption" that judicial review of administrative action is available only after a challenged action is "final." *Bell v. New Jersey*, 461 U.S. 773, 778 (1983). Indeed, "final agency action" is a prerequisite to most causes of action under the APA. *See* 5 U.S.C. § 704; *Lujan v. Nat'l Wildlife Fed'n*, 497 U.S. at 882. The APA's finality requirement is not jurisdictional, however. *See Reliable Automatic Sprinkler Co. v. Consumer Prod. Safety Comm'n*, 324 F.3d 726, 731 (D.C. Cir. 2003). Rather, § 704 merely limits causes of action under the APA, as does, for example, § 706(1)'s provision that the "reviewing court shall ... compel agency action unlawfully withheld or unreasonably delayed." *See Ctr. for Auto Safety v. Nat'l Highway Traffic Safety Admin.*, 452 F.3d 798, 805–06 (D.C. Cir. 2006).

Some enabling statutes are fairly precise in describing the types of agency orders and regulations that constitute final actions subject to judicial review. *See, e.g.*, 47 U.S.C. § 402(b) (describing orders and decisions of the FCC that are subject to review under the Communications Act of 1934); 42 U.S.C. § 7607(b)(1) (describing actions of the Administrator of the EPA that are subject to review under the Clean Air Act). "Such statutes," the Court has said, may "permit judicial review directly, even before the concrete effects normally required for APA review are felt." *Whitman v. Am. Trucking Ass'ns*, 531 U.S. 457, 479–80 (2001) (citing *Lujan v. Nat'l Wildlife Fed'n*, 497 U.S. at 891).

In the absence of a clear directive in an authorizing statute prescribing when judicial review is appropriate, the courts enforce the finality requirement "pragmatically ... , focusing on whether judicial review at the time will disrupt the administrative process." *Bell v. New Jersey*, 461 U.S. at 779. Under this "flexible view of finality," *FTC v. Standard Oil Co. of Cal.*, 449 U.S. 232, 240 (1980), agency orders and regulations will be deemed final if, for example, they are issued or promulgated in a formal manner, are clearly definitive, and are not merely the ruling of a subordinate agency official. *See, e.g., Abbott Labs. v. Gardner*, 387 U.S. 136, 151 (1967).

In *Abbott Laboratories v. Gardner*, the Supreme Court held that publication of regulations by the Food and Drug Commissioner, after announcement in the Federal Register and consideration of comments by interested parties, was final agency action properly subject to declaratory and injunctive relief even though the agency had yet to institute an enforcement action against the complaining drug manufacturers. The Court relied on the fact that the regulations, which required prescription drug manufacturers to include certain information on drug labels and in advertisements, were "definitive" statements of the Commission's position "made effective upon publication." *Id.* The Court pointed to a statement of the Assistant General Counsel for Food and Drugs announcing that compliance was expected and noted that violation of the regulations, which carried the "status of law," was subject to "heavy criminal and civil sanctions." *Id.* at 151–52. Based on these factors, the Court concluded that the regulations amounted to "final agency action within the meaning of ... the Administrative Procedure Act, 5 U.S.C. § 704." *Id.* at 149.

The Court's pragmatic approach to finality does not mean that every agency action that has an immediate effect on a party will be considered final. In *FTC v. Standard Oil Co. of Cal.*, for example, an oil company challenged a Federal Trade Commission complaint prior to the FTC's adjudication of the charges contained therein. 449 U.S. at 234–35. The company alleged that the FTC had no reason to believe that the company was violating the Federal Trade Commission Act. The Court held that mere issuance of the complaint was not "final agency action" or otherwise "directly reviewable" under § 704 of the APA, *id.* at 238, because, among other things, the FTC's averment that the company was violating the Act was "not a definitive statement of position," *id.* at 241.

Contrasting the regulations at issue in *Abbott Laboratories*, the Court in *Standard Oil* held that the FTC's complaint reflected only a "threshold determination" that further inquiry was warranted through enforcement proceedings. *Id.* The Court reasoned that the statutory and regulatory provisions allowing the oil company to challenge the charges against it and to appeal any adverse decision prior to being bound by it demonstrated that the complaint had "no legal force comparable to that of the regulation at issue in *Abbott Laboratories*, nor any comparable effect upon [the oil company's] daily business." *Id.* at 241–42. The Court rejected the argument that the expense and disruption of protracted adjudicatory proceedings would have the same sort of legal and practical effect on the oil company that the regulation in *Abbott Laboratories* had on the complaining drug manufacturers. Because the legal force and practical effect upon the company's "daily business" was no greater "than the disruptions that accompany any major litigation," the Court found that the issuance of the complaint was "not a definitive ruling or regulation." *Id.* at 243.

The Supreme Court's decision in *Bennett v. Spear* importantly amplifies the finality doctrine embodied in § 704 of the APA. The Court held that,

> [a]s a general matter, two conditions must be satisfied for agency action to be final: First, the action must mark the consummation of the agency's decisionmaking process – it must not be of a merely tentative or interlocutory nature. And second, the action must be one by which rights or obligations have been determined, or from which legal consequences will flow.

520 U.S. at 177–78. *Bennett v. Spear* involved an action under the citizen suit provision of the Endangered Species Act. The Act requires the Secretary of the Interior to specify, by regulation, species that are threatened or endangered. Federal agencies must ensure that any actions they authorize, fund, or carry out likely will not jeopardize a listed

species or adversely modify a critical habitat. When an agency determines that a proposed action may adversely affect an endangered species, it must formally consult with the Fish and Wildlife Service. If the Service concludes that the proposed action will jeopardize an endangered species, it issues a "Biological Opinion" outlining reasonable and prudent alternatives. In 1992, the Bureau of Reclamation notified the Service that the operation of the Klamath Project – an irrigation system consisting of a series of lakes, rivers, dams, and irrigation canals – might affect two endangered species of fish. The Service issued a Biological Opinion, concluding that the proposed long-term operation of the project was likely to jeopardize the species and recommending the maintenance of minimum water levels on certain specified reservoirs. The Bureau subsequently notified the Service that it would operate the project in compliance with the Biological Opinion.

Two Oregon irrigation districts that received water from the Klamath Project and the operators of two ranches within those districts filed an action, contending, among other things, that the imposition of minimum water levels violated the APA's prohibition of agency action that is "arbitrary, capricious, an abuse of discretion, or otherwise not in accordance with law." *See* 5 U.S.C. § 706(2)(A). The government argued that the petitioners could not obtain judicial review under the APA, because the Biological Opinion did not conclusively determine the manner in which Klamath Project water would be allocated and thus was not a "final agency action" within the meaning of § 704. The Supreme Court rejected this argument, finding that the Biological Opinion not only marked the consummation of the agency's decisionmaking process, but it also "alter[ed] the legal regime to which the [agency] is subject, authorizing it to take the endangered species if (but only if) it complies with the prescribed conditions." *Bennett v. Spear*, 520 U.S. at 178. In other words, the Biological Opinion was final and reviewable, because it had "direct and appreciable legal consequences." *Id.*

2. THE RIPENESS DOCTRINE

Even when an agency has taken final action, a court may refrain from reviewing a challenge to the action if the case is unripe for review. *Toilet Goods Ass'n v. Gardner*, 387 U.S. 158 (1967). The ripeness inquiry springs from the Article III case or controversy requirement that prohibits courts from issuing advisory opinions on speculative claims. *See Reg'l Rail Reorganization Act Cases*, 419 U.S. 102, 138 (1974). In other words, if a claim challenging final agency action is not concrete, it may be unfit for judicial review without regard to whether the complaining party has standing to pursue the claim. Normally, no such issue arises in cases in which an agency has taken direct enforcement action against a party. Rather, the ripeness issue normally arises in cases in which a regulated party faces the *threat* of future agency enforcement action.

"*Abbott Laboratories* inaugurated an era in which pre-enforcement review is the common pattern of [agency] rulemaking review." STRAUSS,

RAKOFF & FARINA, GELLHORN & BYSE'S ADMINISTRATIVE LAW CASES & COMMENTS 1252 (2003). The decision sets forth the framework for assessing the ripeness of cases in which pre-enforcement review is sought. Under *Abbott Laboratories*, the courts look to "both the fitness of the issues for judicial decision and the hardship to the parties of withholding court consideration." 387 U.S. at 149.

In applying the fitness prong of the *Abbott Laboratories* test, appellate courts consider (1) whether the issue is "purely legal," rather than one reliant on agency expertise, *id.*, (2) whether the challenged action is "final," *id.*, and (3) whether "the impact . . . upon the petitioners is sufficiently direct and immediate as to render the issue appropriate for judicial review," *id.* at 152. In other words, the "fitness" of the issue for judicial review turns on whether a court's consideration of the case "would benefit from further factual development" and "whether judicial intervention would inappropriately interfere with further administrative action." *Ohio Forestry Ass'n v. Sierra Club*, 523 U.S. 726, 733 (1998); *see also Whitman v. Am. Trucking Ass'ns*, 531 U.S. at 479–80. These considerations protect "the agency's interest in crystallizing its policy before that policy is subjected to judicial review and the court's interests in avoiding unnecessary adjudication and in deciding issues in a concrete setting." *Eagle-Picher Indus., Inc. v. EPA*, 759 F.2d 905, 915 (D.C. Cir. 1985).

The hardship prong requires a court to determine whether a delay in judicial review of the agency's allegedly unlawful action will cause a "direct and immediate" impact on the complaining party's "primary conduct." *Better Gov't Ass'n v. Dep't of State*, 780 F.2d 86, 93 (D.C. Cir. 1986). The Supreme Court fleshed out this notion of hardship in *Toilet Goods Ass'n v. Gardner*, 387 U.S. 158, a case decided the same day as *Abbott Laboratories*. It also made clear that it is against the institutional interests protected by the fitness prong that a petitioner's interest in prompt consideration of allegedly unlawful action must be balanced.

In *Toilet Goods*, an association of cosmetics manufacturers and several individual manufacturers and distributors sought declaratory and injunctive relief from certain regulations that allegedly exceeded the statutory authority of the Secretary of Health, Education, and Welfare and the Commissioner of Food and Drugs. Applying the first prong of the ripeness test, the Court noted that there could "be no question that [the] regulation – promulgated in a formal manner after notice and evaluation of submitted comments – [was] a 'final agency action' under" § 704 of the APA. *Id.* at 162. It also found that the issue presented "a purely legal question" of the type "that courts have occasionally dealt with without requiring a specific attempt at enforcement." *Id.* at 163.

Despite the fact that these first two factors suggested that the issue was one fit for judicial review, the Court concluded that they were "outweighed by other considerations," including the fact that the regulation did no more than "serve[] notice . . . that the Commissioner *may* under certain circumstances order inspection of certain facilities and data." *Id.* The Court noted that it had "no idea whether or when such an inspection [would] be ordered and what reasons the Commissioner [might] give to justify his order." *Id.* Since the statute authorized the agencies "to promulgate regulations 'for the efficient enforcement' of the Act," the Court found that its ability to review the regulation would benefit from facts regarding the enforcement issues faced by the agency, and that review was "likely to stand on a much surer footing in the context of a specific application of [the] regulation than could be the case in the framework of the generalized challenge made here." *Id.* at 163–64.

Having found that a challenge to an application of the regulation would put the case on surer footing for purposes of judicial review, the Court nevertheless went on to consider the regulation's effect on petitioners, noting that "the test of ripeness . . . depends not only on how adequately a court can deal with the legal issue presented, but also on the degree and nature of the regulation's present effect on those seeking relief." *Id.* at 164. The Court found that the impact of the cosmetics regulation could not "be said to be felt immediately by those subject to it in conducting their day-to-day affairs." *Id.* As the Court explained, the regulation did not involve "a situation in which primary conduct is affected – when contracts must be negotiated, ingredients tested or substituted, or special records compiled." *Id.* All the regulation did was allow the Commissioner to authorize certain inspections. No change in behavior or action in advance of those inspections was required of cosmetics manufacturers, who had for many years been under a statutory duty to permit reasonable inspections. The Court concluded that none of the adverse consequences that might flow from requiring a later challenge could be considered substantial enough to support a finding of ripeness. A refusal to allow the inspections at issue would not, as the Court explained, result in a seizure of goods, heavy fines, adverse publicity, or the possibility of criminal liability. "[R]efusal to admit an inspector here would at most lead only to a suspension of certification services to the particular party, a determination that can then be promptly challenged through an administrative procedure, which in turn is reviewable by a court." *Id.* at 165.

Amplifying *Toilet Goods* and *Abbott Laboratories*, the Supreme Court has held that hardship will not be found when a complaining party "is not required to engage in, or to refrain from, any conduct." *Texas v. United States*, 523 U.S. 296, 301 (1998). The Court has also stated "that mere uncertainty as to the validity of a legal rule [does not] constitute[ ] a hardship for purposes of the ripeness analysis." *Nat'l Park Hospitality Ass'n v. Dep't of Interior*, 538 U.S. 803, 811 (2003). It is important to note, however, that "the 'hardship' prong of the *Abbott Laboratories* test is not an independent requirement divorced from the consideration of the institutional interests of the court and agency." *City of Houston v. HUD*, 24 F.3d 1421, 1431 n.9 (D.C. Cir. 1994). Thus, when there are no institutional interests favoring postponement of review, a complaining party need not prove hardship. *See, e.g., Consol. Rail Corp. v. United States*, 896 F.2d 574, 577–78 (D.C. Cir. 1990); *see also Venetian Casino*

Resort, L.L.C. v. EEOC, 409 F.3d 359, 365–66 (D.C. Cir. 2005). It is not clear, however, whether judicial review may still be had if a complaining party can satisfy the "hardship" prong of the ripeness doctrine, but the case is "unfit" for review under the *Abbott Laboratories* test.

3.   EXHAUSTION OF ADMINISTRATIVE REMEDIES

A requirement that a party exhaust available administrative remedies before seeking judicial review may be either jurisdictional or nonjurisdictional. *Avocados Plus Inc. v. Veneman*, 370 F.3d 1243, 1247 (D.C. Cir. 2004). Jurisdictional exhaustion "arises when Congress requires resort to the administrative process as a predicate to judicial review. This [type of] exhaustion is rooted, not in prudential principles, but in Congress' power to control the jurisdiction of the federal courts." *Id.* In contrast, nonjurisdictional exhaustion "is a judicially created doctrine requiring parties who seek to challenge agency action to exhaust available administrative remedies before bringing their case to court." *Id.* If a party fails to exhaust administrative remedies that are jurisdictional, "a court cannot excuse it" – judicial review is foreclosed. *Id.* at 1247–48. If an exhaustion requirement is nonjurisdictional, "a district court [may] dismiss plainly meritless claims without first addressing what may be a much more complex question, namely, whether the [plaintiff] did in fact properly exhaust available administrative remedies." *See Woodford v. Ngo*, ___ U.S. ___, ___,126 S.Ct. 2378, 2392 (2006).

Whether a statute requires exhaustion as a jurisdictional prerequisite to judicial review "is purely a question of statutory interpretation." *Avocados Plus*, 370 F.3d at 1247. The courts presume that exhaustion requirements are nonjurisdictional "unless Congress states in clear, unequivocal terms that the judiciary is barred from hearing an action until the administrative agency has come to a decision." *Id.* at 1248; *see also Arbaugh*, 546 U.S. at 516 ("[W]hen Congress does not rank a statutory [requirement] as jurisdictional, courts should treat the restriction as nonjurisdictional in character."). This is true even when a statutory provision can fairly be described as an "exhaustion requirement" making certain administrative remedies "mandatory." *See Ngo*, ___ U.S. at ___, 126 S.Ct. at 2382–83, 2392 (describing the Prison Litigation Reform Act "exhaustion requirement" as "mandatory," but not jurisdictional).

Nonjurisdictional exhaustion "serves the twin purposes of protecting administrative agency authority and promoting judicial efficiency." *McCarthy v. Madigan*, 503 U.S. 140, 145 (1992). It gives an agency a chance to correct its own errors, promotes efficiency in grievance processing, gives parties and courts the benefit of agency expertise, and allows for the creation of a record adequate for judicial review. *See Ngo*, ___ U.S. at ___, 126 S.Ct. at 2385; *Avocados Plus*, 370 F.3d at 1247. Nonjurisdictional "exhaustion requirements are designed to deal with parties who do not want to exhaust." *Ngo*, ___ U.S. at ___, 126 S.Ct. at

2385. And the doctrine allowing courts to enforce these provisions "creates an incentive for these parties to do what they would otherwise prefer not to do, namely, to give the agency a fair and full opportunity to adjudicate their claims. Administrative law does this by requiring proper exhaustion of administrative remedies, which means using all steps that the agency holds out, and doing so *properly* (so that the agency addresses the issues on the merits)." *Id.* (holding that the Prison Litigation Reform Act's nonjurisdictional exhaustion requirement, 42 U.S.C. § 1997e(a), is not satisfied by the filing of an untimely or otherwise procedurally defective administrative grievance); *see also Jones v. Bock*, ___ U.S. ___, ___ 127 S.Ct. 910, 919, 921 (2007) (because the "usual practice under the Federal Rules is to regard exhaustion as an affirmative defense," the Prison Litigation Reform Act does not require that inmates "specially plead or demonstrate exhaustion in their complaints").

"Administrative law, however, contains well established exceptions to [nonjurisdictional] exhaustion." *Ngo*, ___ U.S. at ___, 126 S.Ct. at 2393 (Breyer, J., concurring in the judgment) (citing, as examples, *Shalala v. Ill. Council on Long Term Care, Inc.*, 529 U.S. 1, 13 (2000) (futility); *McCarthy*, 503 U.S. at 147–48 (inadequate or unavailable administrative remedies); *McKart v. United States*, 395 U.S. 185, 197–201 (1969) (hardship)). These exceptions exist, because there are times when requiring exhaustion of administrative remedies will not fulfill the ends it is designed to serve. "There may be no facts in dispute, the disputed issue may be outside the agency's expertise, or the agency may not have the authority to change its decision in a way that would satisfy the challenger's objections." *Avocados Plus*, 370 F.3d at 1247. In addition, a party's case may be prejudiced by requiring resort to the administrative process, or the process may be otherwise unfair because of agency bias. "In these circumstances, the ... court may, in its discretion, excuse exhaustion if the litigant's interests in immediate judicial review outweigh the government's interests in the efficiency or administrative autonomy that the [prudential] exhaustion doctrine is designed to further." *Id.*

If exhaustion is jurisdictional, a party may not avoid the jurisdictional requirements of an authorizing statute by seeking judicial review of agency action under the general federal question jurisdiction provision in 28 U.S.C. § 1331. *See id.* at 1248 n.3 (holding that "[g]eneral federal question jurisdiction under 28 U.S.C. § 1331 does not empower the court to proceed to the merits in a jurisdictional exhaustion case"). "In a nonjurisdictional exhaustion case, if the court decides not to require exhaustion, the case may proceed under § 1331. If the court rules that the plaintiff must exhaust, and the plaintiff proceeds to do so, judicial review of the agency's decision will be under the relevant provision for review of that agency's action." *Id.*

Claimants seeking judicial review of administrative action under the APA face slightly different considerations with respect to exhaustion. Section 704 of the APA provides:

Agency action made reviewable by statute and final agency action for which there is no other adequate remedy in a court are subject to judicial review. A preliminary, procedural, or intermediate agency action or ruling not directly reviewable is subject to review on the review of the final agency action. *Except as otherwise expressly required by statute, agency action otherwise final is final for the purposes of this section whether or not there has been presented or determined an application for a declaratory order, for any form of reconsideration, or, unless the agency otherwise requires by rule and provides that the action meanwhile is inoperative, for an appeal to superior agency authority.*

5 U.S.C. § 704 (emphasis added). In *Darby v. Cisneros*, 509 U.S. 137 (1993), the Supreme Court considered whether the APA, "by providing the conditions under which agency action becomes final for the purposes of judicial review, limits the authority of courts to impose additional exhaustion requirements as a prerequisite to judicial review." *Id.* at 145. The Court found that § 704, "by its very terms, has limited the availability of the doctrine of exhaustion of administrative remedies to that which the statute or rule clearly mandates." *Id.* at 146. Thus, "[w]hen an aggrieved party [seeking review under the APA] has exhausted all administrative remedies expressly prescribed by statute or agency rule, the agency action is final for the purposes of [§ 704] and therefore subject to judicial review." *Id.* In other words, in an action under the APA, no exhaustion, beyond what is prescribed by statute or rule, may be required by a reviewing court. *Id.* at 146–47.

Darby also noted that "the exhaustion doctrine continues to apply as a matter of judicial discretion in cases not governed by the APA," meaning nonjurisdictional cases not governed by the APA. *Id.* at 153–54. It is unclear, however, whether *Darby* means to foreclose judicial discretion to excuse a litigant's failure to exhaust administrative remedies that are within the compass of § 704 but are not otherwise "jurisdictional." The last sentence of § 704 allows an agency to prescribe by rule that there will be no operative agency action until the matter in dispute has been addressed by "superior agency authority." It would appear, then, that when an agency has availed itself of this option, there is no "final agency action" sufficient to secure judicial review pursuant to § 704 until an appeal has been taken to the designated superior agency authority and that authority has rendered judgment on the matter.

4. ISSUE WAIVER

In *United States v. L.A. Tucker Truck Lines, Inc.*, 344 U.S. 33 (1952), the Supreme Court held that "[s]imple fairness to those who are engaged in the tasks of administration, and to litigants, requires as a general rule that courts should not topple over administrative decisions unless the administrative body not only has erred but has erred against objection made at the time appropriate under its practice." *Id.* at 37. This means that, "[a]s a general matter, it is inappropriate for courts reviewing appeals of agency decisions to consider arguments not raised before the administrative agency involved." *1000 Friends of Md. v. Browner*, 265 F.3d 216, 227 (4th Cir. 2001). *L.A. Tucker Truck Lines* involved an agency adjudication, but the principle followed by the Court is routinely applied in cases involving agency rulemaking proceedings. *See, e.g., Appalachian Power Co. v. EPA*, 251 F.3d 1026, 1036 (D.C. Cir. 2001) ("It is black-letter administrative law that absent special circumstances, a party must initially present its comments to the agency during the rulemaking in order for the court to consider the issue."); *Mich. Dep't of Envtl. Quality v. Browner*, 230 F.3d 181, 183 n.1 (6th Cir. 2000) (concluding that issues not raised during notice-and-comment period were waived for purposes of appellate review).

This black-letter law was called into question by the Supreme Court's decision in *Sims v. Apfel*, 530 U.S. 103 (2000). Sims, a Social Security claimant, was denied disability benefits by the Social Security Appeals Council. Sims then filed suit in federal district court where she lost. She also lost before the Fifth Circuit, which held that two of the three arguments pressed by Sims were not reviewable on the merits, because they had never been raised before the Appeals Council. Reversing, the Supreme Court found that "[t]he basis for a judicially imposed issue-exhaustion requirement is an analogy to the rule that appellate courts will not consider arguments not raised before trial courts." *Id.* at 108–09. Thus, the Court reasoned, the application "of issue exhaustion depends on the degree to which the analogy to normal adversarial litigation applies in a particular administrative proceeding." *Id.* at 109. "Where the parties are expected to develop the issues in an adversarial administrative proceeding, . . . the rationale for requiring issue exhaustion is at its greatest." *Id.* at 110. When an administrative proceeding is nonadversarial, however, "the reasons for a court to require issue exhaustion are much weaker." *Id.*

The Social Security proceedings at issue in *Sims* were "inquisitorial rather than adversarial" and highly informal, and they typically involved claimants who were not represented by attorneys. *Id.* at 110–12. Thus, although the Court held that issue exhaustion was inapposite in this particular setting, *Sims* seems to have had little effect on the general principle enunciated in *L.A. Tucker Truck Lines*, namely, that courts reviewing administrative actions normally do not consider arguments not raised before the agency. Indeed, in a decision issued after *Sims*, the Supreme Court cited *L.A. Tucker Truck Lines* with approval. *See Ngo*, ___ U.S. at ___, 126 S. Ct. at 2385; *see also Advocates for Highway & Auto Safety v. Fed. Motor Carrier Safety Admin.*, 429 F.3d 1136, 1150 (D.C. Cir. 2005) (holding that, because the petitioner had not raised certain issues during the agency's rulemaking proceeding, and because the issues were not so clear that the agency should have considered them *sua sponte*, petitioner "forfeited the opportunity to seek judicial review of [those] claims.").

There are a few exceptions to the doctrine enunciated in *L.A. Tucker Truck Lines*. First, it is not always necessary "that the party seeking judicial review of an issue be the party that provided the [agency] with the opportunity to pass on the issue." *Bartholdi Cable Co. v. FCC*, 114 F.3d 274, 280 (D.C. Cir. 1997). Thus, a reviewing court may consider an issue that was addressed by the agency after being presented by someone other than the petitioner. *See, e.g., Nat'l Black Media Coal. v. FCC*, 791 F.2d 1016, 1021–22 (2d Cir. 1986); *Office of Commc'n of the United Church of Christ v. FCC*, 779 F.2d 702, 707 (D.C. Cir. 1985); *see also Office of Commc'n of the United Church of Christ v. FCC*, 465 F.2d 519, 523–24 (D.C. Cir. 1972) (considering issue raised by dissenting members of the Commission). Moreover, "where issues by their nature could not have been raised before the agency (*e.g.*, a material change in circumstances or a serious impropriety in the administrative process), a remand to the agency may be appropriate." *Wash. Ass'n for Television & Children v. FCC*, 712 F.2d 677, 682 (D.C. Cir. 1983). And in some cases, courts consider "arguments that it would have been futile to raise before the agency," for example, when the agency's views are already well-known. *Id.* at 682 & n.9. Finally, it bears noting that if an agency does not argue that an issue was waived, the objection may be lost. *See, e.g., Colo. Wild; Heartwood v. Forest Serv.*, 435 F.3d 1204, 1216 n.3 (10th Cir. 2006).

Chapter XII

THE PRESUMPTION OF REVIEWABILITY
AND ITS EXCEPTIONS

If a party challenging agency action satisfies the requirements of Article III and zone-of-interest standing, and if statutory review is not barred by sovereign immunity or foreclosed by the mootness, finality, ripeness, exhaustion, or waiver doctrines, there is a "strong presumption that Congress intends judicial review." *Bowen v. Mich. Acad. of Family Physicians*, 476 U.S. 667, 670 (1986). The Administrative Procedure Act "embodies the basic presumption of judicial review to one suffering legal wrong because of agency action, or adversely affected or aggrieved by agency action within the meaning of a relevant statute, 5 U.S.C. § 702, so long as no statute precludes such relief or the action is not one committed by law to agency discretion, 5 U.S.C. § 701(a)." *Abbott Labs. v. Gardner*, 387 U.S. 136, 140 (1967). The APA "provides specifically not only for review of agency action made reviewable by statute but also for review of final agency action for which there is no other adequate remedy in a court, 5 U.S.C. § 704." *Abbott Labs.*, 387 U.S. at 140. In light of the APA's language and legislative history, the Court has made it clear that the Act's "generous review provisions must be given a hospitable interpretation." *Id.* at 140–41. Therefore, "only upon a showing of clear and convincing evidence of a contrary legislative intent should the courts restrict access to judicial review." *Id.* at 141. The limited circumstances in which this presumption is overcome are discussed below.

A. STATUTORY PRECLUSION OF JUDICIAL REVIEW

Section 701(a)(1) of the APA bars judicial review of administrative agency action to the extent that it is precluded by statute. 5 U.S.C. § 701(a)(1). Thus, the Supreme Court has held that the strong presumption in favor of judicial review "may be overcome by specific language or specific legislative history that is a reliable indicator of congressional intent." *Block v. Cmty. Nutrition Inst.*, 467 U.S. 340, 349 (1984). When an agency's authorizing statute does not expressly preclude judicial review, the congressional intent necessary to overcome the presumption of reviewability may be "inferred from contemporaneous judicial construction barring review and the congressional acquiescence in it, or from the collective import of legislative and judicial history behind a particular statute." *Id.*

In *Block v. Community Nutrition Institute*, the Supreme Court held that consumers of dairy products could not obtain judicial review of milk market orders issued by the Secretary of Agriculture under the Agricultural Marketing Agreement Act. The Act provided for agreements among the Secretary, milk producers, and milk handlers; for hearings involving these parties; for votes by producers and handlers; and for administrative appeals by handlers. But the Act did not provide for participation by consumers in any proceeding. The Court held that, "[i]n a complex scheme of this type, the omission of such a provision is sufficient reason to believe that Congress intended to foreclose consumer participation in the regulatory process." *Id.* at 347. "Had Congress intended to allow consumers to attack provisions of marketing orders, it surely would have required them to pursue the administrative remedies [covering handlers]. The restriction of the administrative remedy to handlers strongly suggests that Congress intended a similar restriction of judicial review of market orders." *Id.* The Court concluded that "[p]reclusion of [consumer] suits does not pose any threat to realization of the statutory objectives; it means only that those objectives must be realized through the specific remedies provided by Congress and at the behest of the parties directly affected by the statutory scheme." *Id.* at 352–53.

Block thus makes it clear that "when a statute provides a detailed mechanism for judicial consideration of particular issues at the behest of particular persons, judicial review of those issues at the behest of other persons may be found to be impliedly precluded." *Id.* at 349. However, "[a]s a general matter, the mere fact that some acts are made reviewable should not suffice to support an implication of exclusion as to others. The right to review is too important to be excluded on such slender and indeterminate evidence of legislative intent." *Mich. Acad.*, 476 U.S. at 674. In other words, the decision in *Block* rests on and requires strong evidence of preclusion.

It is significant that § 701(a)(1) "does not repeal the review of *ultra vires* actions that was recognized long before [enactment of the APA]." *Aid Ass'n for Lutherans v. Postal Serv.*, 321 F.3d 1166, 1173 (D.C. Cir. 2003). Thus, even when a statute purports to preclude judicial review, a party may still seek review if an agency acts "in excess of its delegated powers and contrary to a specific prohibition." *Leedom v. Kyne*, 358 U.S. 184, 188 (1958); *see also Harmon v. Brucker*, 355 U.S. 579, 581–82 (1958) (per curiam) ("Generally, judicial relief is available to one who has been injured by an act of a government official which is in excess of his express or implied powers."); *Stark v. Wickard*, 321 U.S. 288, 310 (1944) ("The responsibility of determining the limits of statutory grants of authority . . . is a judicial function entrusted to the courts by Congress by the statutes establishing courts and marking their jurisdiction."); *Am. Sch. of Magnetic Healing v. McAnnulty*, 187 U.S. 94, 108, 110 (1902) ("The acts of [agency] officers must be justified by some law, and in case an official violates the law to the injury of an individual the courts generally have jurisdiction to grant relief.... Otherwise, the individual is left to the absolutely uncontrolled and arbitrary action of a public and administrative officer, whose action is unauthorized by any law and is in violation of the rights of the individual."). In short, "[w]hen an executive acts *ultra vires*, courts are normally available to reestablish the limits on his authority." *Aid Ass'n for Lutherans*, 321 F.3d at 1173; *see also Chamber of Commerce of the U.S. v. Reich*, 74 F.3d 1322, 1327–28 (D.C. Cir. 1996).

B.   THE NO–LAW–TO–APPLY EXCEPTION

Section 701(a)(2)'s bar against judicial review of agency action "committed to agency discretion by law," 5 U.S.C. § 701(a)(2), provides a second, "very narrow exception" to the presumption of reviewability. *Citizens to Pres. Overton Park, Inc. v. Volpe*, 401 U.S. 402, 410 (1971). In *Overton Park,* the Supreme Court explained that "[t]he legislative history of the Administrative Procedure Act indicates that [§ 701(a)(2)] is applicable in those rare instances where statutes are drawn in such broad terms that in a given case there is no law to apply." *Id.* Under the no-law-to-apply test, agency action is deemed unreviewable where there is no legal standard against which to judge the agency action or to evaluate the petitioner's challenge. *Heckler v. Chaney*, 470 U.S. 821, 830 (1985). In contrast to the preclusion provision of § 701(a)(1), which rests on statutory foreclosure of review, the § 701(a)(2) no-law-to-apply exception rests on the lack of cognizable standards against which to test agency action.

Webster v. Doe, 486 U.S. 592 (1988), provides a good example of an application of the no-law-to-apply standard. In *Doe*, the plaintiff was dismissed from his position with the CIA because of his sexual orientation, and he challenged the dismissal on statutory and constitutional grounds. The Supreme Court held that Doe's claim was not reviewable because the dismissal decision was committed to agency discretion by law. Looking to the controlling statutory provision, which allowed the Director to dismiss an employee whenever the Director "shall *deem* such termination necessary or advisable in the interests of the United States," the Court concluded, "[t]his standard fairly exudes deference to the Director, and appears to us to foreclose the application of any meaningful judicial standard of review." *Id.* at 600. In other words, the Court found that the statute provided "no basis on which a reviewing court could properly assess an Agency termination decision." *Id.*

A variation of the no-law-to-apply test applies when an agency decides not to undertake an individual enforcement action. In *Heckler v. Chaney*, the Supreme Court reasoned that an "agency is far better equipped than the courts to deal with the many variables involved in the proper ordering of its priorities" with respect to enforcement actions. 470 U.S. at 831–32. Looking to the common-law tradition predating enactment of the APA, the Court concluded that an agency's decision not to take an enforcement action should be presumed to be immune from judicial review. It emphasized, however, that such a "decision is only presumptively unreviewable; the presumption may be rebutted where the substantive statute has provided guidelines for the agency to follow in exercising its enforcement powers." *Id.* at 832–33.

In contrast, "an agency's statement of a *general enforcement policy* may be reviewable for legal sufficiency where the agency has expressed the policy as a formal regulation after the full rulemaking process ... or has otherwise articulated it in some form of universal policy statement." *Crowley Caribbean Transp., Inc. v. Peña*, 37 F.3d 671, 676 (D.C. Cir. 1994). However, the cases supporting this view "do not involve an agency's decision to decline enforcement in the context of an individual case." *Id.* Indeed, the Supreme Court has pointedly said that an otherwise unreviewable individual enforcement action does not become reviewable merely because "the agency gives a 'reviewable' reason." *ICC v. Bhd. of Locomotive Eng'rs*, 482 U.S. 270, 283 (1987). For example, "a common reason for failure to prosecute an alleged criminal violation is the prosecutor's belief (sometimes publicly stated) that the law will not sustain a conviction. That is surely an eminently 'reviewable' proposition, in the sense that courts are well qualified to consider the point; yet it is entirely clear that the refusal to prosecute cannot be the subject of judicial review." *Id.*

Although *Heckler v. Chaney* instructs that nonenforcement decisions are presumptively unreviewable, it bears emphasis that "refusals to institute rulemaking proceedings remain outside *Chaney*'s core and are subject to a judicial check." *Nat'l Customs Brokers & Forwarders Ass'n of Am. v. United States*, 883 F.2d 93, 96 (D.C. Cir. 1989). However, such review is "extremely limited" and "highly deferential." *Id.* A court "will overturn an agency's decision not to initiate a rulemaking only for compelling cause, such as plain error of law or a fundamental change in the factual premises previously considered by the agency." *Id.* at 96–97.

C. REVIEWABILITY OF AGENCY POLICY STATEMENTS AND INTERPRETATIVE RULES

"A general statement of policy is the outcome of neither a rulemaking nor an adjudication." *Pacific Gas & Elec. Co. v. Fed. Power Comm'n*, 506 F.2d 33, 38 (D.C. Cir. 1974). Rather, policy statements – which may be variously labeled directives, guidances, opinion letters, press releases, advisories, warnings, or manuals – "are statements issued by an agency to advise the public prospectively of the manner in which the agency proposes to exercise a discretionary power." *Chrysler Corp. v. Brown*, 441 U.S. 281, 302 n.31 (1979). Some policy statements are issued for the information of the general public; some are issued as generic pronouncements to a class of regulated parties; and still others give notice to particular parties regarding the agency's concerns over their compliance with a statute.

As an informational device, the general statement of policy serves several beneficial functions. By providing a formal method by which an agency can express its views, the general statement of policy encourages public dissemination of the agency's policies prior to their actual application in particular situations. Thus the agency's initial views do not remain secret but are disclosed well in advance of their actual application. Additionally, the publication of a general statement of policy facilitates long range planning within the regulated industry and promotes uniformity in areas of national concern.

Pac. Gas & Elec. Co., 506 F.2d at 38. Under the Freedom of Information Act, agencies are required to publish statements of general policy in the Federal Register. 5 U.S.C. § 552(a)(1)(D). However, such statements are exempt from the APA's notice-and-comment requirements. *See id.* § 553(b)(A).

A true policy statement, meaning one that does not establish a binding norm and is not finally determinative of the issues or rights to which it is addressed, is not subject to judicial review under the APA. *Ctr. for Auto Safety v. Nat'l Highway Traffic Safety Admin.*, 452 F.3d 798, 800 (D.C. Cir. 2006). This is because true policy statements do not constitute "final agency action," which is normally a prerequisite to APA review. *See* 5 U.S.C. § 704; *see also Lujan v. Nat'l Wildlife Fed'n*, 497 U.S. 871, 882 (1990). There are, however, some exceptions to the general rule that policy statements are not subject to judicial review.

First, a policy statement is subject to review when it is relied upon or applied to support an agency action in a particular case. *See, e.g., Christensen v. Harris County*, 529 U.S. 576 (2000). In other words, when an "agency applies [its] policy in a particular situation, it must be prepared to support the policy just as if the policy statement had never been issued. An agency cannot escape its responsibility to present evidence and reasoning supporting its substantive rules by announcing binding precedent in the form of a general statement of policy." *Pac. Gas & Elec. Co.*, 506 F.2d at 38–39; *see also Bechtel v. FCC*, 10 F.3d 875, 887 (D.C. Cir. 1993) (finding that the FCC denied a license based on a policy the rationality of which the agency was unable to defend, and therefore ordering "the Commission [to] consider[] [the license] application ... under standards free of that policy"); *United States v. F/V Alice Amanda*, 987 F.2d 1078 (4th Cir. 1993) (reversing forfeiture order, because penalty was based on a policy that was found to be arbitrary and capricious and not supported by substantial evidence).

A policy statement also will be subject to judicial review if it "mark[s] the consummation of the agency's decisionmaking process" *and* either determines "rights or obligations" or results in discernible "legal consequences" for the parties seeking judicial review. *See Bennett v. Spear*, 520 U.S. 154, 177–78 (1997). In other words, so-called policy statements that in fact amount to final agency action will be subject to judicial review. Thus, for example, in *Barrick Goldstrike Mines Inc. v.*

Browner, 215 F.3d 45 (D.C. Cir. 2000), it was held that an EPA guidance creating new reporting requirements for regulated entities was reviewable final agency action, because "if [petitioner] refuse[d] to abide by [it], the company [would] be subject to an enforcement action." *Id.* at 49; *see also id.* at 50 (explaining that the third reporting requirement had "[l]egal consequences," because "[petitioner] must keep records and report to EPA unless it wishes to risk an enforcement action"). The court firmly "rejected the proposition that if an agency labels its action an 'informal' guideline it may thereby escape judicial review under the APA." *Id.* at 48; *see also W. Ill. Home Health Care, Inc. v. Herman*, 150 F.3d 659, 663 (7th Cir. 1998) (holding that the agency's statement of its view of plaintiffs' status under the Fair Labor Standards Act in a letter closing an investigation constituted reviewable final agency action, because "[l]egal consequences flow from it, both with respect to [petitioners'] obligations to their employees and with respect to their vulnerability to penalties should they disregard the [agency's] determination").

It should be noted, however, that practical consequences, without more, normally do not amount to the sort of legal consequences or determination of rights and obligations justifying judicial review. *See, e.g., Ctr. for Auto Safety*, 452 F.3d at 811 (holding that "*de facto* compliance is not enough to establish that the guidelines have had *legal* consequences"); *Nat'l Ass'n of Home Builders v. Norton*, 415 F.3d 8, 14–16 (D.C. Cir. 2005) (rejecting argument that practical consequences establish final agency action absent showing of legal coercion); *Air Brake Sys., Inc. v. Mineta*, 357 F.3d 632, 645 (6th Cir. 2004) (noting that "adverse economic effects accompany many forms of indisputably non-final government action"). "[I]f the practical effect of the agency action is not a certain change in the legal obligations of a party, the action is non-final for the purpose of judicial review." *Nat'l Ass'n of Home Builders*, 415 F.3d at 15.

If a purported policy statement amounts to final agency action that is ripe for review, a claim may be made that the agency issued a legislative rule in violation of the notice-and-comment requirements contained in § 553 of the APA. *See, e.g., Am. Hosp. Ass'n v. Bowen*, 834 F.2d 1037, 1044–48, 1052–57 (D.C. Cir. 1987). As noted above, true policy statements are exempt from the APA's notice-and-comment requirements. *See* 5 U.S.C. § 553(b)(A). However, "[t]he perimeters of the exemption for general statements of policy ... are fuzzy." *Am. Hosp. Ass'n*, 834 F.2d at 1046. And "[c]ases interpreting the § 553 exemption for general statements of policy ... tend to turn on the distinctive facts of the case." *Id.* at 1047. At bottom, a genuine general statement of policy (1) "does not impose any rights and obligations" and (2) "genuinely leaves the agency and its decisionmakers free to exercise discretion." *Id.* at 1046–47.

The decision in *General Electric Co. v. EPA*, 290 F.3d 377 (D.C. Cir. 2002), offers a good example of facts supporting the conclusion that a purported policy statement is, in reality, a final legislative rule subject to the APA's notice-and-comment requirements. In that case, the agency's self-described policy statement was a "Guidance Document" prescribing permissible risk assessment techniques for parties wishing to use alternative methods for disposal of PCBs other than those laid out in regulations issued under the Toxic Substances Control Act. *Id.* at 379. In assessing the Guidance Document, the court first stated a perceived "common standard" for review in cases of this sort:

> If a document expresses a change in substantive law or policy (that is not an interpretation) which the agency intends to make binding, or administers with binding effect, the agency may not rely upon the statutory exemption for policy statements, but must observe the APA's legislative rulemaking procedures.

Id. at 382–83. The court then ruled that the disputed Guidance Document was a legislative rule, not a policy statement:

> [E]ven though the Guidance Document gives applicants the option of calculating risk in either of two ways (assuming both are practical) it still requires them to conform to one or the other, that is, not to submit an application based upon a third way. And if an applicant does choose to calculate cancer and non-cancer risks separately, then it must consider the non-cancer risks specified in the Guidance Document. To the applicant reading the Guidance Document the message is clear: in reviewing applications the Agency will not be open to considering approaches other than those prescribed in the Document.

Id. at 384; *see also McLouth Steel Prods. Corp. v. Thomas*, 838 F.2d 1317, 1319, 1321–22 (D.C. Cir. 1988) (finding that the "vertical and horizontal spread" model used by EPA to predict "leachate" levels of hazardous components of waste was a legislative rule rather than a general statement of policy, because the model constrained the agency's discretion and was applied as a binding norm).

Courts are often "guided by two lines of inquiry" in distinguishing between situations in which "an agency has issued a binding norm" and situations in which an agency has merely announced an unreviewable statement of policy. *Wilderness Soc'y v. Norton*, 434 F.3d 584, 595 (D.C. Cir. 2006).

> One line of analysis focuses on the effects of the agency action, asking whether the agency has (1) imposed any rights and obligations, or (2) genuinely left the agency and its decisionmakers free to exercise discretion. The language actually used by the agency is often central to making such determinations. The second line of analysis focuses on the agency's expressed intentions. The analysis ... looks to three factors: (1) the agency's own characterization of the action; (2) whether the action was published in the Federal Register or the Code of Federal Regulations; and (3) whether the action has binding effects on private parties or on the agency.

Id. These two lines of analysis overlap at the third step in the second line of analysis, pursuant to which "the court determines whether the agency action binds private parties or the agency itself with the force of law." *CropLife Am. v. EPA*, 329 F.3d 876, 883 (D.C. Cir. 2003). Courts also place great weight on how the agency has disseminated its views.

> *Failure* to publish in the Federal Register is indication that the statement in question was *not* meant to be a regulation, since the [APA] requires regulations to be so published. The converse, however, is not true: *Publication* in the Federal Register does *not* suggest that the matter published *was* meant to be a regulation, since the APA requires general statements of policy to be published as well. *See* 5 U.S.C. § 552(a)(1)(D). The real dividing point between regulations and general statements of policy is publication in the Code of Federal Regulations, which the statute authorizes to contain only documents "having general applicability *and legal effect*," 44 U.S.C. § 1510 (1982) (emphasis added), and which the governing regulations provide shall contain only "each Federal *regulation* of general applicability and current or future effect," 1 C.F.R. § 8.1 (1986) (emphasis added).

Brock v. Cathedral Bluffs Shale Oil Co., 796 F.2d 533, 538–39 (D.C. Cir. 1986); *see also Am. Paper Inst., Inc. v. EPA*, 882 F.2d 287, 288–89 (7th Cir. 1989) (holding EPA's pronouncement to be an unreviewable policy statement partly on the basis of *Brock*).

Like agency policy statements, "interpretative rules" that do not establish a binding norm are not subject to judicial review under the APA. *Compare Syncor Int'l Corp. v. Shalala*, 127 F.3d 90, 96 (D.C. Cir. 1997) (rejecting the government's claim that the rule in question qualified as an interpretative rule), *with Am. Mining Cong. v. Mine Safety & Health Admin.*, 995 F.2d 1106 (D.C. Cir. 1993) (dismissing action challenging agency interpretative rule). As with policy statements, interpretative rules are also exempt from the notice-and-comment requirements of the APA. 5 U.S.C. § 553(b)(A). And interpretative rules, no less than policy statements, are subject to judicial review when they are relied upon or applied to support agency action in a particular case. *See, e.g., Barnhart v. Walton*, 535 U.S. 212 (2002). The difficulty lies in determining whether a rule is interpretative or substantive.

> While the spectrum between a clearly interpretive rule and a clearly substantive one is a hazy continuum, our cases, deploying different verbal tests, have generally sought to distinguish cases in which an agency is merely explicating Congress' desires from those cases in which the agency is adding substantive content of its own. Substantive rules are ones which grant rights, impose obligations, or produce other significant effects on private interests, or which effect a change in existing law or policy. Interpretive rules, by contrast, are those which merely clarify or explain existing law or regulations, are essentially

hortatory and instructional, and do not have the full force and effect of a substantive rule but are in the form of an explanation of particular terms.

Determining whether a given agency action is interpretive or legislative is an extraordinarily case-specific endeavor.

Am. Hosp. Ass'n, 834 F.2d at 1045.

As the decision in *Syncor* makes clear, the distinction between policy statements and interpretative rules defies easy explanation:

[There is a] tendency [on the part] of courts and litigants to lump interpretative rules and policy statements together in contrast to substantive rules.... That causes added confusion because interpretative rules and policy statements are quite different agency instruments. An agency policy statement does not seek to impose or elaborate or interpret a legal norm. It merely represents an agency position with respect to how it will treat – typically enforce – the governing legal norm. By issuing a policy statement, an agency simply lets the public know its current enforcement or adjudicatory approach. The agency retains the discretion and the authority to change its position – even abruptly – in any specific case because a change in its policy does not affect the legal norm. We thus have said that policy statements are binding on neither the public nor the agency. The primary distinction between a substantive rule – really any rule – and a general statement of policy, then, turns on whether an agency intends to bind itself to a particular legal position.

An interpretative rule, on the other hand, typically reflects an agency's construction of a statute that has been entrusted to the agency to administer. The legal norm is one that Congress has devised; the agency does not purport to modify that norm, in other words, to engage in lawmaking.... [I]n such a situation the agency does not claim to be exercising authority to itself make positive law. Instead, it is construing the product of congressional lawmaking based on specific statutory provisions. That is why we have said that the distinction between an interpretative rule and substantive rule ... likely turns on how tightly the agency's interpretation is drawn linguistically from the actual language of the statute.

127 F.3d at 93–94.

*

Chapter XIII

THE DEFERENCE DUE AN AGENCY'S CONSTRUCTION OF ITS AUTHORIZING STATUTE

Under the APA framework for judicial review of administrative agency actions, a court may "hold unlawful and set aside agency action, findings, and conclusions found to be ... in excess of statutory jurisdiction, authority, or limitations, or short of statutory right." 5 U.S.C. § 706(2)(C). In applying § 706(2)(C), the courts have developed a body of case law defining the applicable standards of review, including the amount of deference due an agency's construction of its authorizing statute. This section reviews that case law.

In 1985, just after the Supreme Court issued its seminal decision in *Chevron U.S.A. Inc. v. Natural Resources Defense Council, Inc.*, 467 U.S. 837 (1984), Professor Colin Diver published a thoughtful article describing the dominant modes of statutory interpretation in American administrative law. *See Statutory Interpretation in the Administrative State*, 133 U. Pa. L. Rev. 549 (1985). The article says very little about *Chevron*, probably because the decision was handed down just before the article was published and neither Professor Diver nor anyone else had reason to know that *Chevron* would become one of the most important decisions ever issued in administrative law. *See* Strauss, Rakoff & Farina, Gellhorn & Byse's Administrative Law Cases & Comments 1032–33 (2003). Nonetheless, in reflecting on judicial review of administrative action, Professor Diver offered some useful insights that give context to the many judicial decisions, like *Chevron* and its progeny, that address the deference due an agency's construction of its authorizing statute.

Two competing traditions in American jurisprudence address the issue of the appropriate allocation of interpretive authority between agencies and courts. One ... views matters of statutory interpretation as questions of "law" reserved for independent determination by the judiciary.... Under this conception, a court must independently examine an administrative agency's claimed authority to inflict harm upon a plaintiff, just as it would assess the legal authority of a private entity to do so.

137

The alternative view of the judicial function ... views agencies as delegates, empowered by the legislature to exercise legislative power to articulate and implement public goals. Legislation, so conceived, is as much a mandate as a constraint. Under this conception, courts involved in statutory interpretation must provide enough leeway for agencies to give shape to that legislative mandate.

These two traditions have coexisted uneasily throughout the modern era of administrative law.

Diver, *Statutory Interpretation in the Administrative State*, 133 U. PA. L. REV. 549, 551 (1985). These observations set the stage for a discussion of the case law that addresses the deference due an agency's construction of its authorizing statute.

———————

Chevron is truly seminal, because so many of the most important decisions that address the question of the appropriate deference due an agency's interpretation of its authorizing statute emanate from *Chevron*. It is therefore important to understand what was at stake and the precise terms of the Supreme Court's holding in that case. The Court described the controversy as follows:

In the Clean Air Act Amendments of 1977, Congress enacted certain requirements applicable to States that had not achieved the national air quality standards established by the Environmental Protection Agency (EPA) pursuant to earlier legislation. The amended Clean Air Act required these "nonattainment" States to establish a permit program regulating "new or modified major stationary sources" of air pollution. Generally, a permit may not be issued for a new or modified major stationary source unless several stringent conditions are met. The EPA regulation promulgated to implement this permit requirement allows a State to adopt a plantwide definition of the term "stationary source." Under this definition, an existing plant that contains several pollution-emitting devices may install or modify one piece of equipment without meeting the permit conditions if the alteration will not increase the total emissions from the plant. The question presented ... is whether EPA's decision to allow States to treat all of the pollution-emitting devices within the same industrial grouping as though they were encased within a single "bubble" is based on a reasonable construction of the statutory term "stationary source."

Chevron, 467 U.S. at 839–40. Before EPA adopted the regulations embodying the bubble concept, individual pieces of process equipment within a plant were considered to be a source. In other words, EPA changed its interpretation of the authorizing statute when it adopted the bubble concept. And it was undisputed that EPA changed the regulatory definition of "source" expressly to cut back on the coverage of nonattainment area new source review. The court of appeals set aside EPA's new regulations as contrary to legislative intent, on the ground that the bubble concept was "inappropriate" in programs enacted to improve air quality. *Natural Res. Def. Council, Inc. v. Gorsuch*, 685 F.2d 718, 726 (D.C. Cir. 1982). The Supreme Court reversed.

With the benefit of hindsight, it is easy to recite the important legal principles established by *Chevron*:

> "The basic legal error of the Court of Appeals was to adopt a static judicial definition of the term 'stationary source' when it had decided that Congress itself had not commanded that definition." 467 U.S. at 842.

––––––––

> "[T]he Court of Appeals misconceived the nature of its role in reviewing the regulations at issue. Once it determined, after its own examination of the legislation, that Congress did not actually have an intent regarding the applicability of the bubble concept to the permit program, the question before it was not whether in its view the concept is "inappropriate" in the general context of a program designed to improve air quality, but whether the Administrator's view that it is appropriate in the context of this particular program is a reasonable one." *Id.* at 845.

Chevron "Step One"

> "When a court reviews an agency's construction of the statute which it administers, it is confronted with two questions. First, always, is the question whether Congress has directly spoken to the precise question at issue. If the intent of Congress is clear, that is the end of the matter; for the court, as well as the agency, must give effect to the unambiguously expressed intent of Congress." *Id.* at 842–43.

––––––––

> "The judiciary is the final authority on issues of statutory construction and must reject administrative constructions which are contrary to clear congressional intent. If a court, employing traditional tools of statutory construction, ascertains that Congress had an intention on the precise question at issue, that intention is the law and must be given effect." *Id.* at 843 n.9.

Chevron "Step Two"

> "If ... [a] court determines Congress has not directly addressed the precise question at issue, the court does not simply impose

its own construction on the statute, as would be necessary in the absence of an administrative interpretation. Rather, if the statute is silent or ambiguous with respect to the specific issue, the question for the court is whether the agency's answer is based on a permissible construction of the statute." *Id.* at 843.

––––––––

"The power of an administrative agency to administer a congressionally created ... program necessarily requires the formulation of policy and the making of rules to fill any gap left, implicitly or explicitly, by Congress." *Id.*

––––––––

"If Congress has explicitly left a gap for the agency to fill, there is an express delegation of authority to the agency to elucidate a specific provision of the statute by regulation. Such legislative regulations are given controlling weight unless they are arbitrary, capricious, or manifestly contrary to the statute." *Id.* at 843–44.

––––––––

"Sometimes the legislative delegation to an agency on a particular question is implicit rather than explicit. In such a case, a court may not substitute its own construction of a statutory provision for a reasonable interpretation made by the administrator of an agency." *Id.* at 844.

––––––––

Initially, there was some confusion and much debate over the meaning of *Chevron. See* Strauss, Rakoff & Farina, Gellhorn & Byse's Administrative Law Cases & Comments 1033–34 (2003). *Chevron* "does, of course, contain some very broad, general language concerning deference to agency legal interpretations." Lawson, Federal Administrative Law 442 (2007). And from this, it was initially assumed by some courts and scholars that "the [Supreme] Court was instructing lower courts to replace the long-standing distinction between pure legal questions (generally reviewed *de novo*) and questions of law application (generally reviewed deferentially) with a single, uniform principle of deference." *Id.* Over the years, however, *Chevron* has been amplified and moderated by later Supreme Court decisions, the most important of which include *Gonzales v. Oregon*, 546 U.S. 243 (2006), and *United States v. Mead Corp.*, 533 U.S. 218 (2001). In other words, the framework for judicial review under § 706(2)(C) has evolved over time and the standards of review have gained clarity.

The § 706(2)(C) framework sometimes lacks precision in application, but it is not unclear. Under the *Chevron/Mead/Gonzales* paradigm, an agency's power to regulate "is limited to the scope of the authority Congress has delegated to it." *Am. Library Ass'n v. FCC*, 406 F.3d 689, 698 (D.C. Cir. 2005). Pursuant to *Chevron* Step One, if the intent of Congress is clear, the reviewing court must give effect to that unambiguously expressed intent. If Congress has not directly addressed the precise question at issue, the reviewing court proceeds to *Chevron* Step Two. Under Step Two, "[i]f Congress has explicitly left a gap for the agency to fill, there is an express delegation of authority to the agency to elucidate a specific provision of the statute by regulation. Such legislative regulations are given controlling weight unless they are ... manifestly contrary to the statute." *Chevron*, 467 U.S. at 843–44. Where a "legislative delegation to an agency on a particular question is implicit rather than explicit," the reviewing court must uphold any "reasonable interpretation made by the administrator of [that] agency." *Id.* at 844. But deference to an agency's interpretation of its enabling statute "is due only when the agency acts pursuant to delegated authority." *Am. Library Ass'n*, 406 F.3d at 699.

There are a number of important questions that courts have been required to address in cases implicating § 706(2)(C):

(1) Has the agency acted pursuant to congressionally delegated authority?

(2) Has Congress directly spoken to the precise question at issue?

(3) When an agency purports to act pursuant to an express delegation of authority, is the disputed action manifestly contrary to the statute?

(4) When an agency purports to act pursuant to an implicit delegation of authority, is the agency's interpretation of the statute reasonable?

(5) If an administrative action is within the area in which Congress has authorized an agency to act, was the action taken pursuant to congressionally delegated authority to make rules carrying the force of law and in the exercise of that authority, or, alternatively, was it simply one of the many sorts of interpretative choices that an agency charged with applying a statute necessarily must make in the course of administering it?

Judicial dispositions of these and related issues have given content to the scope and standard of review under § 706(2)(C). These matters are addressed in the succeeding sections.

A. DID THE AGENCY ACT PURSUANT TO CONGRESSIONALLY DELEGATED AUTHORITY?

1. GENERAL PRINCIPLES

A federal agency "literally has no power to act ... unless and until Congress confers power upon it." *La. Pub. Serv. Comm'n v. FCC*, 476 U.S. 355, 374 (1986). An agency "has no constitutional or common law existence or authority, but only those authorities conferred upon it by Congress." *Michigan v. EPA*, 268 F.3d 1075, 1081 (D.C. Cir. 2001). Therefore, "[i]t is axiomatic that an administrative agency's power to promulgate legislative regulations is limited to the authority delegated by Congress." *Bowen v. Georgetown Univ. Hosp.*, 488 U.S. 204, 208 (1988).

The crucial point here is that any inquiry into the legality of administrative action always involves a determination as to whether the agency acted pursuant to delegated authority. *See Gonzales*, 546 U.S. at 258. And a court decides *de novo* whether an agency has acted within the bounds of congressionally delegated authority. If an agency acts outside of its delegated authority, it makes no difference whether the action is also contrary to the plain language of the agency's authorizing statute and therefore unlawful under *Chevron* Step One, or implausible under the statute and thus impermissible under the deferential standard of *Chevron* Step Two. Why? Because deference under *Chevron* Step Two is required only when " 'Congress [has] delegated authority to [an] agency generally to make rules carrying the force of law, and ... the agency interpretation claiming deference was promulgated in the exercise of that authority.' " *Gonzales*, 546 U.S. at 255–56 (quoting *Mead*, 533 U.S. at 226–27). In short, deference under *Chevron* Step Two is premised on either an "express delegation of authority" or an "implicit" "legislative delegation to an agency." *Chevron*, 467 U.S. at 843–44.

The Supreme Court has been consistent and clear in holding that a "precondition to deference under *Chevron* is a congressional delegation of administrative authority." *Adams Fruit Co. v. Barrett*, 494 U.S. 638, 649 (1990). If no delegation of authority is evident in the agency's authorizing statute, it is inappropriate for a court "to consult [agency] interpretations of [a disputed statute] to resolve ambiguities surrounding the scope [of the statute]." *Id.* at 650. "*Chevron* deference ... is not accorded merely because the statute is ambiguous and an administrative official is involved." *Gonzales*, 546 U.S. at 258. An agency's legislative "rule must be promulgated pursuant to authority Congress has delegated to the official. . . . The starting point for this inquiry is, of course, the language of the delegation provision itself." *Id.* When a statute gives an agency official "limited powers, to be exercised in specific ways," it cannot be assumed that Congress meant to delegate to the official "authority to carry out or effect all provisions of the [authorizing statute]." *Id.* at 259. These principles animated the Supreme Court's decisions in *FDA v. Brown & Williamson Tobacco Corp.*, 529 U.S. 120

(2000), and *MCI Telecommunications Corp. v. American Telephone & Telegraph Co.*, 512 U.S. 218 (1994).

MCI involved a challenge to the FCC's interpretation of the term "modify" in § 203(b) of the Communications Act of 1934. The agency argued that, because the Act gave it the discretion to "modify any requirement" imposed under the statute, the Commission possessed the authority to render voluntary an otherwise mandatory requirement that long-distance carriers file their rates. The Supreme Court rejected the agency's construction of the statute, finding "not the slightest doubt" that Congress had directly addressed the question. *MCI*, 512 U.S. at 228. In reaching this result, the Court stated the obvious: "an agency's interpretation of a statute is not entitled to deference when it goes beyond the meaning that the statute can bear." *Id.* at 229. The Court also tellingly observed that "[i]t is highly unlikely that Congress would leave the determination of whether an industry will be entirely, or even substantially, rate-regulated to agency discretion – and even more unlikely that it would achieve that through such a subtle device as permission to 'modify' rate-filing requirements." *Id.* at 231. In other words, the language of the statutory delegation provision simply did not support the agency's claim of authority.

The decision in *Brown & Williamson* echoes the holding in *MCI*. In *Brown & Williamson*, tobacco manufacturers, retailers, and advertisers brought an action challenging the Food and Drug Administration's regulation of tobacco products. The Supreme Court held that the FDA lacked authority to regulate tobacco products as customarily marketed: "Congress has clearly precluded the FDA from asserting jurisdiction to regulate tobacco products. Such authority is inconsistent with the intent that Congress has expressed in the [Federal Food, Drug, and Cosmetic Act's] overall regulatory scheme and in the tobacco-specific legislation that it has enacted subsequent to the FDCA. In light of this clear intent, the FDA's assertion of jurisdiction is impermissible." *Brown & Williamson*, 529 U.S. at 126. The Court then added: "As in *MCI*, we are confident that Congress could not have intended to delegate a decision of such economic and political significance to an agency in so cryptic a fashion." *Id.* at 160. The Court concluded with a powerful reminder that, no matter how well intentioned its motives, an agency cannot act without congressional authority:

> By no means do we question the seriousness of the problem that the FDA has sought to address. The agency has amply demonstrated that tobacco use, particularly among children and adolescents, poses perhaps the single most significant threat to public health in the United States. Nonetheless, no matter how important, conspicuous, and controversial the issue, and regardless of how likely the public is to hold the Executive Branch politically accountable, an administrative agency's power to regulate in the public interest must always be grounded in a valid grant of authority from Congress.

Id. at 161.

2. DELEGATED AUTHORITY AS A PART OF THE *CHEVRON* STEP ONE INQUIRY

A court's inquiry into whether an agency has acted pursuant to congressionally delegated authority is often conflated with the inquiry under *Chevron* Step One. The decisions in *Brown & Williamson* and *MCI* demonstrate this. In each case, the Supreme Court ruled that the agency had acted without congressionally delegated authority and also that the agencies' constructions of their authorizing statutes were contrary to clear congressional intent.

3. DELEGATED AUTHORITY AS A PART OF THE *CHEVRON* STEP TWO INQUIRY

The question of delegated authority also arises in cases in which an agency claims that it is due deference under *Chevron* Step Two. This is unsurprising, since deference under Step Two is premised on either an "express delegation of authority" or an "implicit" "legislative delegation to an agency." *Chevron*, 467 U.S. at 843–44. A good example of a case in which the Supreme Court rejected the agency's claim of deference for want of delegated authority is *Sullivan v. Zebley*, 493 U.S. 521 (1990). At issue were regulations issued by the Secretary of Health and Human Services to determine whether a child was "disabled" and therefore eligible for benefits under the Social Security Act. The Court first acknowledged that, because the Social Security Act expressly granted the Secretary rulemaking power, the standard of review was governed by *Chevron* Step Two. But the Court held that "the Secretary's child-disability regulations [could not] be reconciled with the statute they purport[ed] to implement." *Id.* at 528. Using the *Chevron* Step Two standard of review, the Court concluded: "[T]he Secretary's approach to child disability is *manifestly contrary to the statute, Chevron*, 467 U.S. at 844, *and exceeds his statutory authority*." *Zebley*, 493 U.S. at 541 (emphasis added). In other words, the Court rejected the agency's interpretation under *Chevron* Step Two, in part, because the Secretary had acted in excess of delegated authority. *See also Maislin Indus., U.S., Inc. v. Primary Steel, Inc.*, 497 U.S. 116, 134–35 (1990) (rejecting the ICC's argument for *Chevron* deference, because the agency "[did] not have the power to adopt a policy that directly conflicts with its governing statute").

The decision in *Ragsdale v. Wolverine World Wide, Inc.*, 535 U.S. 81 (2002), offers another good example of a confluence of the *Chevron* Step Two inquiry and the question of delegated authority. In that case, the Supreme Court rejected a Department of Labor regulation interpreting the Family and Medical Leave Act. Qualifying employees were guaranteed 12 weeks of unpaid leave each year under the Act. Respondent Wolverine World Wide had granted petitioner Tracy Ragsdale 30 consecutive weeks of leave when cancer kept her from working in 1996.

Ragsdale nevertheless brought suit under the Act, claiming that, "because Wolverine was in technical violation of certain Labor Department regulations, she was entitled to more leave." *Id.* at 84. The Supreme Court agreed that the Department's regulations required the company to grant Ragsdale 12 more weeks of leave, "because it had not informed her that the 30–week absence would count against her [statutory entitlement]." *Id.* After analyzing the statute in detail, the Court held that the disputed regulation "effects an impermissible alteration of the statutory framework" and, therefore, the regulation could not be justified as "necessary to carry out" the Act. *Id.* at 96. In so holding, the Court added that "[w]hatever the bounds of the Secretary's discretion on this matter, they were exceeded here." *Id.*

The important point here is that, in considering the permissibility of an agency's construction of a statute, a court must determine not just whether the agency's interpretation is founded on reasonable policy goals, but also whether the agency has acted within the realm of its authority under the statute. In other words, an agency action cannot be "permissible" under *Chevron* Step Two if the agency acts in excess of its authority under the applicable statute. *See, e.g., Am. Bar Ass'n v. FTC*, 430 F.3d 457, 468 (D.C. Cir. 2005) (For an agency to suggest "that *Chevron* step two is implicated any time a statute does not expressly *negate* the existence of a claimed administrative power . . . is both flatly unfaithful to the principles of administrative law . . . and refuted by precedent."); *Motion Picture Ass'n of Am. v. FCC*, 309 F.3d 796, 805 (D.C. Cir. 2002) (finding "entirely untenable" "[t]he FCC's position . . . that the adoption of rules mandating video description is permissible because Congress did not expressly foreclose the possibility"). *Chevron* deference "comes into play . . . only as a consequence of statutory ambiguity, and then *only* if the reviewing court finds a[] . . . delegation of authority to the agency." *Sea-Land Serv., Inc. v. Dep't of Transp.*, 137 F.3d 640, 645 (D.C. Cir. 1998) (emphasis added); *see also Michigan v. EPA*, 268 F.3d at 1082 ("Mere ambiguity in a statute is not evidence of congressional delegation of authority."); *Natural Res. Def. Council v. Reilly*, 983 F.2d 259, 266 (D.C. Cir. 1993) ("It is only legislative intent to delegate such authority that entitles an agency to advance its own statutory construction for review under the deferential second prong of *Chevron*."); *City of Kansas City v. HUD*, 923 F.2d 188, 191–92 (D.C. Cir. 1991) (holding that "delegation of interpretive authority," as well as ambiguity, are required before *Chevron* Step Two deference is appropriate).

4. IS DELEGATED AUTHORITY A THRESHOLD INQUIRY?

Since an inquiry into the legality of an administrative action necessarily involves a determination as to whether an agency acted within the limits of its delegated authority, *see Gonzales*, 546 U.S. at 255–69; *Mead*, 533 U.S. at 226–27, it might seem curious that the requirement of "delegated authority" is often incorporated into the *Chevron* analysis. In other words, it might reasonably be assumed that delegated authority is a threshold inquiry that *precedes* the *Chevron* inquiry. Indeed, the Supreme Court seemed to suggest as much in *Gonzales*, where it held that the Attorney General did not have the authority under the federal Controlled Substances Act to adopt a rule declaring that physician-assisted suicide authorized under the Oregon Death With Dignity Act violated the federal statute. In its discussion of *Chevron* and *Mead*, the *Gonzales* decision states that "[t]he starting point . . . is, of course, the language of the delegation provision itself." 546 U.S. at 258. The Court found that, although the Attorney General had rulemaking authority to fulfill his duties under the federal statute, "[t]he specific respects in which he is authorized to make rules" indicate "that he is not author-ized to make a rule declaring illegitimate a medical standard for care and treatment of patients that is specifically authorized under state law." *Id.* In rejecting the government's position, the *Gonzales* Court did not rest on *Chevron* Step One. Nor did the Court focus on the "permissible construction of the statute" formulation of *Chevron* Step Two. Rather, in the section of the opinion addressing *Chevron* and *Mead*, the focal point of the Court's decision is the Attorney General's lack of delegated authority.

In practice, it does not appear to matter whether delegated authority is viewed as a threshold inquiry. If a court finds that an agency interpretation of a statute must be sustained under *Chevron* Step One, it necessarily concludes that the agency acted pursuant to delegated au-thority. *See, e.g.*, *EchoStar Satellite L.L.C. v. FCC*, 457 F.3d 31 (D.C. Cir. 2006). If a court holds illegal an agency action under Step One, it necessarily finds that the agency acted "without authority." *See, e.g.*, *Sierra Club v. EPA*, 294 F.3d 155, 160–62 (D.C. Cir. 2002). If a case cannot be resolved under Step One and the matter is analyzed under Step Two, a court cannot uphold an agency's interpretation of a statute if it finds that the agency acted in excess of its authority. *See, e.g.*, *Zebley*, 493 U.S. at 541.

5. AN AGENCY'S INTERPRETATION OF A STATUTE THAT IT IS NOT SOLELY RESPONSIBLE FOR ADMINISTERING

In considering whether administrative action is within an agency's delegated authority, one final point should be mentioned. A court does not defer to an agency's interpretation of a statute that it is not charged with administering. *See Metro. Stevedore Co. v. Rambo*, 521 U.S. 121, 138 n.9 (1997); *see also Adams Fruit*, 494 U.S. at 649–50. Relatedly, when a statute is administered by several different agencies, "the interpretation of any one of them is not entitled to *Chevron* deference." *Collins v. Nat'l Transp. Safety Bd.*, 351 F.3d 1246, 1253 (D.C. Cir. 2003). The reason is that no one of the several agencies has the delegated authority from Congress to speak with the level of authority to which a court must defer. However, as the court in *Collins* noted, the issue of "shared authority" admits of nuances:

> We may ... reasonably distinguish three types of shared-enforcement schemes. For generic statutes like the APA ... the broadly sprawling applicability undermines any basis for deference, and courts must therefore review interpretative questions de novo. For statutes [with respect to which] the agencies have specialized enforcement responsibilities but their authority potentially overlaps – thus creating risks of inconsistency or uncertainty – de novo review may also be necessary. But for statutes where expert enforcement agencies have mutually exclusive authority over separate sets of regulated persons, the above concerns don't work against application of *Chevron* deference.

Id.

One additional shared-enforcement category is suggested by the Supreme Court's decision in *Martin v. Occupational Safety & Health Review Commission*, 499 U.S. 144 (1991). In that case, the Court addressed the enforcement regime under the Occupational Safety and Health Act and held that regulatory deference was owed only to interpretations of the Secretary of Labor, the primary executive branch enforcer under the statute, and not to the Occupational Safety and Health Review Commission, an independent review board. The Court concluded that Congress intended "to make a single administrative actor accountable for the overall implementation of the Act's policy objectives by combining legislative and enforcement powers in the Secretary." *Id.* at 156. In the Court's view, that goal would be frustrated if the Commission could substitute its own interpretations of the Act for those of the Secretary. The Commission's function was to exercise "the type of nonpolicymaking adjudicatory powers typically exercised by a *court* in the agency-review context," reviewing "the Secretary's interpretations only for consistency with the regulatory language and for reasonableness." *Id.* at 154–55.

B. *CHEVRON* STEP ONE

Under *Chevron* Step One, when a court "ascertains that Congress had an intention on the precise question at issue, that intention is the law and must be given effect." *Chevron*, 467 U.S. at 843 n.9. An agency's construction of the statute that it administers is entitled to no deference if the reviewing court determines that Congress has directly spoken to the precise question at issue. "The judiciary is the final authority on issues of statutory construction and must reject administrative constructions which are contrary to clear congressional intent." *Id.* The Step One formulation is easier to read than it is to apply, however.

Before a court may invoke *Chevron* Step One, it must find that "the intent of Congress is clear," meaning that the statutory provision at issue is "unambiguous[]" with respect to the question presented. *Id.* at

842–43. As explained by the Supreme Court, this requires that the governing statute, read "as a whole," give clear meaning regarding congressional intent, *see, e.g., Dunn v. Commodity Futures Trading Comm'n,* 519 U.S. 465, 466–67, 479 n.14 (1997), or that "the text [of the statute] and reasonable inferences from it give a clear answer," *Brown v. Gardner,* 513 U.S. 115, 116, 120 (1994). And the Court has made it plain that "[a]mbiguity [in a statute] is a creature not of definitional possibilities but of statutory context." *Id.* at 118. Simply stated, statutory text must be read in context in order to derive the meaning of words.

In some cases, the application of Step One is straightforward. *See, e.g., Friends of the Earth, Inc. v. EPA,* 446 F.3d 140 (D.C. Cir. 2006); *Holly Sugar Corp. v. Johanns,* 437 F.3d 1210 (D.C. Cir. 2006); *Cal. Indep. Sys. Operator Corp. v. FERC,* 372 F.3d 395 (D.C. Cir. 2004). In others, however, the search for a statute's plain meaning is not so easy. Indeed, the Supreme Court has issued many decisions resting on *Chevron* Step One that have been opposed by dissenting opinions. *See, e.g., Rapanos v. United States,* ___ U.S. ___, 126 S. Ct. 2208 (2006) (plurality opinion) (holding that certain Michigan wetlands are not "waters of the United States" under the Clean Water Act); *Gen. Dynamics Land Sys., Inc. v. Cline,* 540 U.S. 581 (2004) (holding that discrimination against the relatively young is outside the protection of the Age Discrimination in Employment Act); *Utah v. Evans,* 536 U.S. 452 (2002) (holding that the Census Bureau's use of "hot-deck imputation" does not violate a statutory provision forbidding use of "the statistical method known as sampling"); *Barnhart v. Sigmon Coal Co.,* 534 U.S. 438 (2002) (holding that, under the Coal Industry Retiree Health Benefit Act, the Commissioner of Social Security may not assign premium responsibility for retired miners to the "successors in interest of out-of-business signatory operators"); *Solid Waste Agency of N. Cook County v. Army Corps of Eng'rs,* 531 U.S. 159 (2001) (holding that the authority granted to the Army Corps of Engineers under the Clean Water Act does not include the regulation of a sand and gravel pit which provides habitat for migratory birds); *Brown & Williamson,* 529 U.S. 120 (holding that the FDA has no authority to regulate tobacco products as customarily marketed); *MCI,* 512 U.S. 218 (holding that the FCC's "decision to make tariff filing optional for all nondominant long-distance carriers is [not] a valid exercise of its modification authority"); *City of Chicago v. Envtl. Def. Fund,* 511 U.S. 328 (1994) (holding that under the Solid Waste Disposal Act, "the ash generated by a resource recovery facility's incineration of municipal solid waste is [not] exempt from regulation as a hazardous waste"); *Norfolk & W. Ry. Co. v. Am. Train Dispatchers' Ass'n,* 499 U.S. 117 (1991) (holding that under the Interstate Commerce Act, the exemption "from all other law" for carriers taking necessary steps to carry out an ICC-approved transaction includes legal obligations under a collective bargaining agreement); *Dole v. United Steelworkers of Am.,* 494 U.S. 26 (1990) (holding that the Office of Management and Budget does not have authority under the Paperwork Reduction Act to review the Department of Labor's disclosure regulations). Many of the dissenting Justices in these cases argued that the agencies' authorizing statutes were ambiguous and that the Court should have deferred to the agencies' interpretations under *Chevron* Step Two.

In framing the standard governing review under *Chevron* Step One, the Supreme Court importantly has directed that courts must "employ[] traditional tools of statutory construction" in their search for a statute's plain meaning. *Chevron*, 467 U.S. at 842–43 & n.9. Shortly after *Chevron* was issued, the Court indicated in *NLRB v. United Food & Commercial Workers Union, Local 23*, 484 U.S. 112 (1987), that "traditional tools of statutory construction" normally include consideration of the "words, structure, and history" of the agency's authorizing statute. *Id.* at 123–24. After closely examining the text, statutory framework, and legislative history of the National Labor Relations Act, the Court held that a federal court has no authority to review a "decision of the National Labor Relations Board's General Counsel dismissing an unfair labor practice complaint pursuant to an informal settlement in which the charging party refused to join." *Id.* at 114. However, four Justices joined a separate concurring opinion arguing that the Court's examination of the statute's words, structure, and history merely confirmed that the NLRB's interpretation was entitled to deference under *Chevron* Step Two, not that the Court had spoken "conclusively and authoritatively" under *Chevron* Step One. *Id.* at 133–34 (Scalia, J., concurring). Although it is not clear whether the opinion for the Court in *United Food & Commercial Workers Union* meant to invoke Step One or apply Step Two, the decision appears to have set the stage for the use of traditional tools of statutory construction to resolve future challenges under *Chevron* Step One.

Supreme Court precedent now plainly establishes that a court may look to the "text, structure, purpose, and history" of an agency's authorizing statute, as well as "its relationship to other federal statutes," to determine whether the statutory provision at issue admits of a congressional intent on the precise question at issue. *Gen. Dynamics Land Sys.*, 540 U.S. at 600; *see also Cal. Dental Ass'n v. FTC*, 526 U.S. 756 (1999) (relying on plain meaning, structure, and purpose of the statute, as well as the absence of contrary legislative history, in finding that the FTC's "jurisdiction under the Federal Trade Commission Act . . . extends to an association that . . . provides substantial economic benefit to its for-profit members"); *Nat'l Credit Union Admin. v. First Nat'l Bank & Trust Co.*, 522 U.S. 479 (1998) (relying on plain meaning and canons of construction that similar language in the same statutory section must be accorded a consistent meaning and statutory terms should not be rendered surplusage or read out of the statute entirely, in holding "that the *same* common bond of occupation must unite each member of an occupationally defined federal credit union"); *Gardner*, 513 U.S. 115 (relying on statutory scheme, meaning of the same term in other statutes, and the canon of construction that a statutory term should be accorded a consistent meaning, in holding that Department of Veteran Affairs regulation was inconsistent with the controlling statute);

Mobil Oil Exploration & Producing S.E., Inc. v. United Distrib. Cos., 498 U.S. 211 (1991) (relying on plain meaning and statutory structure, in finding that FERC has authority under the Natural Gas Policy Act to set a single ceiling price for old gas); *Adams Fruit*, 494 U.S. 638 (relying on statutory plain meaning, structure, and purpose, in holding that "exclusivity provisions in state workers' compensation laws do not bar migrant workers from availing themselves of a private right of action under the Migrant and Seasonal Agricultural Worker Protection Act"). It is well understood, however, that courts tend to be cautious in relying on legislative history to determine the plain meaning of a statute, as it can be "extremely murky and a slender reed on which to place reliance." *Nat'l Credit Union Admin.*, 522 U.S. at 503 n.10; *see also Dunn*, 519 U.S. at 480–81 (Scalia, J., concurring in part and in the judgment).

Finally, it should be noted that, when statutory language is clear in requiring certain regulatory action, a reviewing court will not defer to an agency's "judgment" to ignore the statute. This point was emphasized by the Supreme Court in *Massachusetts v. EPA*, __ U.S. __, 127 S. Ct. 1438 (2007). In that case, the Commonwealth of Massachusetts, along with other parties, petitioned the agency to regulate greenhouse gases pursuant to the Clean Air Act. The Court held that, "[b]ecause greenhouse gases fit well within the Clean Air Act's capacious definition of 'air pollutant,' . . . EPA has the statutory authority to regulate the emission of such gases from new motor vehicles." *Id.* at 1462. EPA argued, however, that "even if it [had] statutory authority to regulate greenhouse gases, it would be unwise to do so at [that] time." *Id.* The Court rejected this argument, stating:

> EPA's decision . . . rests on reasoning divorced from the statutory text. While the statute does condition the exercise of EPA's authority on its formation of a "judgment," that judgment must relate to whether an air pollutant "cause[s], or contribute[s] to, air pollution which may reasonably be anticipated to endanger public health or welfare." Put another way, the use of the word "judgment" is not a roving license to ignore the statutory text. It is but a direction to exercise discretion within defined statutory limits.

> If EPA makes a finding of endangerment, the Clean Air Act requires the agency to regulate emissions of the deleterious pollutant from new motor vehicles. EPA no doubt has significant latitude as to the manner, timing, content, and coordination of its regulations with those of other agencies. But once EPA has responded to a petition for rulemaking, its reasons for action or inaction must conform to the authorizing statute. Under the clear terms of the Clean Air Act, EPA can avoid taking further action only if it determines that greenhouse gases do not contribute to climate change or if it provides some reasonable explanation as to why it cannot or will not exercise its discretion to determine whether they do. To the extent that this constrains agency discretion to pursue other priorities of

the Administrator or the President, this is the congressional design.

Id.

The Court's rejection of the government's position offers a telling counterpoint to its decision in *Brown & Williamson*, 529 U.S. 120, on which the EPA relied to support its position. *Massachusetts v. EPA*, ___ U.S. at ___, 127 S. Ct. at 1461. In *Brown & Williamson*, the Court held that tobacco products are not "drugs" or "devices" subject to Food and Drug Administration regulation under the Federal Food, Drug, and Cosmetic Act. In distinguishing that case, the Court said: "However much a ban on tobacco products clashed with the 'common sense' intuition that Congress never meant to remove those products from circulation, there is nothing counterintuitive to the notion that EPA can curtail the emission of substances that are putting the global climate out of kilter." *Id.*

C. *CHEVRON* STEP TWO

If a challenge to an agency's interpretation of its authorizing statute cannot be resolved pursuant to *Chevron* Step One – in other words, if Congress has not addressed the precise question at issue – then *Chevron* Step Two deference may apply. As noted above, the standard of review under Step Two entails the following considerations:

> If ... [a] court determines Congress has not directly addressed the precise question at issue, the court does not simply impose its own construction on the statute, as would be necessary in the absence of an administrative interpretation. Rather, if the statute is silent or ambiguous with respect to the specific issue, the question for the court is whether the agency's answer is based on a permissible construction of the statute.
>
> The power of an administrative agency to administer a congressionally created ... program necessarily requires the formulation of policy and the making of rules to fill any gap left, implicitly or explicitly, by Congress. If Congress has explicitly left a gap for the agency to fill, there is an express delegation of authority to the agency to elucidate a specific provision of the statute by regulation. Such legislative regulations are given controlling weight unless they are arbitrary, capricious, or manifestly contrary to the statute. Sometimes the legislative delegation to an agency on a particular question is implicit rather than explicit. In such a case, a court may not substitute its own construction of a statutory provision for a reasonable interpretation made by the administrator of an agency.

Chevron, 467 U.S. at 843–44.

1. AN AGENCY MUST ACT WITH THE FORCE OF LAW

The Supreme Court has explained that Step Two deference only comes into play when an agency has acted within the area in which Congress has authorized it to act, *and* the action at issue was taken pursuant to congressionally delegated authority to make law and with the intent on the part of the agency to act with the force of law. *Mead*, 533 U.S. at 226–27. As *Mead* explains, "[i]t is fair to assume generally that Congress contemplates administrative action with the effect of law when it provides for a relatively formal administrative procedure tending to foster the fairness and deliberation that should underlie a pronouncement of such force." *Id.* at 230. The absence of rulemaking or adjudicatory procedures is not dispositive, however, for the Court has "sometimes found reasons for *Chevron* deference even when no such administrative formality was required and none was afforded." *Id.* at 231; *see also Barnhart v. Walton*, 535 U.S. 212, 221 (2002) ("[T]he fact that the Agency . . . reached its interpretation through means less formal than 'notice and comment' rulemaking does not automatically deprive that interpretation of the judicial deference otherwise its due."). Moreover, the mere existence of "general rulemaking authority does not mean that [every] rule the agency promulgates is a valid exercise of that authority." *Colo. River Indian Tribes v. Nat'l Indian Gaming Comm'n*, 466 F.3d 134, 139 (D.C. Cir. 2006).

In determining whether *Chevron* deference is due, courts also may look to "the face of the statute" to see whether "the terms of the congressional delegation" give any indication that Congress meant to delegate authority to the agency to issue rulings with the force of law. *Mead*, 533 U.S. at 231–32; *see also Gonzales*, 546 U.S. at 258 (indicating that "[t]he starting point for this inquiry is, of course, the language of the delegation provision itself"). A reviewing court must consider whether the enabling statute bespeaks a congressional intention to authorize the agency to undertake a "legislative type of activity that would naturally bind more than the parties" to a particular action; whether the agency's action is subject to review by a higher authority; whether the agency had "a lawmaking pretense in mind"; and whether the challenged agency ruling is of a type that routinely emanates from a central agency authority rather than from "scattered offices" in a vast administrative bureaucracy. *Mead*, 533 U.S. at 232–33. When there is no persuasive evidence that Congress delegated authority to an agency to take a particular action with the force of law, or when the agency action for which deference is claimed was not taken in the exercise of such authority, then the action is "beyond the *Chevron* pale." *Id.* at 234.

2. THE "PERMISSIBLE CONSTRUCTION OF THE STATUTE" STANDARD

A reviewing court applies a *de novo* standard of review in determining whether an agency has acted pursuant to delegated authority and whether Congress has directly spoken to the precise question at issue. Under this *de novo* standard of review, "[t]he judiciary is the final authority on issues of statutory construction and must reject administrative constructions which are contrary to clear congressional intent." *Chevron*, 467 U.S. at 843 n.9. *Chevron* Step Two, however, is less precise in what it requires. Step Two does not purport to embrace any of the traditional standards of review – *de novo*, clearly erroneous, substantial evidence, arbitrary and capricious, or abuse of discretion. Rather, "[a]s *Chevron* itself illustrates, the resolution of ambiguity in a statutory text is often more a question of policy than of law." *Pauley v. BethEnergy Mines, Inc.*, 501 U.S. 680, 696 (1991). Thus, the Supreme Court has said that, in applying *Chevron* Step Two, "the question for the court is whether the agency's answer is based on a permissible construction of the statute." *Chevron*, 467 U.S. at 843.

In explaining Step Two's "permissible construction" standard of review, the Supreme Court carefully distinguishes between two types of agency actions. One type includes agency actions based on "express delegation[s] of authority," which must be upheld unless "manifestly contrary to the statute." The other type includes agency actions based on "implicit" delegations, which must be upheld if they reflect "a reasonable interpretation" of the statute. *Id.* at 843–44.

3. THE "MANIFESTLY CONTRARY TO THE STATUTE" TEST: REVIEW OF AGENCY INTERPRETATIONS RESTING ON "EXPRESS" DELEGATIONS OF AUTHORITY

Agency action taken pursuant to an *express* delegation of authority can be measured pursuant to the terms of the delegation and thus rarely poses serious difficulties for a reviewing court. Explicit delegations of authority are typically found when "Congress has expressly delegated to [an agency] the authority to prescribe regulations containing such classifications, differentiations, or other provisions as, in the judgment of the [agency], are necessary or proper to effectuate the purposes of [the authorizing statute], to prevent circumvention or evasion thereof, or to facilitate compliance therewith," *Household Credit Servs., Inc. v. Pfennig*, 541 U.S. 232, 238 (2004), or when "Congress confer[s] on [an agency] exceptionally broad authority to prescribe standards for applying certain sections of [its authorizing statute]," *Atkins v. Rivera*, 477 U.S. 154, 162 (1986). "[W]henever Congress has explicitly left [such] gap[s] for the agency to fill, the agency's regulation is given controlling weight unless it is arbitrary, capricious, or manifestly contrary to the statute." *Household Credit Servs.*, 541 U.S. at 239. If the agency action is not "manifestly contrary to the statute" or, more specifically, to the terms of the delegation, it will survive Step Two review. The "manifestly contrary to the statute" test is thus an intelligible, easy to apply standard of review. Several case examples illustrate the point.

Agency Actions Found Not to Be Manifestly
Contrary to Statute

Household Credit Servs., Inc. v. Pfennig, 541 U.S. 232 (2004): The Court upheld the Federal Reserve Board's determination that the term "finance charge" in the Truth in Lending Act excluded fees imposed for exceeding a credit limit.

————

United States v. O'Hagan, 521 U.S. 642 (1997): The Court upheld the SEC's "disclose or abstain from trading requirement," concluding that Congress had authorized the SEC to prohibit acts that were not themselves fraudulent under the common law or § 10(b), if the prohibition is reasonably designed to prevent acts and practices that are fraudulent.

————

ABF Freight Sys., Inc. v. NLRB, 510 U.S. 317 (1994): The Court upheld the NLRB's decision to rely on other civil and criminal remedies for false testimony, rather than create a rule prohibiting a victim of an unfair labor practice who submits false testimony from winning reinstatement with back pay.

————

Atkins v. Rivera, 477 U.S. 154 (1986): The Court upheld the Secretary of Health and Human Services' regulation instructing states to "use a prospective period of not more than 6 months to compute income" of the medically needy.

Agency Actions Found to Be Manifestly
Contrary to Statute

Sullivan v. Zebley, 493 U.S. 521 (1990): The Court concluded that the Secretary's child disability regulations were manifestly contrary to the statute, because they (1) did not cover all illnesses and abnormalities that actually can be disabling; (2) contained criteria setting a higher level of severity than the statutory standard; (3) excluded any claimant whose impairment would not prevent any and all persons from doing any kind of work, but which actually precluded the particular claimant from working; and (4) excluded claimants who have unlisted impairments or combinations of impairments.

————

Ragsdale v. Wolverine World Wide, Inc., 535 U.S. 81 (2002): The Court held that an agency regulation creating a "categorical penalty" under the Family and Medical Leave Act was contrary to the statute and beyond the authority of the Secretary of Labor.

4. THE "REASONABLENESS" TEST: AGENCY INTERPRETATIONS RESTING ON "IMPLICIT" DELEGATIONS OF AUTHORITY

The hard cases for the courts involve petitions to review agency actions that are purportedly based on implicit delegations of authority. Review in these cases to determine whether agency constructions are "reasonable," and thus "permissible" under Step Two, can be challenging. In *Mead*, the Court attempted to explain what is meant by an *implicit* delegation of authority:

> Congress ... may not have expressly delegated authority or responsibility to implement a particular provision or fill a particular gap. Yet it can still be apparent from the agency's generally conferred authority and other statutory circumstances that Congress would expect the agency to be able to speak with the force of law when it addresses ambiguity in the statute or fills a space in the enacted law, even one about which Congress did not actually have an intent as to a particular result.

533 U.S. at 229. A year later in *Barnhart v. Walton*, 535 U.S. 212 (2002), the Supreme Court lent some clarity to *Mead*'s definition of an implicit delegation. The claimant in *Barnhart* sought judicial review after his application for disability benefits and supplemental income was denied. At issue was the Social Security Administration's interpretation of the statutory definition of "inability." The Supreme Court held that the Social Security Administration's interpretation – requiring that a claimant's "inability to engage in any substantial gainful activity" last, or be expected to last, for at least 12 months – was based on a permissible construction of the statute. In reaching this conclusion, the Court stated: "In this case, the interstitial nature of the legal question, the related expertise of the Agency, the importance of the question to administration of the statute, the complexity of that administration, and the careful consideration the Agency has given the question over a long period of time all indicate that *Chevron* provides the appropriate legal lens through which to view the legality of the Agency interpretation here at issue." *Id.* at 222 (citing *Mead*, 533 U.S. 218); *see also Nat'l Cable & Telecomms. Ass'n v. Gulf Power Co.*, 534 U.S. 327, 339 (2002) (noting that, "as a general rule, agencies have authority to fill gaps" where their authorizing statutes are silent and the subject matter is "technical, complex, and dynamic").

But the premise "that a statute's ambiguity constitutes an implicit delegation from Congress to the agency to fill in the statutory gaps" is not inviolate. *Brown & Williamson*, 529 U.S. at 159. In some cases, a court will have good "reason to hesitate before concluding that Congress has intended such an implicit delegation." *Id.* Thus, for example, a court may " 'ask whether the legal question is an important one. Congress is more likely to have focused upon, and answered, major questions, while leaving interstitial matters to answer themselves in the course of the statute's daily administration.' " *Id.* (quoting Breyer, *Judicial Review of Questions of Law and Policy*, 38 ADMIN. L. REV. 363, 370 (1986)). In addition, it must be remembered that "[a]mbiguity is a creature not of definitional possibilities but of statutory context." *Gardner*, 513 U.S. at 118. This means that an agency may not offer an implausible interpretation of its authorizing statute in order to create an "ambiguity" justifying deference under *Chevron* Step Two. Finally, it cannot be assumed that congressional silence, without more, equals a congressional delegation of authority. Thus, the argument that "disputed regulations are permissible because the statute [did] not expressly foreclose the construction advanced by the agency" has been rejected as "entirely untenable under well-established case law." *Aid Ass'n for Lutherans v. Postal Serv.*, 321 F.3d 1166, 1174 (D.C. Cir. 2003). This makes sense, for if courts "[w]ere . . . to *presume* a delegation of power absent an express *withholding* of such power, agencies would enjoy virtually limitless hegemony, a result plainly out of keeping with *Chevron* and quite likely with the Constitution as well." *Ry. Labor Executives' Ass'n v. Nat'l Mediation Bd.*, 29 F.3d 655, 671 (D.C. Cir. 1994) (en banc).

The inquiry as to whether there is an implicit delegation of authority often overlaps with the inquiry as to whether the agency's interpretation is reasonable. This is seen in *Goldstein v. SEC*, 451 F.3d 873 (D.C. Cir. 2006). In that case, an investment advisory firm and a hedge fund petitioned for review of an order of the Securities and Exchange Commission regulating "hedge funds" under the Investment Advisers Act. The Act exempts advisers with fewer than 15 clients from registering with the SEC. The court held that an SEC rule requiring that hedge fund investors be counted as clients of the fund's adviser was invalid as conflicting with purposes underlying the statute. The decision indicates that the agency's interpretation both exceeded congressionally delegated authority and fell outside the bounds of reasonableness:

> The Act does not define "client." Relying on *Chevron*, the Commission believes this renders the statute ambiguous as to a method for counting clients. There is no such rule of law. The lack of a statutory definition of a word does not necessarily render the meaning of a word ambiguous, just as the presence of a definition does not necessarily make the meaning clear. A definition only pushes the problem back to the meaning of the defining terms.

> If Congress employs a term susceptible of several meanings, as many terms are, it scarcely follows that Congress has authorized an agency to choose *any* one of those meanings. As always, the words of the statute should be read in context, the statute's

place in the overall statutory scheme should be considered, and the problem Congress sought to solve should be taken into account to determine whether Congress has foreclosed the agency's interpretation.

. . . .

... [I]t may be that ... the strict dichotomy between clarity and ambiguity is artificial, that what we have is a continuum, a probability of meaning. Here, even if the [statute] does not foreclose the Commission's interpretation, the interpretation falls outside the bounds of reasonableness....

The "reasonableness" of an agency's construction depends, in part, on the construction's fit with the statutory language, as well as its conformity to statutory purposes. As described above, the Commission's interpretation of the word "client" comes close to violating the plain language of the statute. At best it is counterintuitive to characterize the investors in a hedge fund as the "clients" of the adviser.

Id. at 878, 880–81; *see also Am. Library Ass'n*, 406 F.3d at 705 (agency construction of its authorizing statute rejected under *Chevron* Step Two because it was both in excess of congressionally delegated authority and unreasonable); *Aid Ass'n for Lutherans*, 321 F.3d at 1178 (same).

The "reasonableness" test governing judicial review of agency interpretations resting on implicit delegations of authority can be elusive. This may explain why, in a number of cases, common sense guides judicial judgment. Thus, for example, in *American Bar Ass'n v. FTC*, 430 F.3d 457, the court held that the FTC exceeded its statutory authority when it determined "that attorneys engaged in the practice of law are covered by the federal Gramm–Leach–Bliley Act." *Id.* at 458. In analyzing the FTC's arguments that the Act authorized it to regulate the practice of law, the court first found that Congress's failure to negate the regulation of lawyers under the statute could not, without more, support the agency's claim for deference. "[I]f there is the sort of ambiguity that supports an implicit congressional delegation of authority to the agency to make a deference-worthy interpretation of the statute, we must look elsewhere than the failure to negate regulation of attorneys." *Id.* at 468. The court then found that "the existence of ambiguity [in the statute was] not enough per se to warrant deference to the agency's interpretation. The ambiguity must be such as to make it appear that Congress either explicitly or implicitly delegated authority to cure that ambiguity." *Id.* at 469. Finally, the court held that "[t]o find [the FTC's] interpretation deference-worthy, [it] would have to conclude that Congress not only had hidden a rather large elephant in a rather obscure mousehole, but had buried the ambiguity in which the pachyderm lurks beneath an incredibly deep mound of specificity, none of which bears the footprints of the beast or any indication that Congress even suspected its presence." *Id.* Having examined a statutory "scheme of the length, detail, and intricacy of the one before [it]," the court found it "difficult to believe that Congress, by any remaining ambiguity, intended to undertake the regulation of the profession of law – a profession never before regulated by federal functional regulators – and never mentioned in the statute." *Id.* Because the FTC's claim for deference made no sense in light of the statute's words and purpose, it did not survive judicial scrutiny.

Agencies sometimes contend that regulations promulgated pursuant to a statutory grant of broad rulemaking authority should be deemed reasonable under *Chevron* Step Two so long as they are reasonably related to the purposes of the agency's authorizing statute. This view comes from the Court's pre-*Chevron* decision in *Mourning v. Family Publications Service, Inc.*, 411 U.S. 356 (1973). The Court has, however, made it clear that *Mourning* has only limited precedential value in the *Chevron/Mead/Gonzales* regime. *See Ragsdale*, 535 U.S. at 92 ("Our previous decisions, *Mourning* included, do not authorize agencies to contravene Congress' will in this manner."). In short, "[a]n agency's general rulemaking authority does not mean that the specific rule the agency promulgates is a valid exercise of that authority." *Colo. River Indian Tribes*, 466 F.3d at 139. Nor does a statute's "general declaration of policy" determine the legality of regulations promulgated to implement specific provisions of an authorizing statute. *Id.* "Agencies are ... bound, not only by the ultimate purposes Congress has selected, but by the means it has deemed appropriate, and prescribed, for the pursuit of those purposes." *Id.*

5. THE MEANING OF DEFERENTIAL REVIEW UNDER *CHEVRON* STEP TWO

Once a court determines that Congress either explicitly or implicitly delegated to an agency the authority to fill a gap in its authorizing statute, the court must accept the agency's position if it is based on a "permissible" interpretation of the statute. *Chevron*, 467 U.S. at 843. As the Supreme Court made clear in *National Cable & Telecommunications Ass'n v. Brand X Internet Services*, 545 U.S. 967 (2005), this deference is due without regard to whether the agency's interpretation of its authorizing statute differs from what a court believes is the best interpretation of the statute. In *Brand X*, the Court reviewed an FCC ruling that cable companies providing broadband Internet access were not telecommunications carriers and thus were exempt from regulation under Title II of the Communications Act. The court of appeals had held that the FCC's construction of the statute was foreclosed by a conflicting interpretation that the court had adopted in an earlier decision. The Supreme Court reversed, holding that the appellate court erred in failing to follow the dictates of *Chevron*.

> A court's prior judicial construction of a statute trumps an agency construction otherwise entitled to *Chevron* deference only if the prior court decision holds that its construction

follows from the unambiguous terms of the statute and thus leaves no room for agency discretion. This principle follows from *Chevron* itself. *Chevron* established a presumption that Congress, when it left ambiguity in a statute meant for implementation by an agency, understood that the ambiguity would be resolved, first and foremost, by the agency, and desired the agency (rather than the courts) to possess whatever degree of discretion the ambiguity allows. Yet allowing a judicial precedent to foreclose an agency from interpreting an ambiguous statute, as the Court of Appeals assumed it could, would allow a court's interpretation to override an agency's. *Chevron*'s premise is that it is for agencies, not courts, to fill statutory gaps. The better rule is to hold judicial interpretations contained in precedents to the same demanding *Chevron* step one standard that applies if the court is reviewing the agency's construction on a blank slate: Only a judicial precedent holding that the statute unambiguously forecloses the agency's interpretation, and therefore contains no gap for the agency to fill, displaces a conflicting agency construction.

Id. at 982–83.

The decision in *Brand X* also reaffirms *Chevron*'s holding that when an agency acts within the compass of its delegated authority to fill "gaps" in its authorizing statute, it is not bound by its own earlier interpretations of the statute. In other words, over time, an agency may lawfully change its construction of the authorizing statute, so long as the new interpretation carries the force of law, does not flaunt the statute's plain meaning, remains within the range of the agency's delegated authority, is permissible under *Chevron* Step Two, and is not otherwise arbitrary and capricious. *See Chevron*, 467 U.S. at 863–64. Under both *Chevron* Step Two review and arbitrary and capricious review, discussed in Part Two, Chapter XV, *infra*, an agency must offer a reasonable explanation for any changed construction of its statute. *See Rust v. Sullivan*, 500 U.S. 173, 186–87 (1991). But the agency is not bound by notions of *stare decisis* when it elects to revise its interpretation of its authorizing statute. As the decision in *Rust* makes clear, the Supreme Court

has rejected the argument that an agency's interpretation is not entitled to deference because it represents a sharp break with prior interpretations of the statute in question. In *Chevron*, [the court] held that a revised interpretation deserves deference because an initial agency interpretation is not instantly carved in stone and the agency, to engage in informed rulemaking, must consider varying interpretations and the wisdom of its policy on a continuing basis. An agency is not required to establish rules of conduct to last forever, but rather must be given ample latitude to adapt its rules and policies to the demands of changing circumstances.

Id.

6. NO DEFERENCE IS DUE AN AGENCY'S LITIGATION POSITION

Chevron deference is accorded only when a court finds a permissible construction *"made by the administrator of an agency." Chevron*, 467 U.S. at 844 (emphasis added). In other words, deference under *Chevron* Step Two is due to an agency's interpretation of its authorizing statute, not to agency counsel's litigation position. This point was made clear by the Supreme Court in *Bowen v. Georgetown University Hospital*:

> We have never applied [*Chevron* deference] to agency litigating positions that are wholly unsupported by regulations, rulings, or administrative practice. To the contrary, we have declined to give deference to an agency counsel's interpretation of a statute where the agency itself has articulated no position on the question, on the ground that Congress has delegated to the administrative official and not to appellate counsel the responsibility for elaborating and enforcing statutory commands.

488 U.S. at 212; *see also City of Kansas City v. HUD*, 923 F.2d at 192 ("That counsel advances a particular statutory interpretation during the course of trial does not confer upon that interpretation any special legitimacy. Deference under *Chevron*, even in the context of informal adjudication, can be accorded only to a judgment of the agency itself.").

D. *SKIDMORE* DEFERENCE

If an administrative action is within the area in which Congress has authorized an agency to act, a question may arise as to whether it was taken pursuant to congressionally "delegated authority to ... make rules carrying the force of law" and "in the exercise of that authority," or, alternatively, whether it was simply one of the many "sorts of interpretative choices" that an agency "charged with applying a statute necessarily" must make in the course of administering it. *Mead*, 533 U.S. at 226–27. If an action falls within the former category, it will be reviewed under the *Chevron* framework. If the action falls within the latter category, the agency's interpretation will be entitled only to a level of deference commensurate with its inherent power to persuade. *See id.* at 227–28 (citing *Skidmore v. Swift & Co.*, 323 U.S. 134 (1944)). This is the so-called "*Skidmore*" standard of review.

In distinguishing between actions carrying the force of law and mere interpretive choices, *Mead* reaffirmed the Court's prior holding that agency interpretations contained in opinion letters, enforcement guidelines, policy statements, manuals, and other such documents – "all of which lack the force of law – do not warrant *Chevron*-style deference." *Christensen v. Harris County*, 529 U.S. 576, 587 (2000); *see also Mead*, 533 U.S. at 234. In other words, "interpretative rules and enforcement guidelines are not entitled to the same deference as norms that derive from the exercise of [an agency's] delegated lawmaking powers." *Christensen*, 529 U.S. at 587.

When the *Skidmore* standard controls, the final judgment on the legality of any contested administrative action rests with the court. *See Gonzales*, 546 U.S. at 268–69. This does not mean that no deference is due an agency's interpretation under the *Skidmore* standard of review. Both *Mead* and *Skidmore* recognize that an agency's interpretation, though not carrying the force of law, may nevertheless merit some respect (and therefore some deference) in light of the "specialized experience and broader investigations and information available to the agency" and the uniformity that agency interpretations can bring to the enforcement of law. *Mead*, 533 U.S. at 234–35. The deference due under *Skidmore* is thus variable, but in all events less deferential than under *Chevron* Step Two. A very good example of a court's application of *Skidmore* may be seen in *Public Citizen, Inc. v. Dep't of Health & Human Servs.*, 332 F.3d 654 (D.C. Cir. 2003).

*

Chapter XIV

THE DEFERENCE DUE AN AGENCY'S INTERPRETATION OF ITS OWN REGULATIONS

Judicial review of an agency's interpretation of its own regulations is governed by 5 U.S.C. § 706(2)(A), which requires courts to set aside agency action that is "arbitrary, capricious, an abuse of discretion, or otherwise not in accordance with law." *See Allentown Mack Sales & Serv., Inc. v. NLRB*, 522 U.S. 359, 377 (1998); *see also Thomas Jefferson Univ. v. Shalala*, 512 U.S. 504, 512 (1994). Pursuant to this standard, a court accords "substantial deference" to an agency's views. *See, e.g., Allentown Mack*, 522 U.S. at 377; *Thomas Jefferson Univ.*, 512 U.S. at 512. Thus, an agency interpretation that "does not violate the Constitution or a federal statute ... must be given controlling weight unless it is plainly erroneous or inconsistent with the regulation." *Stinson v. United States*, 508 U.S. 36, 45 (1993). "In other words," deference to an agency's interpretation of its regulation is required "unless an alternative reading is compelled by the regulation's plain language or by other indications of the [agency's] intent at the time of the regulation's promulgation." *Thomas Jefferson Univ.*, 512 U.S. at 512. The substantial deference due agency interpretations of ambiguous regulations is "all the more warranted when ... the regulation concerns a complex and highly technical regulatory program, in which the identification and classification of relevant criteria necessarily require significant expertise and entail the exercise of judgment grounded in policy concerns." *Id.*

A court need not conclude that an agency's construction was the only one possible, or even the one that the court would adopt were it reviewing *de novo*. Rather, when "the meaning of regulatory language is not free from doubt, the reviewing court should give effect to the agency's interpretation so long as it is reasonable, that is, so long as the interpretation sensibly conforms to the purpose and wording of the regulations." *Martin v. Occupational Safety & Health Review Comm'n*, 499 U.S. 144, 150–51 (1991).

It has been suggested that the deference due an agency's interpretation of its own regulations is similar to the *Chevron* Step Two deference afforded an agency's interpretation of its authorizing statute. *See Paralyzed Veterans of Am. v. D.C. Arena L.P.*, 117 F.3d 579, 584 (D.C. Cir. 1997) ("*Chevron* requires a reviewing court to affirm a permissible (or reasonable) interpretation of an ambiguous statute, and we very much doubt that we would defer to an *unreasonable* agency interpretation of an ambiguous regulation."). This is not surprising, since, in each situation, the governing standard of review is shaped by similar concerns regarding the proper role of the courts. *Compare Pauley v. BethEnergy Mines, Inc.*, 501 U.S. 680, 696 (1991) ("Judicial deference to an agency's interpretation of ambiguous provisions of the statutes it is authorized to implement reflects a sensitivity to the proper roles of the political and judicial branches."), *with Martin*, 499 U.S. at 151 ("Because applying an agency's regulation to complex or changing circumstances calls upon the agency's unique expertise and policymaking prerogatives, we presume that the power authoritatively to interpret its own regulations is a component of the agency's delegated lawmaking powers.").

Chevron deference and the deference due an agency's interpretation of its regulations are not identical, however. While courts review with "near indifference" an agency interpretation of an ambiguous statute that is "advanced for the first time in a litigation brief," *see United States v. Mead Corp.*, 533 U.S. 218, 228 (2001) (citing *Bowen v. Georgetown Univ. Hosp.*, 488 U.S. 204, 212–13 (1988)), there is no categorical bar against deferring to an agency's interpretation of its own regulation when it is first articulated in the course of litigation, *Auer v. Robbins*, 519 U.S. 452, 462 (1997). In *Auer*, the Supreme Court held that the agency's interpretation of its regulations was not "unworthy of deference" merely because it came to the court "in the form of a legal brief." *Id.* The Court found that, although the regulation was ambiguous, it could "comfortably bear[]" the meaning assigned by the agency. *Id.* at 461. The Court additionally found that the interpretation reasonably resolved the ambiguity without distorting the meaning of the regulation, and that it was "in no sense a *post hoc* rationalization advanced by an agency seeking to defend past agency action against attack," *id.* at 462. The Court also noted that there was "no reason to suspect that the interpretation [did] not reflect the agency's fair and considered judgment on the matter in question." *Id.*

In *Christensen v. Harris County*, 529 U.S. 576 (2000), the Court emphasized that "*Auer* deference is warranted only when the language of the regulation is ambiguous.... To defer to [an] agency's position [when a disputed regulation is plainly permissive, not ambiguous,] would be to permit the agency, under the guise of interpreting a regulation, to create *de facto* a new regulation.... *Auer* deference is unwarranted [in such circumstances]." *Id.* at 588; *see also Humanoids Group v. Rogan*, 375 F.3d 301, 306 (4th Cir. 2004); *Drake v. FAA*, 291 F.3d 59, 68 (D.C. Cir. 2002).

Although the deference afforded an agency's interpretation of its own regulations is significant, it is not without limits. First, no deference is due to an agency's interpretation of its regulations when "the underlying regulation does little more than restate the terms of the statute itself." *Gonzales v. Oregon*, 546 U.S. 243, 257 (2006). In such a situation, the "language the [interpretation] addresses comes from Congress, not the [agency], and the near-equivalence of the statute and regulation belies the Government's argument for *Auer* deference." *Id.* Second, any regulation that is the subject of an agency interpretation "must have sufficient content and definitiveness as to be a meaningful exercise in agency lawmaking. It is certainly not open to an agency to promulgate mush and then give it concrete form only through subsequent less formal interpretations." *Paralyzed Veterans of Am.*, 117 F.3d at 584. Such an approach would violate the notice-and-comment requirements of the APA. *See* 5 U.S.C. § 553. Moreover, if an agency's present interpretation of a regulation effectively amends the contested regulation, then "the modification can only be made in accordance with the notice and comment requirements of the APA." *SBC Inc. v. FCC*, 414 F.3d 486, 498 (3d Cir. 2005); *see also Shell Offshore Inc. v. Babbitt*, 238 F.3d 622, 629 (5th Cir. 2001); *Alaska Prof'l Hunters Ass'n v. FAA*, 177 F.3d 1030, 1036 (D.C. Cir. 1999). Finally, when an agency interpretation of a regulation conflicts with a prior interpretation of that same regulation, it is, at the very least, "entitled to considerably less deference than a consistently held agency view." *Thomas Jefferson Univ.*, 512 U.S. at 515.

The substantial deference afforded an agency's interpretations of its own regulations generally does not extend "to one agency's interpretation of a regulation issued and administered by another agency." *Sec'y of Labor v. Excel Mining, LLC*, 334 F.3d 1, 7 (D.C. Cir. 2003). However, an agency need not have drafted a regulation in order for its interpretation of that regulation to be afforded deference. Courts "do not defer . . . to an administrative agency's interpretation of its regulation solely because its employees are the drafters and presumably have superior knowledge as to what they intended. . . . [T]he doctrine of deference is based primarily on the agency's statutory role as the sponsor of the regulation, not necessarily on its drafting expertise." *Paralyzed Veterans of Am.*, 117 F.3d at 585. Thus, if an agency properly adopts a regulation initially promulgated by another agency and, through that regulation, acts within the compass of its own congressionally delegated authority, the adopting agency's interpretation of the regulation will be given controlling weight unless plainly erroneous or inconsistent with the regulatory text. *Excel Mining*, 334 F.3d at 6–7 (rejecting the argument that deference must be denied the Labor Department's construction of a regulation, properly adopted by it pursuant to its authority to regulate under the Mine Act, simply because the regulation was originally drafted as a joint finding by the Secretary of Health, Education, and Welfare and the Secretary of the Interior).

*

Chapter XV

THE REQUIREMENT OF REASONED DECISIONMAKING: ARBITRARY AND CAPRICIOUS REVIEW UNDER THE APA

Section 706(2)(A) of the APA provides that a reviewing court shall "hold unlawful and set aside agency action, findings, and conclusions found to be ... arbitrary, capricious, an abuse of discretion, or otherwise not in accordance with law." 5 U.S.C. § 706(2)(A). This is the APA's "catch-all" provision governing the scope and standards of review, and the courts rarely draw any meaningful distinctions between acts that are "arbitrary, capricious, or an abuse of discretion." *Block v. Pitney Bowes Inc.*, 952 F.2d 1450, 1454 (D.C. Cir. 1992). "[A]rbitrary, capricious, [or] an abuse of discretion" review under § 706(2)(A) is now routinely applied by the courts as one standard under the heading of "arbitrary and capricious" review. And it encompasses both review of the factual basis of an agency's action, *see Citizens to Preserve Overton Park, Inc. v. Volpe*, 401 U.S. 402, 416 (1971), and review of an agency's reasoning as distinguished from its factfinding, *see Bowman Transp., Inc. v. Ark.-Best Freight Sys., Inc.*, 419 U.S. 281, 285–86 (1974). Moreover, the arbitrary and capricious standard governs review of *all* proceedings that are subject to challenge under the APA. *See Consumers Union of U.S., Inc. v. FTC*, 801 F.2d 417, 422 (D.C. Cir. 1986). Thus, if an action is subject to review under the APA, it does not matter whether it is a formal or informal adjudication or a formal or informal rulemaking proceeding – all are subject to arbitrary and capricious review under § 706(2)(A).

As the Supreme Court made clear in its seminal *State Farm* decision, the touchstone of arbitrary and capricious review is reasoned decisionmaking:

> Normally, an agency rule would be arbitrary and capricious if the agency has relied on factors which Congress has not intended it to consider, entirely failed to consider an important aspect of the problem, offered an explanation for its decision that runs counter to the evidence before the agency, or is so implausible that it could not be ascribed to a difference in view or the product of agency expertise.

Motor Vehicle Mfrs. Ass'n of the U.S. v. State Farm Mut. Auto. Ins. Co., 463 U.S. 29, 43 (1983). *State Farm* involved a judicial challenge to an agency's action taken pursuant to informal rulemaking procedures.

167

However, in *Allentown Mack Sales & Service, Inc. v. NLRB*, 522 U.S. 359 (1998), the Supreme Court made it clear that the requirement of reasoned decisionmaking also applies in situations involving judicial review of agency adjudicatory actions.

> The Administrative Procedure Act, which governs the proceedings of administrative agencies and related judicial review, establishes a scheme of "reasoned decisionmaking." Not only must an agency's decreed result be within the scope of its lawful authority, but the process by which it reaches that result must be logical and rational. Courts enforce this principle with regularity when they set aside agency regulations which, though well within the agencies' scope of authority, are not supported by the reasons that the agencies adduce. The National Labor Relations Board, uniquely among major federal administrative agencies, has chosen to promulgate virtually all the legal rules in its field through adjudication rather than rulemaking. But adjudication is subject to the requirement of reasoned decisionmaking as well.

Id. at 374. "Reasoned decisionmaking ... promotes sound results, and unreasoned decisionmaking the opposite." *Id.* at 375.

As the decision in *Allentown Mack* demonstrates, the application of the arbitrary and capricious standard is somewhat different in situations involving judicial review of agency adjudications as opposed to informal rulemakings. In the informal rulemaking context, agency actions often involve fundamental legislative-type policy judgments. *See Vermont Yankee Nuclear Power Corp. v. Natural Res. Def. Council, Inc.*, 435 U.S. 519, 557–58 (1978). Judicial review of agency adjudications, on the other hand, tends to focus on the adequacy of the evidence in the record to support the agency's judgment, the agency's adherence to precedent, and the agency's application of its standard of proof. *See Allentown Mack*, 522 U.S. at 374 ("It is hard to imagine a more violent breach of [the reasoned decisionmaking] requirement than [when an agency] appl[ies] a rule of primary conduct or a standard of proof which is in fact different from the rule or standard formally announced.").

It is generally understood that arbitrary and capricious review is applied most frequently in cases involving judicial challenges to informal rulemakings. In this context, "[t]he function of the court is to assure that the agency has given reasoned consideration to all the material facts and issues." *Greater Boston Television Corp. v. FCC*, 444 F.2d 841, 851 (D.C. Cir. 1970). Although the arbitrary and capricious standard does not allow for *de novo* review, it does permit a court to take what has been characterized as a "hard look" at agency actions emanating from informal rulemaking proceedings and other agency actions based on less than full trial-type records. *Nat'l Lime Ass'n v. EPA*, 627 F.2d 416, 451 n.126 (D.C. Cir. 1980).

The *State Farm* opinion enunciates in detail the principles governing arbitrary and capricious review. *State Farm* involved a challenge by insurance companies to an order of the National Highway Traffic Safety Administration rescinding a regulation requiring that new motor vehicles be equipped with passive restraints designed to protect vehicle occupants. The Supreme Court held that the agency's revocation of the regulation was arbitrary and capricious, because the agency failed to present an adequate factual basis and reasoned explanation for rescinding the passive restraint requirement and altogether failed to consider the efficacy of air bag technology. In reaching this result, the Court explained:

> [Under the "arbitrary and capricious" standard,] a reviewing court may not set aside an agency rule that is rational, based on consideration of the relevant factors, and within the scope of the authority delegated to the agency by the statute.... The scope of review under the "arbitrary and capricious" standard is narrow and a court is not to substitute its judgment for that of the agency. Nevertheless, the agency must examine the relevant data and articulate a satisfactory explanation for its action including a rational connection between the facts found and the choice made. In reviewing that explanation, we must consider whether the decision was based on a consideration of the relevant factors and whether there has been a clear error of judgment.... The reviewing court ... may not supply a reasoned basis for the agency's action that the agency itself has not given. We will, however, uphold a decision of less than ideal clarity if the agency's path may reasonably be discerned.
>
> . . . .
>
> Nor [may a court] broadly require an agency to consider all policy alternatives in reaching decision. [A] rulemaking cannot be found wanting simply because the agency failed to include every alternative [policy option] and thought conceivable by ... the mind of man regardless of how uncommon or unknown that alternative may have been....

State Farm, 463 U.S. at 42–43, 51.

State Farm clarified certain issues regarding arbitrary and capricious review about which there previously had been some question. First, the decision made clear that the standard is not inconsistent with the dictates of *Vermont Yankee*. *See id.* at 50–51. *Vermont Yankee* prohibits courts from imposing any procedural requirements upon an agency beyond those required by the APA, the agency's authorizing statute, and the agency's properly adopted rules. 435 U.S. at 524–25. In *State Farm*, the Court rebuked the government for invoking *Vermont Yankee* "as though it were a talisman under which any agency decision is by definition unimpeachable." *State Farm*, 463 U.S. at 50. In concluding that the agency acted arbitrarily and capriciously when it failed to consider a regulation requiring air bags in new cars, the Court noted that it did "not require ... any specific procedures which [the agency] must follow." *Id.* at 50–51. Rather, the Court "h[e]ld only that given the judgment made [by the agency] in 1977 that airbags are an effective and cost-beneficial life-saving technology, the mandatory passive restraint rule may not be abandoned without any consideration whatsoever of an airbags-only requirement." *Id.* at 51.

Second, *State Farm* rejected the government's suggestion "that the arbitrary-and-capricious standard requires no more than the minimum rationality a statute must bear in order to withstand analysis under the Due Process Clause." *Id.* at 43 n.9. As explained in *FCC v. Beach Communications, Inc.*, 508 U.S. 307 (1993), the constitutional requirement of "equal protection is not a license for courts to judge the wisdom, fairness, or logic of legislative choices. In areas of social and economic policy, a statutory classification that neither proceeds along suspect lines nor infringes fundamental constitutional rights must be upheld against equal protection challenge if there is any reasonably conceivable state of facts that could provide a rational basis for the classification." *Id.* at 313. Thus, on rational basis review, a statutory classification is presumed valid, and those challenging its rationality must negate "every conceivable basis [that] might support it." *Id.* at 314–15. In other words, under the rational basis test, congressional social and economic policy is not subject to the same degree of appellate scrutiny as courtroom factfinding, but may be upheld on the basis of rational speculation, even when that speculation is unsupported by evidence or empirical data. In *State Farm*, the Court roundly rejected the suggestion that arbitrary and capricious review encompasses no more searching an inquiry than that which is permitted under the rational basis test. The Court made clear that it did "not view as equivalent the presumption of constitutionality afforded legislation drafted by Congress and the presumption of regularity afforded an agency in fulfilling its statutory mandate." *State Farm*, 463 U.S. at 43 n.9.

Finally, *State Farm* holds that "the rescission or modification" of a regulation "is subject to the same [arbitrary and capricious] test" pursuant to which an agency's promulgation of a regulation is reviewed. *Id.* at 41. The Court explained:

> Revocation [of a regulation] constitutes a reversal of the agency's former views as to the proper course. A settled course of behavior embodies the agency's informed judgment that, by pursuing that course, it will carry out the policies committed to it by Congress. There is, then, at least a presumption that those policies will be carried out best if the settled rule is adhered to. Accordingly, an agency changing its course by rescinding a rule is obligated to supply a reasoned analysis for the change beyond that which may be required when an agency does not act in the first instance.

Id. at 41–42.

State Farm also suggests that the "standard a court would use to judge an agency's refusal to promulgate a rule in the first place" is "considerably narrower than the traditional arbitrary-and-capricious test." *Id.* at 41. In *Massachusetts v. EPA*, ___ U.S. ___, 127 S.Ct. 1438 (2007), the Court confirmed that review of an agency's denial of a petition for rulemaking is very narrow:

> There are key differences between a denial of a petition for rulemaking and an agency's decision not to initiate an enforcement action. In contrast to nonenforcement decisions, agency refusals to initiate rulemaking are less frequent, more apt to involve legal as opposed to factual analysis, and subject to special formalities, including a public explanation. They moreover arise out of denials of petitions for rulemaking which (at least in the circumstances here) the affected party had an undoubted procedural right to file in the first instance. Refusals to promulgate rules are thus susceptible to judicial review, though such review is extremely limited and highly deferential.

Id. at 1459 (citing and quoting *Nat'l Customs Brokers & Forwarders Ass'n of Am. v. United States*, 883 F.2d 93, 96 (D.C. Cir. 1989)). The issue in *Massachusetts v. EPA* was whether the agency had authority to regulate greenhouse gas emissions from new motor vehicles under the Clean Air Act. EPA denied the petition for rulemaking on the grounds that it lacked authority to regulate because greenhouse gases are not "air pollutants" as that term is defined in the statute. The Court rejected the agency's statutory interpretation and held that EPA had erred in assuming that it lacked authority to regulate. Because EPA had authority to grant the relief sought in the petition for rulemaking, and had offered no good reason for its refusal to regulate, the Court held that the agency's denial of the petition could not survive arbitrary and capricious review under § 706(2)(A).

Under the arbitrary and capricious standard, judicial review of agency action normally must be based on the existing administrative record, "not some new record made initially in the reviewing court." *Camp v. Pitts*, 411 U.S. 138, 142 (1973) (per curiam). And a reviewing court must confine itself to the grounds upon which the record discloses that the agency's action was based. *SEC v. Chenery Corp.*, 318 U.S. 80, 87–88 (1943). "If those grounds are inadequate or improper, the court is powerless to affirm the administrative action by substituting what it considers to be a more adequate or proper basis." *SEC v. Chenery Corp.*, 332 U.S. 194, 196 (1947). In other words, the court may not enter "the domain which Congress has set aside exclusively for the administrative agency." *Id.* This means that a reviewing court may not supply a reasoned basis for the agency action that the agency itself did not give in the record under review. *Chenery Corp.*, 318 U.S. at 88. Nor may a court consider "*post hoc* rationalizations by agency counsel." *Williams Gas Processing—Gulf Coast Co. v. FERC*, 373 F.3d 1335, 1345 (D.C. Cir. 2004).

There is a close connection between judicial review of the adequacy of the record compiled during rulemaking procedures and review of the substance of rules promulgated by administrative agencies. The decision in *United States v. Nova Scotia Food Products Corp.*, 568 F.2d 240 (2d Cir. 1977), is recognized as one of the leading cases amplifying this point. In that case, the Food and Drug Administration established rules governing the processing of smoked fish. Several years after the rulemaking, the agency brought action in district court to enforce its rules against Nova Scotia, a whitefish processor. The district court enjoined Nova Scotia from processing hot smoked whitefish except in accordance with the agency's regulations. On review, Nova Scotia contended that the administrative record, upon which the FDA's rules were predicated, was inadequate for judicial review, and that the FDA's "failure to disclose to interested persons the factual material upon which the agency was relying vitiates the element of fairness which is essential to any kind of administrative action." *Id.* at 248.

In sustaining the challenge to the FDA rule, the *Novia Scotia* decision first notes that, "when the pertinent research material is readily available and the agency has no special expertise on the precise parameters involved, there is [no] reason to conceal the scientific data relied upon from the interested parties." *Id.* at 251. The decision adds that, "[i]f the failure to notify interested persons of the scientific research upon which the agency was relying actually prevented the presentation of relevant comment, the agency may be held not to have considered all the relevant factors." *Id.* For an agency "[t]o suppress meaningful comment by failure to disclose the basic data relied upon is akin to rejecting comment altogether. . . . The inadequacy of comment in turn leads in the direction of arbitrary decision-making." *Id.* at 252.

It is important to understand that, even though the decisions in *Overton Park*, *State Farm*, and their progeny indicate that, under the arbitrary and capricious standard, a court must "engage in a substantial inquiry" that involves "a thorough, probing, in-depth review," *Overton Park*, 401 U.S. at 415, the standard is, nonetheless, fundamentally deferential. This is particularly true in administrative actions that involve legislative-type policy judgments, *see, e.g., Vermont Yankee*, 435 U.S. at 557–58, matters on the cutting edge of scientific knowledge, *see, e.g., Balt. Gas & Elec. Co. v. Natural Res. Def. Council, Inc.*, 462 U.S. 87, 103 (1983), and judgments regarding agency enforcement priorities, *see, e.g., City of Bedford v. FERC*, 718 F.2d 1164, 1169–70 (D.C. Cir. 1983). The Supreme Court also has made it clear that, in assessing whether an agency action is arbitrary and capricious, a reviewing court should ignore agency errors that have no real bearing on the final agency action and are thus harmless. *National Ass'n of Home Builders v. Defenders of Wildlife*, __ U.S. __, __, 127 S.Ct. 2518, 2530 (2007) (citing 5 U.S.C. § 706, which provides that "due account shall be taken of the rule of prejudicial error" in agency actions reviewed under the APA).

One final point is worth mentioning in connection with judicial review under § 706(2)(A). As noted above, the courts often conflate the four parts of § 706(2)(A) – arbitrary, capricious, abuse of discretion, and not in accordance with law – into a single standard constituting "arbitrary and capricious" review. *See, e.g., Tourus Records, Inc. v. DEA*, 259

F.3d 731, 736 (D.C. Cir. 2001) (holding that a reviewing court must set aside agency action it finds to be "arbitrary, capricious, an abuse of discretion, or otherwise not in accordance with law," and stating that this § 706(2)(A) "standard requires the agency to examine the relevant data and articulate a satisfactory explanation for its action including a rational connection between the facts found and the choice made"). There are times, however, when the "not in accordance with law" standard under § 706(2)(A) is applied apart from arbitrary and capricious review. Thus, for example, in *Holland v. National Mining Ass'n*, 309 F.3d 808 (D.C. Cir. 2002), the court undertook a *Chevron* analysis within the framework of § 706(2)(A)'s "not in accordance with law" provision. *See id.* at 815. Examples of this type are rare, however, as issues relating to *Chevron* and *Mead* are normally raised under § 706(2)(C), which provides that a reviewing court shall "hold unlawful and set aside agency action, findings, and conclusions found to be ... in excess of statutory jurisdiction, authority, or limitations, or short of statutory right." 5 U.S.C. § 706(2)(C).

*

Chapter XVI

FACTUAL DETERMINATIONS MADE IN ON-THE-RECORD PROCEEDINGS: SUBSTANTIAL EVIDENCE REVIEW

Whenever an agency is required to act "on the record after opportunity for an agency hearing," *see* 5 U.S.C. §§ 553(c), 554(a), in other words pursuant to formal rulemaking or adjudicatory procedures, the APA mandates that agency findings and conclusions be supported "by substantial evidence," *id.* § 706(2)(E). Some authorizing statutes also require that an agency's factual findings and conclusions be supported by substantial evidence. *See, e.g.*, National Labor Relations Act, 29 U.S.C. § 160(e)-(f). There is an enormous body of case law construing the substantial evidence standard of review, so this section will only highlight some of the most important principles.

Prior to enactment of the APA, the Supreme Court construed substantial evidence to mean "such relevant evidence as a reasonable mind might accept as adequate to support a conclusion." *Consol. Edison Co. v. NLRB*, 305 U.S. 197, 229 (1938). The pre-APA case law established that in order to be "substantial," evidence "must do more than create a suspicion of the existence of the fact to be established.... [I]t must be enough to justify, if the trial were to a jury, a refusal to direct a verdict when the conclusion sought to be drawn from it is one of fact for the jury." *NLRB v. Columbian Enameling & Stamping Co.*, 306 U.S. 292, 300 (1939). After Congress codified the substantial evidence test in § 706(2)(E) of the APA, the Supreme Court explained the standard in its seminal decision in *Universal Camera Corp. v. NLRB*, 340 U.S. 474 (1951).

Universal Camera clarifies that, as codified in § 706(2)(E) of the APA, substantial evidence review requires a court to consider the *whole* record upon which an agency's factual findings are based. Looking to the language and legislative history of the APA, the Court concluded that the courts could not determine the substantiality of the evidence supporting an agency decision "merely on the basis of evidence which in and of itself justified it, without taking into account contradictory evidence or evidence from which conflicting inferences could be drawn." *Id.* at 487. Rather, reviewing courts must "take into account whatever in the record fairly detracts" from the evidence supporting an agency's decision. *Id.* at 488.

In describing the whole record review of § 706(2)(E), the Court acknowledged that the requirement "does not furnish a calculus of value by which a reviewing court can assess the evidence." *Id.* It also noted that substantial evidence review does not negate the "respect" with which courts are to review decisions based on agency expertise. *Id.* Nor, the Court explained, does whole record review mean that a court can displace an agency's "choice between two fairly conflicting views," even though the reviewing court "would justifiably have made a different choice had the matter been before it *de novo.*" *Id.* Rather, a reviewing court must "ask whether a reasonable mind might accept a particular evidentiary record as adequate to support a conclusion." *Dickinson v. Zurko,* 527 U.S. 150, 162 (1999). Or, put differently, a court must decide whether, on the record under review, "it would have been possible for a reasonable jury to reach the [agency's] conclusion." *Allentown Mack Sales & Serv., Inc. v. NLRB,* 522 U.S. 359, 366–67 (1998).

In a number of agency adjudicatory actions, the agency and its administrative law judge ["ALJ"] will disagree. In such situations, *Universal Camera* instructed that an ALJ's findings should not be given "more weight than in reason and in the light of judicial experience they deserve." 340 U.S. at 496. According to the Court, this means "that evidence supporting a conclusion may be less substantial when an impartial, experienced [ALJ] who has observed the witnesses and lived with the case has drawn conclusions different from the [agency's] than when [the ALJ and the agency have] reached the same conclusion." *Id.* An ALJ's findings "are to be considered along with the consistency and inherent probability of testimony," and the significance of the findings will depend "largely on the importance of credibility in the particular case." *Id.*

At bottom, the decision in *Universal Camera* concluded that, while agency findings are "entitled to respect," they must, pursuant to whole record substantial evidence review, "be set aside when the record before a Court of Appeals clearly precludes [an agency's] decision from being justified by a fair estimate of the worth of the testimony of witnesses or [the agency's] informed judgment on matters within its special competence or both." *Id.* at 490. Substantial evidence review "gives the agency the benefit of the doubt, since it requires not the degree of evidence which satisfies the *court* that the requisite fact exists, but merely the degree which *could* satisfy a reasonable factfinder." *Allentown Mack,* 522 U.S. at 377. And it does not allow a court to "supplant the agency's findings merely by identifying alternative findings that could be supported by substantial evidence." *Arkansas v. Oklahoma,* 503 U.S. 91, 113 (1992); *see also Robinson v. Nat'l Transp. Safety Bd.,* 28 F.3d 210, 215 (D.C. Cir. 1994) (holding that an agency decision "may be supported by substantial evidence even though a plausible alternative interpretation of the evidence would support a contrary view"). As noted above, however, "evidence that is substantial viewed in isolation may become insubstantial when contradictory evidence is taken into account." *Landry v. FDIC,* 204 F.3d 1125, 1140 (D.C. Cir. 2000). This means that an agency cannot ignore evidence that undercuts its judgment or discount such evidence without adequate explanation. *See, e.g., Morall v. DEA*, 412 F.3d 165, 179–80 (D.C. Cir. 2005) (granting the petition for review, because the agency's decision entirely ignored relevant evidence that was favorable to the petitioner); *Lakeland Bus Lines, Inc. v. NLRB*, 347 F.3d 955, 963 (D.C. Cir. 2003) (holding that the Board's "clipped view of the record" did not support the conclusion that the employer had committed unfair labor practices); *Vemco, Inc. v. NLRB*, 79 F.3d 526, 529 (6th Cir. 1996) (granting the petition for review, because the agency did not explain why it credited unsupported testimony and rejected contrary testimony that was supported by other evidence); *Sahara Coal Co. v. Fitts*, 39 F.3d 781, 782 (7th Cir. 1994) (holding that an agency tribunal cannot "base its decision on a mechanical nose count of witnesses").

If agency action is subject to review under the APA, but neither the agency's authorizing statute nor the APA requires the agency to hold a hearing or to make formal findings on the hearing record, then final agency action normally is subject to arbitrary and capricious review under § 706(2)(A) but not substantial evidence review under § 706(2)(E). *See Camp v. Pitts*, 411 U.S. 138, 140–42 (1973). The arbitrary and capricious standard of review governs review of *all* proceedings that are subject to challenge under the APA. *See Consumers Union of U.S., Inc. v. FTC*, 801 F.2d 417, 422 (D.C. Cir. 1986). This means that even when agency action is subject to substantial evidence review, it is also subject to arbitrary and capricious review. The converse is not true, however, because the substantial evidence test is applicable only when an agency is required to hold a hearing or to make formal findings on the hearing record.

Because § 706(2)(A) is a "catch-all" provision, *Block v. Pitney Bowes Inc.*, 952 F.2d 1450, 1454 (D.C. Cir. 1992), an agency action is necessarily arbitrary and capricious under § 706(2)(A) if it is not supported by substantial evidence as required by § 706(2)(E) or by the agency's authorizing statute. This point is highlighted in *Allentown Mack*, 522 U.S. at 374–75, where the Supreme Court made it clear that, in the adjudicatory context – no less than when a challenged administrative action involves an informal rulemaking proceeding or other less than full trial-type records – reasoned decisionmaking requires that the decisional process be logical and rational. Thus, for example, an agency may not announce that one standard of proof controls in an adjudicatory hearing, but then actually apply another in making factual determinations and reaching substantive conclusions. If an agency were able to announce one rule and apply another, it would become a complicated enterprise for a court to determine whether an agency's decision is supported by substantial evidence. "Reviewing courts are entitled to take [the legal standards an agency enunciates in principle] to mean what they say, and to conduct substantial-evidence review on that basis." *Id.* at 376–77. Courts owe no deference to "an agency's eccentric view of what a reasonable factfinder *ought* to demand." *Id.* at 377; *see also Morall*, 412 F.3d at 180 (concluding that an agency decision that could not withstand substantial evidence review because it failed to take into account record evidence contradicting its position was also arbitrary and capricious).

*

Chapter XVII

COMPARING AND CONTRASTING THE PRINCIPAL STANDARDS OF REVIEW

A. THE INTERPLAY OF *CHEVRON* STEP TWO AND ARBITRARY AND CAPRICIOUS REVIEW

In some circumstances, there is an overlap in the analysis required pursuant to the *Chevron* Step Two test, *Chevron U.S.A., Inc. v. Natural Res. Def. Council, Inc.*, 467 U.S. 837, 843–44 (1984), and that required under the arbitrary and capricious standard defined in *Motor Vehicle Manufacturers Ass'n of the U.S., Inc. v. State Farm Mut. Auto. Ins. Co.*, 463 U.S. 29, 42–44 (1983). *See, e.g., Nat'l Ass'n of Regulatory Util. Comm'rs v. ICC*, 41 F.3d 721, 728 (D.C. Cir. 1994) ("The Commission has, in our view, acted unreasonably whether one considers the case as one involving a question of *Chevron* Step II statutory interpretation or a garden variety arbitrary and capricious review or, as we do, a case that overlaps both administrative law concepts."). This overlap is exemplified in *Rust v. Sullivan*, 500 U.S. 173 (1991), where the Court sustained regulations of the Department of Health and Human Services that evidenced a change in the agency's interpretation of its authorizing statute. The Court upheld the change both because the new regulations espoused a permissible interpretation under *Chevron* Step Two *and* because the agency's decision to change its position was supported by the reasoned decisionmaking required by *State Farm*. *Id.* at 186–87. "In such situations, what is 'permissible' under *Chevron* is also reasonable under *State Farm*." *Arent v. Shalala*, 70 F.3d 610, 616 n.6 (D.C. Cir. 1995); *see also id.* at 620 (Wald, J., concurring in the judgment) ("Because both standards require the reviewing court to ask whether the agency has considered all of the factors made relevant by the statute, this court has often found the *State Farm* line of cases relevant to a *Chevron* step two analysis.").

In other circumstances, the application of the *Chevron* Step Two test and the arbitrary and capricious standard involves no overlap. For example, a court may conclude that an agency action is based on a permissible interpretation of its enabling statute, yet, nevertheless find the action an invalid exercise of decisionmaking authority under 5 U.S.C.

§ 706(2)(A), because the agency "entirely failed to consider an important aspect of the problem" or otherwise failed to engage in reasoned decisionmaking. *State Farm*, 463 U.S. at 43.

The occasional analytical overlap between *Chevron* Step Two and arbitrary and capricious review can sometimes make it difficult to determine under which standard a case should be decided. The opinions in *Arent* demonstrate the problem. In that case, public interest groups challenged labeling regulations promulgated by the FDA under the Nutrition Labeling and Education Act. The Act established voluntary guidelines pursuant to which retail stores were to provide certain nutritional information to consumers. The Act also required that if retail stores were not in "substantial compliance" with the guidelines, the FDA was to issue mandatory guidelines. 70 F.3d at 612. The public interest groups alleged that the FDA's regulations set a standard for "substantial compliance" that was so low as to be arbitrary and capricious and a violation of the statute.

Although the court unanimously upheld the regulations, there was a difference of opinion as to whether petitioners' challenges implicated *State Farm*'s arbitrary and capricious test or *Chevron* Step Two. The majority opinion in *Arent* held that the case was controlled by *State Farm*. Characterizing *Chevron* review as "principally concerned with whether an agency has authority to act under a statute," *id.* at 615, the majority concluded that "there is no question that the FDA had authority to define the circumstances constituting food retailers' substantial compliance with the [statute's] voluntary labeling guidelines," *id.* at 616. According to the majority, "[t]he only issue here is whether the FDA's discharge of that authority was reasonable ... [and s]uch a question falls within the province of traditional arbitrary and capricious review under 5 U.S.C. § 706(2)(A)." *Id.*

The concurring judge in *Arent* acknowledged that the reasonableness inquiry governing review of the regulations "arguably falls within [the] area of overlap" between *Chevron* Step Two and *State Farm*. *Id.* at 620. However, she concluded that, because, "[i]n reviewing the FDA's regulations, [the court's] task was to determine whether the agency rationally considered the factors set forth in the [statute] when it defined 'substantial compliance,'" the court was obliged to apply the *Chevron* Step Two standard of review. *Id.* Accordingly, the concurring judge argued that she could not find "*State Farm* applicable to the *exclusion* of *Chevron*." *Id.*

It may matter whether a case is decided under *Chevron* or *State Farm*, or both. When a court finds that an agency action is arbitrary and capricious, it will normally remand the case to the agency for further consideration. *See* Daugirdas, Note, *Evaluating Remand Without Vacatur: A New Judicial Remedy for Defective Agency Rulemakings*, 80 N.Y.U. L. REV. 278 (2005). Thus, when an administrative action is found to be arbitrary and capricious, an agency has an opportunity to revisit its decision and provide an adequate justification or reach a different conclusion. In contrast, when a court concludes that an agency interpretation fails *Chevron*, it has found that the agency acted outside of the compass of its delegated authority or that the agency's action rests on an impermissible construction of its authorizing statute. In such circumstances, the agency's action will be reversed and vacated. *See, e.g., Am. Library Ass'n v. FCC*, 406 F.3d 689 (D.C. Cir. 2005). It is possible, of course, that if a court vacates an agency action as impermissible under *Chevron* Step Two, the agency might later be able to advance a different, "permissible" interpretation of its authorizing statute upon which to rest its previously proposed action. *See Nat'l Cable & Telecomms. Ass'n v. Brand X Internet Servs.*, 545 U.S. 967, 985 (2005) (holding that, "[b]efore a judicial construction of a statute, whether contained in a precedent or not, may trump an agency's, the court must hold that the statute unambiguously requires the court's construction").

Finally, it should be noted that when an agency's interpretation of its authorizing statute is inconsistent with its past practice, the standards of review pursuant to *Chevron* Step Two and *State Farm* appear to merge. In *Brand X*, the Court stated:

> Unexplained inconsistency is, at most, a reason for holding an interpretation to be an arbitrary and capricious change from agency practice under the Administrative Procedure Act. [*State Farm*, 463 U.S. at 46–57.] For if the agency adequately explains the reasons for a reversal of policy, change is not invalidating, since the whole point of *Chevron* is to leave the discretion provided by the ambiguities of a statute with the implementing agency. An initial agency interpretation is not instantly carved in stone. On the contrary, the agency must consider varying interpretations and the wisdom of its policy on a continuing basis, *Chevron*, 467 U.S. at 863–64, for example, in response to changed factual circumstances, or a change in administrations. That is no doubt why in *Chevron* itself, [the] Court deferred to an agency interpretation that was a recent reversal of agency policy.

545 U.S. at 981–82. Likewise, in *Rust v. Sullivan*, the Court held:

> This Court has rejected the argument that an agency's interpretation is not entitled to deference because it represents a sharp break with prior interpretations of the statute in question. In *Chevron*, we held that a revised interpretation deserves deference because an initial agency interpretation is not instantly carved in stone and the agency, to engage in informed rulemaking, must consider varying interpretations and the wisdom of its policy on a continuing basis. An agency is not required to establish rules of conduct to last forever, but rather must be given ample latitude to adapt its rules and policies to the demands of changing circumstances.
>
> We find that the Secretary amply justified his change of interpretation with a "reasoned analysis."

500 U.S. at 186–87 (citing *State Farm*, 463 U.S. at 42, in support of the requirement of "reasoned analysis."). These holdings may suggest that only arbitrary and capricious review is appropriate in situations in which an agency, acting pursuant to delegated authority, adopts a new statutory interpretation resulting in "unexplained inconsistency" with its prior interpretation. Or they may simply mean that the arbitrary and capricious standard is incorporated as a part of the *Chevron* Step Two test in these circumstances. *See, e.g., Ala. Educ. Ass'n v. Chao*, 455 F.3d 386, 397 (D.C. Cir. 2006) (reversing an agency statutory interpretation under Step Two, because the agency "failed to supply a reasoned analysis supporting its change of position"); *see also AFL–CIO. v. Brock*, 835 F.2d 912, 919–20 (D.C. Cir.1987).

B. THE SUBSTANTIAL EVIDENCE TEST VERSUS ARBITRARY AND CAPRICIOUS REVIEW

In *Association of Data Processing Service Organizations, Inc. v. Board of Governors of the Federal Reserve System*, 745 F.2d 677 (D.C. Cir. 1984), then-Judge Scalia suggested that "the distinction between the substantial evidence test and the arbitrary or capricious test is largely semantic." *Id.* at 684. He explained that "[w]hen the arbitrary or capricious standard is performing [the] function of assuring factual support, there is no *substantive* difference between what it requires and what would be required by the substantial evidence test, since it is impossible to conceive of a 'nonarbitrary' factual judgment supported only by evidence that is not substantial in the APA sense." *Id.* at 683–84. The Supreme Court's decision in *Dickinson v. Zurko*, 527 U.S. 150 (1999), noted *Data Processing Service Organizations* without indicating whether it agreed with the proposition that there is "no difference between the APA's 'arbitrary, capricious' standard and its 'substantial evidence' standard as applied to court review of agency factfinding." *Id.* at 158.

The point made in *Data Processing Service Organizations* is not inaccurate, but it is an incomplete comparison of the arbitrary and capricious and substantial evidence standards of review. The arbitrary and capricious standard under § 706(2)(A) is a catchall provision. *See Block v. Pitney Bowes Inc.*, 952 F.2d 1450, 1454 (D.C. Cir. 1992). Thus, there is no doubt that when the formal decisionmaking mandates of §§ 556 and 557 or an agency's authorizing statute require that agency action be predicated on substantial evidence, that action can be found arbitrary and capricious under § 706(2)(A) simply by virtue of the fact that it is not supported by substantial evidence. However, when administrative action results from an informal rulemaking and permissibly rests on a policy judgment or a prediction, it will be upheld if it is supported by reasoned decisionmaking, albeit without substantial evidence. *See, e.g., FCC v. Nat'l Citizens Comm. for Broadcasting*, 436 U.S. 775, 797 (1978) (holding that, because "evidence of specific abuses by common owners is difficult to compile" and "the possible benefits of competition do not lend themselves to detailed forecast," "the Commission was entitled to rely on its judgment, based on experience," in adopting rules prohibiting common ownership of co-located newspapers and broadcast stations). Conversely, an agency action may be arbitrary and capricious even when there is substantial evidence to support it, if, for example, the agency fails to follow required procedures, in violation of § 706(2)(D), or takes an action that is "not in accordance with law," in violation of § 706(2)(A).

It is also worth noting that the substantial evidence standard of review under § 706(2)(E) is sometimes applied in conjunction with the arbitrary and capricious standard of review under § 706(2)(A). For example, in *Morall v. DEA*, 412 F.3d 165 (D.C. Cir. 2005), a case in which a physician sought review of a Drug Enforcement Administration decision to revoke her license to dispense controlled substances, the court granted the petition for review for two independent reasons. The court found no substantial evidence to support the agency's decision to revoke the physician's license based on her drug record-keeping failures and her alleged lying to DEA investigators. But the court also found that, because the revocation constituted an unprecedented and unexplained departure from agency policy and practice, the agency's sanction could not withstand arbitrary and capricious review even if the decision had been supported by substantial evidence.

The differences between arbitrary and capricious and substantial evidence review are not great, but they are more than semantic.

*

APPENDIX

SELECT PROVISIONS DEFINING STANDARDS OF REVIEW GOVERNING APPEAL OF DISTRICT COURT DECISIONS

The standards governing appellate review of trial court decisions are not comprehensively codified either by statute or rule. Rather, the applicable standards of review are found in a variety of sources, including 28 U.S.C. § 2111, certain provisions of the Federal Rules of Civil Procedure, the Federal Rules of Criminal Procedure, and the Federal Rules of Evidence, the wealth of judicial decisions construing and applying these provisions, and the broader body of common law amplifying standards of review generally. Section 2111 and the most relevant rules are excerpted in this statutory appendix.

Rules Informing *De Novo* Review of Certain District Court Conclusions of Law

Federal Rules of Civil Procedure

FED. R. CIV. P. 12. Defenses and Objections: When and How Presented; Motion for Judgment on the Pleadings; Consolidating Motions; Waiving Defenses; Pretrial Hearing

. . . .

(b) How to Present Defenses. Every defense to a claim for relief in any pleading must be asserted in the responsive pleading if one is required. But a party may assert the following defenses by motion:

(1) lack of subject-matter jurisdiction;

(2) lack of personal jurisdiction;

(3) improper venue;

(4) insufficient process;

(5) insufficient service of process;

(6) failure to state a claim upon which relief can be granted; and

(7) failure to join a party under Rule 19.

A motion asserting any of these defenses must be made before pleading if a responsive pleading is allowed. If a pleading sets out a claim for relief that does not require a responsive pleading, an opposing party may assert at trial any defense to that claim. No defense or objection is waived by joining it with one or more other defenses or objections in a responsive pleading or in a motion.

(c) Motion for Judgment on the Pleadings. After the pleadings are closed – but early enough not to delay trial – a party may move for judgment on the pleadings.

(d) Result of Presenting Matters Outside the Pleadings. If, on a motion under Rule 12(b)(6) or 12(c), matters outside the pleadings are presented to and not excluded by the court, the motion must be treated as one for summary judgment under Rule 56. All parties must be given a reasonable opportunity to present all the material that is pertinent to the motion.

(e) Motion for a More Definite Statement. A party may move for a more definite statement of a pleading to which a responsive pleading is allowed but which is so vague or ambiguous that the party cannot reasonably prepare a response. The motion must be made before filing a responsive pleading and must point out the defects complained of and the details desired. If the court orders a more definite statement and the order is not obeyed within 10 days after notice of the order or within the time the court sets, the court may strike the pleading or issue any other appropriate order.

. . . .

(g) Joining Motions.

(1) Right to Join. A motion under this rule may be joined with any other motion allowed by this rule.

(2) Limitation on Further Motions. Except as provided in Rule 12(h)(2) or (3), a party that makes a motion under this rule must not make another motion under this rule raising a defense or objection that was available to the party but omitted from its earlier motion.

(h) Waiving and Preserving Certain Defenses.

(1) When Some Are Waived. A party waives any defense listed in Rule 12(b)(2)-(5) by:

(A) omitting it from a motion in the circumstances described in Rule 12(g)(2); or

(B) failing to either:

(i) make it by motion under this rule; or

(ii) include it in a responsive pleading or in an amendment allowed by Rule 15(a)(1) as a matter of course.

(2) When to Raise Others. Failure to state a claim upon which relief can be granted, to join a person required by Rule 19(b), or to state a legal defense to a claim may be raised:

(A) in any pleading allowed or ordered under Rule 7(a);

(B) by a motion under Rule 12(c); or

(C) at trial.

(3) Lack of Subject–Matter Jurisdiction. If the court determines at any time that it lacks subject-matter jurisdiction, the court must dismiss the action.

(i) Hearing Before Trial. If a party so moves, any defense listed in Rule 12(b)(1)-(7) – whether made in a pleading or by motion – and a motion under Rule 12(c) must be heard and decided before trial unless the court orders a deferral until trial.

Fed. R. Civ. P. 50. Judgment as a Matter of Law in a Jury Trial; Related Motion for a New Trial; Conditional Ruling

(a) Judgment as a Matter of Law.

(1) In General. If a party has been fully heard on an issue during a jury trial and the court finds that a reasonable jury would not have a legally sufficient evidentiary basis to find for the party on that issue, the court may:

(A) resolve the issue against the party; and

(B) grant a motion for judgment as a matter of law against the party on a claim or defense that, under the controlling law, can be maintained or defeated only with a favorable finding on that issue.

(2) Motion. A motion for judgment as a matter of law may be made at any time before the case is submitted to the jury. The motion must specify the judgment sought and the law and facts that entitle the movant to the judgment.

(b) Renewing the Motion After Trial; Alternative Motion for a New Trial. If the court does not grant a motion for judgment as a matter of law made under Rule 50(a), the court is considered to have submitted the action to the jury subject to the court's later deciding the legal questions raised by the motion. No later than 10 days after the entry of judgment – or if the motion addresses a jury issue not decided by a verdict, no later than 10 days after the jury was discharged – the movant may file a renewed motion for judgment as a matter of law and may include an alternative or joint request for a new trial under Rule 59. In ruling on the renewed motion, the court may:

(1) allow judgment on the verdict, if the jury returned a verdict;

(2) order a new trial; or

(3) direct the entry of judgment as a matter of law.

(c) Granting the Renewed Motion; Conditional Ruling on a Motion for a New Trial.

(1) In General. If the court grants a renewed motion for judgment as a matter of law, it must also conditionally rule on any motion for a new trial by determining whether a new trial should be granted if the judgment is later vacated or reversed. The court must state the grounds for conditionally granting or denying the motion for a new trial.

(2) Effect of a Conditional Ruling. Conditionally granting the motion for a new trial does not affect the judgment's finality; if the judgment is reversed, the new trial must proceed unless the appellate court orders otherwise. If the motion for a new trial is conditionally denied, the appellee may assert error in that denial; if the judgment is reversed, the case must proceed as the appellate court orders.

(d) Time for a Losing Party's New–Trial Motion. Any motion for a new trial under Rule 59 by a party against whom judgment as a matter of law is rendered must be filed no later than 10 days after the entry of the judgment.

(e) Denying the Motion for Judgment as a Matter of Law; Reversal on Appeal. If the court denies the motion for judgment as a matter of law, the prevailing party may, as appellee, assert grounds entitling it to a new trial should the appellate court conclude that the trial court erred in denying the motion. If the appellate court reverses the judgment, it may order a new trial, direct the trial court to determine whether a new trial should be granted, or direct the entry of judgment.

Fed. R. Civ. P. 56. Summary Judgment

(a) By a Claiming Party. A party claiming relief may move, with or without supporting affidavits, for summary judgment on all or part of the claim. The motion may be filed at any time after:

(1) 20 days have passed from commencement of the action; or

(2) the opposing party serves a motion for summary judgment.

(b) By a Defending Party. A party against whom relief is sought may move at any time, with or without supporting affidavits, for summary judgment on all or part of the claim.

(c) Serving the Motion; Proceedings. The motion must be served at least 10 days before the day set for the hearing. An opposing party may serve opposing affidavits before the hearing day. The judgment sought should be rendered if the pleadings, the discovery and disclosure materials on file, and any affidavits show that there is no genuine issue as to any material fact and that the movant is entitled to judgment as a matter of law.

(d) Case Not Fully Adjudicated on the Motion.

(1) Establishing Facts. If summary judgment is not rendered on the whole action, the court should, to the extent practicable, determine what material facts are not genuinely at issue. The court should so determine by examining the pleadings and evidence before it and by interrogating the attorneys. It should then issue an order specifying what facts – including items of damages or other relief – are not genuinely at issue. The facts so specified must be treated as established in the action.

(2) Establishing Liability. An interlocutory summary judgment may be rendered on liability alone, even if there is a genuine issue on the amount of damages.

(e) Affidavits; Further Testimony.

(1) In General. A supporting or opposing affidavit must be made on personal knowledge, set out facts that would be admissible in evidence, and show that the affiant is competent to testify on the matters stated. If a paper or part of a paper is referred to in an affidavit, a sworn or certified copy must be attached to or served with the affidavit. The court may permit an affidavit to be supplemented or opposed by depositions, answers to interrogatories, or additional affidavits.

(2) Opposing Party's Obligation to Respond. When a motion for summary judgment is properly made and supported, an opposing party may not rely merely on allegations or denials in its own pleading; rather, its response must – by affidavits or as otherwise provided in this rule – set out specific facts showing a genuine issue for trial. If the opposing party does not so respond, summary judgment should, if appropriate, be entered against that party.

(f) When Affidavits Are Unavailable. If a party opposing the motion shows by affidavit that, for specified reasons, it cannot present facts essential to justify its opposition, the court may:

(1) deny the motion;

(2) order a continuance to enable affidavits to be obtained, depositions to be taken, or other discovery to be undertaken; or

(3) issue any other just order.

(g) Affidavit Submitted in Bad Faith. If satisfied that an affidavit under this rule is submitted in bad faith or solely for delay, the court must order the submitting party to pay the other party the reasonable expenses, including attorney's fees, it incurred as a result. An offending party or attorney may also be held in contempt.

Federal Rules of Criminal Procedure

FED. R. CRIM. P. 29. Motion for a Judgment of Acquittal

(a) Before Submission to the Jury. After the government closes its evidence or after the close of all the evidence, the court on the defendant's motion must enter a judgment of acquittal of any offense for which the evidence is insufficient to sustain a conviction. The court may on its own consider whether the evidence is insufficient to sustain a conviction. If the court denies a motion for a judgment of acquittal at the close of the government's evidence, the defendant may offer evidence without having reserved the right to do so.

(b) Reserving Decision. The court may reserve decision on the motion, proceed with the trial (where the motion is made before the close of all the evidence), submit the case to the jury, and decide the motion either before the jury returns a verdict or after it returns a verdict of guilty or is discharged without having returned a verdict. If the court reserves decision, it must decide the motion on the basis of the evidence at the time the ruling was reserved.

(c) After Jury Verdict or Discharge.

(1) Time for a Motion. A defendant may move for a judgment of acquittal, or renew such a motion, within 7 days after a guilty verdict or after the court discharges the jury, whichever is later.

(2) Ruling on the Motion. If the jury has returned a guilty verdict, the court may set aside the verdict and enter an acquittal. If the jury has failed to return a verdict, the court may enter a judgment of acquittal.

(3) No Prior Motion Required. A defendant is not required to move for a judgment of acquittal before the court submits the case to the jury as a prerequisite for making such a motion after jury discharge.

(d) Conditional Ruling on a Motion for a New Trial.

(1) Motion for a New Trial. If the court enters a judgment of acquittal after a guilty verdict, the court must also conditionally determine whether any motion for a new trial should be granted if the judgment of acquittal is later vacated or reversed. The court must specify the reasons for that determination.

(2) Finality. The court's order conditionally granting a motion for a new trial does not affect the finality of the judgment of acquittal.

(3) Appeal.

(A) Grant of a Motion for a New Trial. If the court conditionally grants a motion for a new trial and an appellate court later reverses the judgment of acquittal, the trial court must proceed with the new trial unless the appellate court orders otherwise.

(B) Denial of a Motion for a New Trial. If the court conditionally denies a motion for a new trial, an appellee may assert that the denial was erroneous. If the appellate court later reverses the judgment of acquittal, the trial court must proceed as the appellate court directs.

Clearly Erroneous Review of Findings of Fact Made in Connection with Judgments Rendered in Civil Bench Trials

FED. R. CIV. P. 52. Findings and Conclusions by the Court; Judgment on Partial Findings

(a) Findings and Conclusions.

(1) In General. In an action tried on the facts without a jury or with an advisory jury, the court must find the facts specially and state its conclusions of law separately. The findings and conclusions may be stated on the record after the close of the evidence or may appear in an opinion or a memorandum of decision filed by the court. Judgment must be entered under Rule 58.

(2) For an Interlocutory Injunction. In granting or refusing an interlocutory injunction, the court must similarly state the findings and conclusions that support its action.

(3) For a Motion. The court is not required to state findings or conclusions when ruling on a motion under Rule 12 or 56 or, unless these rules provide otherwise, on any other motion.

(4) Effect of a Master's Findings. A master's findings, to the extent adopted by the court, must be considered the court's findings.

(5) Questioning the Evidentiary Support. A party may later question the sufficiency of the evidence supporting the findings, whether or not the party requested findings, objected to them, moved to amend them, or moved for partial findings.

(6) Setting Aside the Findings. Findings of fact, whether based on oral or other evidence, must not be set aside unless clearly erroneous, and the reviewing court must give due regard to the trial court's opportunity to judge the witnesses' credibility.

(b) Amended or Additional Findings. On a party's motion filed no later than 10 days after the entry of judgment, the court may amend its findings – or make additional findings – and may amend the judgment accordingly. The motion may accompany a motion for a new trial under Rule 59.

(c) Judgment on Partial Findings. If a party has been fully heard on an issue during a nonjury trial and the court finds against the party on that issue, the court may enter judgment against the party on a claim or defense that, under the controlling law, can be maintained or defeated only with a favorable finding on that issue. The court may, however, decline to render any judgment until the close of the evidence. A judgment on partial findings must be supported by findings of fact and conclusions of law as required by Rule 52(a).

Harmless Error, Plain Error Review, and Rules Prescribing When and How to Object to Avoid Plain Error Review

Title 28, U.S. Code, Judiciary and Judicial Procedure

28 U.S.C. § 2111. Harmless Error

On the hearing of any appeal or writ of certiorari in any case, the court shall give judgment after an examination of the record without regard to errors or defects which do not affect the substantial rights of the parties.

Federal Rules of Civil Procedure

FED. R. CIV. P. 46. Objecting to a Ruling or Order

A formal exception to a ruling or order is unnecessary. When the ruling or order is requested or made, a party need only state the action that it wants the court to take or objects to, along with the grounds for the request or objection. Failing to object does not prejudice a party who had no opportunity to do so when the ruling or order was made.

FED. R. CIV. P. 51. Instructions to the Jury; Objections; Preserving a Claim of Error

(a) Requests.

    (1) Before or at the Close of the Evidence. At the close of the evidence or at any earlier reasonable time that the court orders, a party may file and furnish to every other party written requests for the jury instructions it wants the court to give.

    (2) After the Close of the Evidence. After the close of the evidence, a party may:

        (A) file requests for instructions on issues that could not reasonably have been anticipated by an earlier time that the court set for requests; and

        (B) with the court's permission, file untimely requests for instructions on any issue.

(b) Instructions. The court:

    (1) must inform the parties of its proposed instructions and proposed action on the requests before instructing the jury and before final jury arguments;

    (2) must give the parties an opportunity to object on the record and out of the jury's hearing before the instructions and arguments are delivered; and

    (3) may instruct the jury at any time before the jury is discharged.

(c) Objections.

(1) How to Make. A party who objects to an instruction or the failure to give an instruction must do so on the record, stating distinctly the matter objected to and the grounds for the objection.

(2) When to Make. An objection is timely if:

(A) a party objects at the opportunity provided under Rule 51(b)(2); or

(B) a party was not informed of an instruction or action on a request before that opportunity to object, and the party objects promptly after learning that the instruction or request will be, or has been, given or refused.

(d) Assigning Error; Plain Error.

(1) Assigning Error. A party may assign as error:

(A) an error in an instruction actually given, if that party properly objected; or

(B) a failure to give an instruction, if that party properly requested it and – unless the court rejected the request in a definitive ruling on the record – also properly objected.

(2) Plain Error. A court may consider a plain error in the instructions that has not been preserved as required by Rule 51(d)(1) if the error affects substantial rights.

FED. R. CIV. P. 61. Harmless Error

Unless justice requires otherwise, no error in admitting or excluding evidence – or any other error by the court or a party – is ground for granting a new trial, for setting aside a verdict, or for vacating, modifying, or otherwise disturbing a judgment or order. At every stage of the proceeding, the court must disregard all errors and defects that do not affect any party's substantial rights.

Federal Rules of Criminal Procedure

FED. R. CRIM. P. 11. Pleas

. . . .

(h) Harmless Error. A variance from the requirements of this rule is harmless error if it does not affect substantial rights.

FED. R. CRIM. P. 30. Jury Instructions

(a) In General. Any party may request in writing that the court instruct the jury on the law as specified in the request. The request must be made at the close of the evidence or at any earlier time that the court reasonably sets. When the request is made, the requesting party must furnish a copy to every other party.

(b) Ruling on a Request. The court must inform the parties before closing arguments how it intends to rule on the requested instructions.

(c) Time for Giving Instructions. The court may instruct the jury before or after the arguments are completed, or at both times.

(d) Objections to Instructions.

A party who objects to any portion of the instructions or to a failure to give a requested instruction must inform the court of the specific objection and the grounds for the objection before the jury retires to deliberate. An opportunity must be given to object out of the jury's hearing and, on request, out of the jury's presence. Failure to object in accordance with this rule precludes appellate review, except as permitted under Rule 52(b).

Fed. R. Crim. P. 51. Preserving Claimed Error

(a) Exceptions Unnecessary. Exceptions to rulings or orders of the court are unnecessary.

(b) Preserving a Claim of Error. A party may preserve a claim of error by informing the court – when the court ruling or order is made or sought – of the action the party wishes the court to take, or the party's objection to the court's action and the grounds for that objection. If a party does not have an opportunity to object to a ruling or order, the absence of an objection does not later prejudice that party. A ruling or order that admits or excludes evidence is governed by Federal Rule of Evidence 103.

Fed. R. Crim. P. 52. Harmless and Plain Error

(a) Harmless Error. Any error, defect, irregularity, or variance that does not affect substantial rights must be disregarded.

(b) Plain Error. A plain error that affects substantial rights may be considered even though it was not brought to the court's attention.

Federal Rules of Evidence

Fed. R. Evid. 103. Rulings on Evidence

(a) Effect of Erroneous Ruling. – Error may not be predicated upon a ruling which admits or excludes evidence unless a substantial right of the party is affected, and

> **(1) Objection.** – In case the ruling is one admitting evidence, a timely objection or motion to strike appears of record, stating the specific ground of objection, if the specific ground was not apparent from the context; or

(2) Offer of Proof. – In case the ruling is one excluding evidence, the substance of the evidence was made known to the court by offer or was apparent from the context within which questions were asked.

Once the court makes a definitive ruling on the record admitting or excluding evidence, either at or before trial, a party need not renew an objection or offer of proof to preserve a claim of error for appeal.

(b) Record of Offer and Ruling. – The court may add any other or further statement which shows the character of the evidence, the form in which it was offered, the objection made, and the ruling thereon. It may direct the making of an offer in question and answer form.

(c) Hearing of Jury. – In jury cases, proceedings shall be conducted, to the extent practicable, so as to prevent inadmissible evidence from being suggested to the jury by any means, such as making statements or offers of proof or asking questions in the hearing of the jury.

(d) Plain Error. – Nothing in this rule precludes taking notice of plain errors affecting substantial rights although they were not brought to the attention of the court.

Rules Pertaining to Waiver of Appellate Review

Federal Rules of Civil Procedure

FED. R. CIV. P. 12. Defenses and Objections: When and How Presented; Motion for Judgment on the Pleadings; Consolidating Motions; Waiving Defenses; Pretrial Hearing

. . . .

(g) Joining Motions.

(1) Right to Join. A motion under this rule may be joined with any other motion allowed by this rule.

(2) Limitation on Further Motions. Except as provided in Rule 12(h)(2) or (3), a party that makes a motion under this rule must not make another motion under this rule raising a defense or objection that was available to the party but omitted from its earlier motion.

(h) Waiving and Preserving Certain Defenses.

(1) When Some Are Waived. A party waives any defense listed in Rule 12(b)(2)-(5) by:

(A) omitting it from a motion in the circumstances described in Rule 12(g)(2); or

(B) failing to either:

(i) make it by motion under this rule; or

(ii) include it in a responsive pleading or in an amendment allowed by Rule 15(a)(1) as a matter of course.

(2) When to Raise Others. Failure to state a claim upon which relief can be granted, to join a person required by Rule 19(b), or to state a legal defense to a claim may be raised:

(A) in any pleading allowed or ordered under Rule 7(a);

(B) by a motion under Rule 12(c); or

(C) at trial.

(3) Lack of Subject – Matter Jurisdiction. If the court determines at any time that it lacks subject-matter jurisdiction, the court must dismiss the action.

. . . .

FED. R. CIV. P. 38. Right to a Jury Trial; Demand

(a) Right Preserved. The right of trial by jury as declared by the Seventh Amendment to the Constitution – or as provided by a federal statute – is preserved to the parties inviolate.

(b) Demand. On any issue triable of right by a jury, a party may demand a jury trial by:

(1) serving the other parties with a written demand – which may be included in a pleading – no later than 10 days after the last pleading directed to the issue is served; and

(2) filing the demand in accordance with Rule 5(d).

(c) Specifying Issues. In its demand, a party may specify the issues that it wishes to have tried by a jury; otherwise, it is considered to have demanded a jury trial on all the issues so triable. If the party has demanded a jury trial on only some issues, any other party may – within 10 days after being served with the demand or within a shorter time ordered by the court – serve a demand for a jury trial on any other or all factual issues triable by jury.

(d) Waiver; Withdrawal. A party waives a jury trial unless its demand is properly served and filed. A proper demand may be withdrawn only if the parties consent.

. . . .

FED. R. CIV. P. 49. Special Verdict; General Verdict and Questions

(a) Special Verdict.

(1) In General. The court may require a jury to return only a special verdict in the form of a special written finding on each issue of fact. The court may do so by:

(A) submitting written questions susceptible of a categorical or other brief answer;

(B) submitting written forms of the special findings that might properly be made under the pleadings and evidence; or

(C) using any other method that the court considers appropriate.

(2) Instructions. The court must give the instructions and explanations necessary to enable the jury to make its findings on each submitted issue.

(3) Issues Not Submitted. A party waives the right to a jury trial on any issue of fact raised by the pleadings or evidence but not submitted to the jury unless, before the jury retires, the party demands its submission to the jury. If the party does not demand submission, the court may make a finding on the issue. If the court makes no finding, it is considered to have made a finding consistent with its judgment on the special verdict.

. . . .

Federal Rules of Criminal Procedure

FED. R. CRIM. P. 12. Pleadings and Pretrial Motions

. . . .

(b) Pretrial Motions.

. . . .

(2) Motions That May Be Made Before Trial. A party may raise by pretrial motion any defense, objection, or request that the court can determine without a trial of the general issue.

(3) Motions That Must Be Made Before Trial. The following must be raised before trial:

(A) a motion alleging a defect in instituting the prosecution;

(B) a motion alleging a defect in the indictment or information – but at any time while the case is pending, the court may hear a claim that the indictment or information fails to invoke the court's jurisdiction or to state an offense;

(C) a motion to suppress evidence;

(D) a Rule 14 motion to sever charges or defendants; and

(E) a Rule 16 motion for discovery.

. . . .

(c) Motion Deadline. The court may, at the arraignment or as soon afterward as practicable, set a deadline for the parties to make pretrial motions and may also schedule a motion hearing.

. . . .

(e) Waiver of a Defense, Objection, or Request. A party waives any Rule 12(b)(3) defense, objection, or request not raised by the deadline the court sets under Rule 12(c) or by any extension the court provides. For good cause, the court may grant relief from the waiver.

. . . .

Conversion Chart:
2007 Amendments to
the Federal Rules of Civil Procedure

Amendments to the Federal Rules of Civil Procedure were forwarded to Congress by the Chief Justice of the United States in the Spring of 2007. *See* Orders of the Supreme Court of the United States Adopting and Amending Rules and Forms, Order 30 (Apr. 30, 2007). Absent contrary congressional action, the amended rules will take effect on December 1, 2007. The Advisory Committee Notes make clear that the amendments affecting the rules cited in our text – which include both stylistic changes and, in some instances, the renumbering of subsections – are not intended to effect substantive changes in the law. On the assumption that Congress is unlikely to reject these uncontroversial amendments, the book references and quotes the rules in the form in which they will appear effective December 1, 2007. The conversion chart below may prove useful to those researching issues pertaining to the renumbered rules.

Renumbered (effective Dec. 1, 2007)	Pre-amendment Numbering
FED. R. CIV. P. 8(d)(1)	FED. R. CIV. P. 8(e)(1)
FED. R. CIV. P. 8(e)	FED. R. CIV. P. 8(f)
FED. R. CIV. P. 12(i)	FED. R. CIV. P. 12(d)
FED. R. CIV. P. 50(b)(1)-(3)	FED. R. CIV. P. 50(b)(1), (2)
FED. R. CIV. P. 50(c)(1), (2)	FED. R. CIV. P. 50(c)(1)
FED. R. CIV. P. 50(e)	FED. R. CIV. P. 50(d)
FED. R. CIV. P. 52(a)(1)-(4), (6)	FED. R. CIV. P. 52(a)
FED. R. CIV. P. 52(a)(5)	FED. R. CIV. P. 52(b)
FED. R. CIV. P. 56(e)(1), (2)	FED. R. CIV. P. 56(e)

PROVIDED FROM THE ADMINISTRATIVE
PROCEDURE ACT

The Administrative Procedure Act, subject only to constitutional precepts and overriding provisions in agency authorizing statutes, generally controls judicial review of agency action. Excerpted below are some of the principal provisions of the APA that set the parameters for the scope and standards of review governing judicial review of agency actions.

---

5 U.S.C. § 551. Definitions

For the purpose of this subchapter –

(1) "agency" means each authority of the Government of the United States, whether or not it is within or subject to review by another agency, but does not include –

(A) the Congress;

(B) the courts of the United States;

(C) the governments of the territories or possessions of the United States;

(D) the government of the District of Columbia;

or except as to the requirements of section 552 of this title –

(E) agencies composed of representatives of the parties or of representatives of organizations of the parties to the disputes determined by them;

(F) courts martial and military commissions;

(G) military authority exercised in the field in time of war or in occupied territory; or

(H) functions conferred by sections 1738, 1739, 1743, and 1744 of title 12; chapter 2 of title 41; subchapter II of chapter 471 of title 49; or sections 1884, 1891–1902, and former section 1641(b)(2), of title 50, appendix;

(2) "person" includes an individual, partnership, corporation, association, or public or private organization other than an agency;

(3) "party" includes a person or agency named or admitted as a party, or properly seeking and entitled as of right to be admitted as a party, in an agency proceeding, and a person or agency admitted by an agency as a party for limited purposes;

(4) "rule" means the whole or a part of an agency statement of general or particular applicability and future effect designed to implement, interpret, or prescribe law or policy or describing the organization, procedure, or practice requirements of an agency and includes the approval or prescription for the future of rates, wages, corporate or financial structures or reorganizations thereof, prices, facilities, appliances, services or allowances therefor or of valuations, costs, or accounting, or practices bearing on any of the foregoing;

(5) "rule making" means agency process for formulating, amending, or repealing a rule;

(6) "order" means the whole or a part of a final disposition, whether affirmative, negative, injunctive, or declaratory in form, of an agency in a matter other than rule making but including licensing;

(7) "adjudication" means agency process for the formulation of an order;

(8) "license" includes the whole or a part of an agency permit, certificate, approval, registration, charter, membership, statutory exemption or other form of permission;

(9) "licensing" includes agency process respecting the grant, renewal, denial, revocation, suspension, annulment, withdrawal, limitation, amendment, modification, or conditioning of a license;

(10) "sanction" includes the whole or a part of an agency –

(A) prohibition, requirement, limitation, or other condition affecting the freedom of a person;

(B) withholding of relief;

(C) imposition of penalty or fine;

(D) destruction, taking, seizure, or withholding of property;

(E) assessment of damages, reimbursement, restitution, compensation, costs, charges, or fees;

(F) requirement, revocation, or suspension of a license; or

(G) taking other compulsory or restrictive action;

(11) "relief" includes the whole or a part of an agency –

(A) grant of money, assistance, license, authority, exemption, exception, privilege, or remedy;

(B) recognition of a claim, right, immunity, privilege, exemption, or exception; or

(C) taking of other action on the application or petition of, and beneficial to, a person;

(12) "agency proceeding" means an agency process as defined by paragraphs (5), (7), and (9) of this section;

(13) "agency action" includes the whole or a part of an agency rule, order, license, sanction, relief, or the equivalent or denial thereof, or failure to act; and

(14) "ex parte communication" means an oral or written communication not on the public record with respect to which reasonable prior notice to all parties is not given, but it shall not include requests for status reports on any matter or proceeding covered by this subchapter.

5 U.S.C. § 553. Rule making

(a) This section applies, according to the provisions thereof, except to the extent that there is involved –

(1) a military or foreign affairs function of the United States; or

(2) a matter relating to agency management or personnel or to public property, loans, grants, benefits, or contracts.

(b) General notice of proposed rule making shall be published in the Federal Register, unless persons subject thereto are named and either personally served or otherwise have actual notice thereof in accordance with law. The notice shall include –

(1) a statement of the time, place, and nature of public rule making proceedings;

(2) reference to the legal authority under which the rule is proposed; and

(3) either the terms or substance of the proposed rule or a description of the subjects and issues involved.

Except when notice or hearing is required by statute, this subsection does not apply –

(A) to interpretative rules, general statements of policy, or rules of agency organization, procedure, or practice; or

(B) when the agency for good cause finds (and incorporates the finding and a brief statement of reasons therefor in the rules issued) that notice and public procedure thereon are impracticable, unnecessary, or contrary to the public interest.

(c) After notice required by this section, the agency shall give interested persons an opportunity to participate in the rule making through submission of written data, views, or arguments with or without opportunity for oral presentation. After consideration of the relevant matter presented, the agency shall incorporate in the rules adopted a concise general statement of their basis and purpose. When rules are required by statute to be made on the record after opportunity for an agency hearing, sections 556 and 557 of this title apply instead of this subsection.

(d) The required publication or service of a substantive rule shall be made not less than 30 days before its effective date, except –

(1) a substantive rule which grants or recognizes an exemption or relieves a restriction;

(2) interpretative rules and statements of policy; or

(3) as otherwise provided by the agency for good cause found and published with the rule.

(e) Each agency shall give an interested person the right to petition for the issuance, amendment, or repeal of a rule.

5 U.S.C. § 554. Adjudications

(a) This section applies, according to the provisions thereof, in every case of adjudication required by statute to be determined on the record after opportunity for an agency hearing, except to the extent that there is involved –

(1) a matter subject to a subsequent trial of the law and the facts de novo in a court;

(2) the selection or tenure of an employee, except a[n] administrative law judge appointed under section 3105 of this title;

(3) proceedings in which decisions rest solely on inspections, tests, or elections;

(4) the conduct of military or foreign affairs functions;

(5) cases in which an agency is acting as an agent for a court; or

(6) the certification of worker representatives.

(b) Persons entitled to notice of an agency hearing shall be timely informed of –

(1) the time, place, and nature of the hearing;

(2) the legal authority and jurisdiction under which the hearing is to be held; and

(3) the matters of fact and law asserted.

When private persons are the moving parties, other parties to the proceeding shall give prompt notice of issues controverted in fact or law; and in other instances agencies may by rule require responsive pleading. In fixing the time and place for hearings, due regard shall be had for the convenience and necessity of the parties or their representatives.

(c) The agency shall give all interested parties opportunity for –

(1) the submission and consideration of facts, arguments, offers of settlement, or proposals of adjustment when time, the nature of the proceeding, and the public interest permit; and

(2) to the extent that the parties are unable so to determine a controversy by consent, hearing and decision on notice and in accordance with sections 556 and 557 of this title.

(d) The employee who presides at the reception of evidence pursuant to section 556 of this title shall make the recommended decision or initial decision required by section 557 of this title, unless he becomes unavailable to the agency. Except to the extent required for the disposition of ex parte matters as authorized by law, such an employee may not –

(1) consult a person or party on a fact in issue, unless on notice and opportunity for all parties to participate; or

(2) be responsible to or subject to the supervision or direction of an employee or agent engaged in the performance of investigative or prosecuting functions for an agency.

An employee or agent engaged in the performance of investigative or prosecuting functions for an agency in a case may not, in that or a factually related case, participate or advise in the decision, recommended decision, or agency review pursuant to section 557 of this title, except as witness or counsel in public proceedings. This subsection does not apply –

(A) in determining applications for initial licenses;

(B) to proceedings involving the validity or application of rates, facilities, or practices of public utilities or carriers; or

(C) to the agency or a member or members of the body comprising the agency.

(e) The agency, with like effect as in the case of other orders, and in its sound discretion, may issue a declaratory order to terminate a controversy or remove uncertainty.

5 U.S.C. § 556. Hearings; presiding employees; powers and duties; burden of proof; evidence; record as basis of decision

(a) This section applies, according to the provisions thereof, to hearings required by section 553 or 554 of this title to be conducted in accordance with this section.

(b) There shall preside at the taking of evidence –

(1) the agency;

(2) one or more members of the body which comprises the agency; or

(3) one or more administrative law judges appointed under section 3105 of this title.

This subchapter does not supersede the conduct of specified classes of proceedings, in whole or in part, by or before boards or other employees specially provided for by or designated under statute. The functions of presiding employees and of employees participating in decisions in accordance with section 557 of this title shall be conducted in an impartial manner. A presiding or participating employee may at any time disqualify himself. On the filing in good faith of a timely and sufficient affidavit of personal bias or other disqualification of a presiding or participating employee, the agency shall determine the matter as a part of the record and decision in the case.

(c) Subject to published rules of the agency and within its powers, employees presiding at hearings may –

(1) administer oaths and affirmations;

(2) issue subpoenas authorized by law;

(3) rule on offers of proof and receive relevant evidence;

(4) take depositions or have depositions taken when the ends of justice would be served;

(5) regulate the course of the hearing;

(6) hold conferences for the settlement or simplification of the issues by consent of the parties or by the use of alternative means of dispute resolution as provided in subchapter IV of this chapter;

(7) inform the parties as to the availability of one or more alternative means of dispute resolution, and encourage use of such methods;

(8) require the attendance at any conference held pursuant to paragraph (6) of at least one representative of each party who has authority to negotiate concerning resolution of issues in controversy;

(9) dispose of procedural requests or similar matters;

(10) make or recommend decisions in accordance with section 557 of this title; and

(11) take other action authorized by agency rule consistent with this subchapter.

(d) Except as otherwise provided by statute, the proponent of a rule or order has the burden of proof. Any oral or documentary evidence may be received, but the agency as a matter of policy shall provide for the exclusion of irrelevant, immaterial, or unduly repetitious evidence. A sanction may not be imposed or rule or order issued except on consideration of the whole record or those parts thereof cited by a party and supported by and in accordance with the reliable, probative, and substantial evidence. The agency may, to the extent consistent with the interests of justice and the policy of the underlying statutes administered by the agency, consider a violation of section 557(d) of this title sufficient grounds for a decision adverse to a party who has knowingly committed such violation or knowingly caused such violation to occur. A party is entitled to present his case or defense by oral or documentary evidence, to submit rebuttal evidence, and to conduct such cross-examination as may be required for a full and true disclosure of the facts. In rule making or determining claims for money or benefits or applications for initial licenses an agency may, when a party will not be prejudiced thereby, adopt procedures for the submission of all or part of the evidence in written form.

(e) The transcript of testimony and exhibits, together with all papers and requests filed in the proceeding, constitutes the exclusive record for decision in accordance with section 557 of this title and, on payment of lawfully prescribed costs, shall be made available to the parties. When an agency decision rests on official notice of a material fact not appearing in the evidence in the record, a party is entitled, on timely request, to an opportunity to show the contrary.

5 U.S.C. § 557. Initial decisions; conclusiveness; review by agency; submissions by parties; contents of decisions; record

(a) This section applies, according to the provisions thereof, when a hearing is required to be conducted in accordance with section 556 of this title.

(b) When the agency did not preside at the reception of the evidence, the presiding employee or, in cases not subject to section 554(d) of this title, an employee qualified to preside at hearings pursuant to section 556 of this title, shall initially decide the case unless the agency requires, either in specific cases or by general rule, the entire record to be certified to it for decision. When the presiding employee makes an initial decision, that decision then becomes the decision of the agency without further proceedings unless there is an appeal to, or review on motion of, the agency within time provided by rule. On appeal from or review of the initial decision, the agency has all the powers which it would have in making the initial decision except as it may limit the issues on notice or by rule. When the agency makes the decision without having presided at the reception of the evidence, the presiding employee or an employee qualified to preside at hearings pursuant to section 556 of this title shall first recommend a decision, except that in rule making or determining applications for initial licenses –

> **(1)** instead thereof the agency may issue a tentative decision or one of its responsible employees may recommend a decision; or

> **(2)** this procedure may be omitted in a case in which the agency finds on the record that due and timely execution of its functions imperatively and unavoidably so requires.

(c) Before a recommended, initial, or tentative decision, or a decision on agency review of the decision of subordinate employees, the parties are entitled to a reasonable opportunity to submit for the consideration of the employees participating in the decisions –

(1) proposed findings and conclusions; or

(2) exceptions to the decisions or recommended decisions of subordinate employees or to tentative agency decisions; and

(3) supporting reasons for the exceptions or proposed findings or conclusions.

The record shall show the ruling on each finding, conclusion, or exception presented. All decisions, including initial, recommended, and tentative decisions, are a part of the record and shall include a statement of –

(A) findings and conclusions, and the reasons or basis therefor, on all the material issues of fact, law, or discretion presented on the record; and

(B) the appropriate rule, order, sanction, relief, or denial thereof.

(d) (1) In any agency proceeding which is subject to subsection (a) of this section, except to the extent required for the disposition of ex parte matters as authorized by law –

(A) no interested person outside the agency shall make or knowingly cause to be made to any member of the body comprising the agency, administrative law judge, or other employee who is or may reasonably be expected to be involved in the decisional process of the proceeding, an ex parte communication relevant to the merits of the proceeding;

(B) no member of the body comprising the agency, administrative law judge, or other employee who is or may reasonably be expected to be involved in the decisional process of the proceeding, shall make or knowingly cause to be made to any interested person outside the agency an ex parte communication relevant to the merits of the proceeding;

(C) a member of the body comprising the agency, administrative law judge, or other employee who is or may reasonably be expected to be involved in the decisional process of such proceeding who receives, or who makes or knowingly causes to be made, a communication prohibited by this subsection shall place on the public record of the proceeding:

(i) all such written communications;

(ii) memoranda stating the substance of all such oral communications; and

(iii) all written responses, and memoranda stating the substance of all oral responses, to the materials described in clauses (i) and (ii) of this subparagraph;

(D) upon receipt of a communication knowingly made or knowingly caused to be made by a party in violation of this subsection, the agency, administrative law judge, or other employee presiding at the hearing may, to the extent consistent with the interests of justice and the policy of the underlying statutes, require the party to show cause why his claim or interest in the proceeding should not be dismissed, denied, disregarded, or otherwise adversely affected on account of such violation; and

(E) the prohibitions of this subsection shall apply beginning at such time as the agency may designate, but in no case shall they begin to apply later than the time at which a proceeding is noticed for hearing unless the person responsible for the communication has knowledge that it will be noticed, in which case the prohibitions shall apply beginning at the time of his acquisition of such knowledge.

(2) This subsection does not constitute authority to withhold information from Congress.

5 U.S.C. § 558. Imposition of sanctions; determination of applications for licenses; suspension, revocation, and expiration of licenses

(a) This section applies, according to the provisions thereof, to the exercise of a power or authority.

(b) A sanction may not be imposed or a substantive rule or order issued except within jurisdiction delegated to the agency and as authorized by law.

(c) When application is made for a license required by law, the agency, with due regard for the rights and privileges of all the interested parties or adversely affected persons and within a reasonable time, shall set and complete proceedings required to be conducted in accordance with sections 556 and 557 of this title or other proceedings required by law and shall make its decision. Except in cases of willfulness or those in which public health, interest, or safety requires otherwise, the withdrawal, suspension, revocation, or annulment of a license is lawful only if, before the institution of agency proceedings therefor, the licensee has been given –

(1) notice by the agency in writing of the facts or conduct which may warrant the action; and

(2) opportunity to demonstrate or achieve compliance with all lawful requirements.

When the licensee has made timely and sufficient application for a renewal or a new license in accordance with agency rules, a license with reference to an activity of a continuing nature does not expire until the application has been finally determined by the agency.

5 U.S.C. § 701. Application; definitions

(a) This chapter applies, according to the provisions thereof, except to the extent that –

(1) statutes preclude judicial review; or

(2) agency action is committed to agency discretion by law.

(b) For the purpose of this chapter –

(1) "agency" means each authority of the Government of the United States, whether or not it is within or subject to review by another agency, but does not include –

(A) the Congress;

(B) the courts of the United States;

(C) the governments of the territories or possessions of the United States;

(D) the government of the District of Columbia;

(E) agencies composed of representatives of the parties or of representatives of organizations of the parties to the disputes determined by them;

(F) courts martial and military commissions;

(G) military authority exercised in the field in time of war or in occupied territory; or

(H) functions conferred by sections 1738, 1739, 1743, and 1744 of title 12; chapter 2 of title 41; subchapter II of chapter 471 of title 49; or sections 1884, 1891–1902, and former section 1641(b)(2), of title 50, appendix; and

(2) "person", "rule", "order", "license", "sanction", "relief", and "agency action" have the meanings given them by section 551 of this title.

5 U.S.C. § 702. Right of review

A person suffering legal wrong because of agency action, or adversely affected or aggrieved by agency action within the meaning of a relevant statute, is entitled to judicial review thereof. An action in a court of the United States seeking relief other than money damages and stating a claim that an agency or an officer or employee thereof acted or failed to act in an official capacity or under color of legal authority shall not be dismissed nor relief therein be denied on the ground that it is against the United States or that the United States is an indispensable party. The United States may be named as a defendant in any such action, and a judgment or decree may be entered against the United States: *Provided*, That any mandatory or injunctive decree shall specify the Federal officer or officers (by name or by title), and their successors in office, personally responsible for compliance. Nothing herein (1) affects other limitations on judicial review or the power or duty of the court to dismiss any action or deny relief on any other appropriate legal or equitable ground; or (2) confers authority to grant relief if any other statute that grants consent to suit expressly or impliedly forbids the relief which is sought.

5 U.S.C. § 703. Form and venue of proceeding

The form of proceeding for judicial review is the special statutory review proceeding relevant to the subject matter in a court specified by statute or, in the absence or inadequacy thereof, any applicable form of legal action, including actions for declaratory judgments or writs of prohibitory or mandatory injunction or habeas corpus, in a court of competent jurisdiction. If no special statutory review proceeding is applicable, the action for judicial review may be brought against the United States, the agency by its official title, or the appropriate officer. Except to the extent that prior, adequate, and exclusive opportunity for judicial review is provided by law, agency action is subject to judicial review in civil or criminal proceedings for judicial enforcement.

5 U.S.C. § 704. Actions reviewable

Agency action made reviewable by statute and final agency action for which there is no other adequate remedy in a court are subject to judicial review. A preliminary, procedural, or intermediate agency action or ruling not directly reviewable is subject to review on the review of the final agency action. Except as otherwise expressly required by statute, agency action otherwise final is final for the purposes of this section whether or not there has been presented or determined an application for a declaratory order, for any form of reconsideration, or, unless the agency otherwise requires by rule and provides that the action meanwhile is inoperative, for an appeal to superior agency authority.

5 U.S.C. § 706. Scope of review

To the extent necessary to decision and when presented, the reviewing court shall decide all relevant questions of law, interpret constitutional and statutory provisions, and determine the meaning or applicability of the terms of an agency action. The reviewing court shall –

(1) compel agency action unlawfully withheld or unreasonably delayed; and

(2) hold unlawful and set aside agency action, findings, and conclusions found to be –

(A) arbitrary, capricious, an abuse of discretion, or otherwise not in accordance with law;

(B) contrary to constitutional right, power, privilege, or immunity;

(C) in excess of statutory jurisdiction, authority, or limitations, or short of statutory right;

(D) without observance of procedure required by law;

(E) unsupported by substantial evidence in a case subject to sections 556 and 557 of this title or otherwise reviewed on the record of an agency hearing provided by statute; or

(F) unwarranted by the facts to the extent that the facts are subject to trial de novo by the reviewing court.

In making the foregoing determinations, the court shall review the whole record or those parts of it cited by a party, and due account shall be taken of the rule of prejudicial error.

5 U.S.C. § 3105. Appointment of administrative law judges

Each agency shall appoint as many administrative law judges as are necessary for proceedings required to be conducted in accordance with sections 556 and 557 of this title. Administrative law judges shall be assigned to cases in rotation so far as practicable, and may not perform duties inconsistent with their duties and responsibilities as administrative law judges.

*

Index

References are to Pages

A

T to Z